S0-AVX-461

THE 1969 MIRACLE METS

THE 1969 MIRACLE METS

The Improbable Story of the World's Greatest Underdog Team

Steven Travers

Foreword by Bud Harrelson

The Lyons Press
Guilford, Connecticut
An imprint of The Globe Pequot Press

The Lyons Press is an imprint of The Globe Pequot Press.

Text design by Libby Kingsbury
Layout Artist: Kim Burdick
Project Manager: John Burbidge

Library of Congress Cataloging-in-Publication Data
Travers, Steven.
1969 miracle Mets / Steven Travers.
p. cm.
ISBN 978-1-59921-410-8
1. New York Mets (Baseball team)—History. I. Title. II. Title: Nineteen sixty nine miracle Mets.
GV875.N45T73 2008
796.357'64097471—dc22
2008045937

Printed in the United States of America

10 9 8 7 6 5 4 3 2 1

To the great Tom Seaver
A Christy Mathewson for our times

CONTENTS

Acknowledgments ix
Foreword by Bud Harrelson xi
Introduction xvii
1 "Can't Anybody Here Play This Game?" 1
2 The Reincarnation of Christy Mathewson 8
3 High Hopes 21
4 In the "Big Inning" 43
5 Meet the Mets 52
6 The Leaping Corpse 62
7 The First Crucial Day 68
8 The Birth of a True New York Sports Icon 73
9 The Wrath of Gil 82
10 Resurrection 88
11 The March to the Sea 106
12 David vs. Goliath 117
13 The Perfect Game 131
14 The Promised Land 140
15 Fall from Grace 150
16 Those Amazin' Mets 156
Appendix A: 1969 Team Roster 165
Appendix B: Batting Statistics 166

Appendix C: Pitching Statistics 168
Appendix D: Fielding Statistics 170
Bibliography 172
Index 176
About the Author 186

ACKNOWLEDGMENTS

My thanks go to Gene Brissie, Tom McCarthy, and Lara Asher at The Globe Pequot Press, as well as project manager John Burbidge and copyeditor Laura Daly. Also to the great Tom Seaver, Buddy Harrelson, Matt Merola, and the New York Mets. Great thanks to Mary at George Brace Photos, and John Horne and Pat Kelly of the Baseball Hall of Fame.

Special thanks to John Rogers and Micah Gulledge of Sports Cards Plus and the John Rogers Photo Archive. The "Surge" in Iraq seems to have been only slightly more difficult to achieve than getting photo issues for this book squared away. You guys are the collective "General David Petraeus" of photo suppliers.

Thanks to Peter Miller and Adrienne Rosado of PMA Literary and Film Management in New York City. As always, thanks to my wonderful daughter, Elizabeth Travers, and my supportive parents. Above all others, my greatest thanks go to Jesus Christ, the source of all that is decent and true in my life.

FOREWORD

I felt the excitement and energy from day one when I walked into Shea Stadium in 1965. Back then, you had these rickety old ballparks, and it stood out as one of the first huge multi-purpose stadiums. I was in awe right from the beginning. And even though this year marks the opening of Citi Field for the New York Mets, Shea will endure in our memories and remain a part of the miracle and lore of 1969. Now when teams rise out of nowhere and win they get compared to "the Amazin' Mets"—the first New York team to experience such a miraculous transformation.

Many things contributed to our unbelievable season in 1969—homerun hitters, strong pitching, a different level of bonding among the players. But the real magic of the 1969 Mets had a lot to do with Gil Hodges. We were barely out of last place in 1968 when Hodges arrived. We did acquire some new players—players that he was very aware of—but he didn't do much in '68 because he didn't really know the players yet, and he didn't want other people's opinions about the players that we had. He just kind of sat back, quietly watched and analyzed, and made a few recommendations. He changed Jerry Grote's stance and the way he held his hands. And then in '69 he came to spring training and he had some suggestions. I remember him

Fellow Californian Bud Harrelson was Tom Seaver's best friend and a hero of the 1969 Mets.
John Rogers Archives

saying *do you guys realize that you lost 36 one-run ballgames? So you lost thirty-six games by one run.* And he was trying to be simplistic here. We had good defense and good pitching, in spite of the fact that we were a young team. He said *if you won half of those games . . . if we can stick in those games and win half of them, all of a sudden, we're going to be a contending ball club. We'll have 18 more wins. And if every pitcher won one more game than they lost, we'd be 10 games over 500.* He had a way of making things simple but also making you think.

Gil Hodges was more than a manager—he was a father figure for me. I really fell in love with him as a person and as a leader and had a lot of respect for him. I used to think that I was the only guy he called into the office to talk to and teach—not criticize. He wasn't that kind of manager. He always said *to err is human, to make a mental mistake is not professional.* He was trying to teach us that we all possessed talent but that other winning teams used their brains and we needed to start using ours. We needed to think. We needed to prepare for situations that occur. So he taught subtly by suggesting.

He once called me in to his office after I was thrown out for trying to steal home. He said, *I'm just wondering what you were thinking when you tried to steal home.* And I replied, *well I got thrown out.* And he said, *no, no I understand you wanted to help and that would have tied up the game.* But then he asked, *why shouldn't you have done that?* And I thought of a few possible reasons. He asked me who was hitting when I tried to steal, and I told him it was Kenny Boswell. At first I thought that maybe because Boswell was a left-handed hitter, it was an advantage to the catcher, because the hitter wouldn't be in the way of his tag when I was coming from third base. But that's not what he meant. Instead he asked, *well how was he hitting?* And I said, *he was hot.* And he said, *well you should have let him hit.* And that was it. That was the lesson. He did this periodically, and it was handled very secretly. One of the coaches would come up to a player and discretely say, *Gil wants to talk to you.* So you'd go into his office and sit down with him, and he would question you. Afterwards I found out he did that with a lot of players. At the time I thought I was special, but that's just how he made you feel. He had quite an impact on every player on that team. He made the difference. He really did.

When we started out the '69 season, we weren't tearing up anything in the beginning. But then we got Donn Clendenon in the second half, a tremendous home-run hitter, and he changed things. For the first time we had the kind of player who could hit three-run homers, so that if we were losing a game by two runs, we suddenly had a winning chance. Before then we didn't have anyone like that who did it consistently. Other teams couldn't pitch around him, and so that gave us a different face. We started beating the western teams—San Francisco, San Diego, and Los Angeles—and in our history, we had never been able to win against those teams in previous seasons. About midway through in the summer, the sense was *we're in this,* we're beating people we never beat before. And suddenly we're watching teams play against us, making the mistakes that the Mets always used to make—mistakes that we were no longer making. And we were winning games two to one, three to two, and two nothing because of our pitching, which was now revered and feared by a lot of people. We had the big three—Tom Seaver, Jerry Koosman, and Gary Gentry. People still didn't take us seriously, because we'd never won in past seasons, but before they knew it, we were still there in the end, having won 38 of our last 49 games. We then stole the division from Chicago, but we had to beat Atlanta for the pennant, which we did. The media didn't think we had a chance against Baltimore in the World Series, because they had won before and were becoming a dynasty. But then they beat us in the first game and then never won another. Many things happened in that year that made it feel as if some kind of higher power was helping us—things just went our way, particularly the World Series.

The team in 1969 was different. You could really feel the camaraderie, and there was a lot of encouragement among the players. Guys would say *pick me up, come on, I struck out but you can do it.* And Gil Hodges was very positive in that little lesson he gave us in spring training. We wore shirts and ties and coats when we flew and that stuck with me. He said *we're not going to be a bunch of slobs walking through the airport and into the hotel.* So we had a dress code, and I don't remember it being that way until he got there. He expected professionalism and class, and that was okay. It makes you feel pretty good about yourself, having everyone dressed well together, because you have that uniformity. That sense of being a team. It's amazing what happens when you win—how the friendships solidify because you were in battle together and you won. You have this common ground and emotional feeling that this was amazing or a miracle, because no one expected it. In fact, Casey Stengel always said *the Mets will win when they put a man on the moon.* He was a real character and was just being comical, but sure enough, you know, in '69 they put a man on the moon. We actually watched that landing—we were stuck in the Montreal airport and it was on television, and the whole team was sitting there watching it together. We weren't on a plane, we didn't see it second hand, we were seeing it live and it seemed like this was all meant to be.

My closest friend on the team was Tom Seaver, and he's another reason we had such an extraordinary year. We were both from California, both went to triple A in Jacksonville, Florida, and both lived in the same complex. I got called up in 1966, one year before him. His rookie year was in 1967, and in that era when you were a first year player, you had to have a roommate when the team traveled. So when it came time to make the first road trip, they asked Tom who he wanted to room with and he chose me because I was the one guy on the team he knew from our days in Jacksonville. And that's how it started. We roomed together for about eight years, and we became like brothers. Even his wife Nancy called me Roomie. To this day, we still call each other Roomie. We had different schedules because I played every day and went to bed early, and he'd stay up late after he pitched a game. But I could sleep through anything—he could have had a party in our room and I wouldn't have heard it. We developed this brothership that has lasted more than forty years.

Many of us formed lasting bonds that year. Seaver, Grote, Nolan Ryan, and I went fishing a lot during spring training. We used to fish until midnight or one o'clock in the morning on a bridge, and we'd catch all of these silver trout. One night Ryan set his pole down, and we heard this rumbling noise from a boat, but we couldn't see where it was in the dark. And all of the sudden that fishing pole Ryan had placed against the side of the bridge just takes off! It caught us all by surprise, but it's a night we'll always remember now. Grote was in charge when we went fishing, so he'd clean the fish we caught and freeze them, and then we'd pick a night to have a big party, and we'd all throw in some money and bring some dessert, and Grote would cook all this fish. We all lived in the same area, so we could walk there. We had good times sitting there and talking and doing something together other than baseball.

In my memory, all the good stuff happened at Shea—we clinched the National League, we won the playoffs against the Braves, and we won the 5th and final game in the World Series. When we beat Atlanta the fans tore up the field, and when we triumphed over Baltimore they took the field. We were caught up in the moment. There's a picture of Gentry and Seaver, out on the field smoking a cigar after the fans left, and it looked like a bomb site. I left the field and went right into the family room and kissed my mom and brought my dad into the clubhouse. He sat down by my locker, and he was the proudest guy in the world. It was a miracle because if we hadn't won those three games at Shea, we would have traveled back to Baltimore for the final two games and he would have returned home and never seen us win the World Series.

Now the once majestic Shea Stadium is gone, replaced by a more modern ballpark with all the amenities. Some traditions are dying, and baseball has become less about entertainment and more about business. But home plate will still remain in the parking lot, so that people can envision where the original ballpark once held cheering fans and the sense of possibility and wonder. I was there on Closing Weekend to take down the number 4 and expose number 3, for the third to last game. There were about forty-five players who were invited to the Diamond Club that weekend from different eras. Some were from the original 1962 team, some were from 1973, but most were from the winning teams from 1986 and 1969. After the last game, we walked out onto the field and were introduced as they showed highlights from our careers on the Diamond Vision screen. And it was sad to say our goodbyes to Shea, to see this piece of history disappear, but also happy to see a new ballpark emerge. Then Seaver threw out a pitch to Mike Piazza, and we all touched home plate one last time.

Everything in baseball is historic if you win. But this was real history, us winning in '69. I think the whole world was rooting for us. I've won and lost as a coach, and I've won and lost as a player, but being a part of the Miracle Mets is the one thing I'll always remember.

—Bud Harrelson

INTRODUCTION

In today's world, celebrity is cheap and comes in many varieties, courtesy of cable TV, the Internet, and the scandal sheets. Hollywood has a refined process of producing, assembly-line style, its celebrities. But beyond this kind of superficiality lies true celebrity status. Few people of any type ever achieve it, even beyond the grave. It is a greatness that eclipses our definition of celebrity when somebody can become a larger-than-life figure in a country as big and full of swagger as America.

There are those lauded for their greatness in Mount Rushmore style—presidents during great crisis, generals in a desperate struggle, astronauts staking claims to space—but there is one very select group of uniquely American celebrity/heroes: the New York Sports Icons. Even this gaudy title does not tell the true story, for many athletes who play in New York City are superstars but do not rise to the heights of the true, recognized-by-history icon. To live in this rarified air, athletes must have achieved things above and beyond mere mortals. They must have done so in the most crucial manner

When Tom Seaver entered the pantheon of the New York Sports Icon, Mets coach Yogi Berra knew what he was seeing. *Brace Photos*

possible and risen to a place in the spotlight—the Arena, as Theodore Roosevelt called it—that minimizes all other accomplishments.

To understand this status, one must understand that very few non–New York athletes achieve this level. In Boston, Ted Williams took years to rise to this place in history, while Bill Russell, Carl Yastrzemski, and Roger Clemens never did. In California, Sandy Koufax did what Willie Mays and Barry Bonds did not. Most of the legends are regional in nature: college football stars at Southern California or Oklahoma; Tony Gwynn toiling away in obscurity in San Diego; Hank Aaron breaking records in comparable silence. A Michael Jordan, a Joe Montana: these kinds of figures achieving their bona fides without benefit of the Big Apple's stage are rarities. In fact, it is usually only when they are recognized by New York—cheering crowds at the Garden, "The Four Horsemen" of Notre Dame at the Polo Grounds, or on Madison Avenue—that the imprimatur comes to them. But New York Sports Icons achieve status in an almost religious manner; their moments in the sun say what words fail to accomplish. Theirs is a truth that, when witnessed in an American arena, is never misunderstood.

Who are these gods of the New Greece, gladiators of the New Rome? In the biggest city, on the biggest stage, the list is oh so short. The Chosen Ones are Christy Mathewson, Babe Ruth, Lou Gehrig, Joe DiMaggio, Jackie Robinson, Yogi Berra, Willie Mays, Frank Gifford, Mickey Mantle, Joe Namath, and Tom Seaver.

It is the list of those who are so close, yet do not make the cut that makes this group all the more impressive. John McGraw, Bill Terry, Mel Ott, Whitey Ford, Casey Stengel, Duke Snider, Walt Frazier, Willis Reed, and Reggie Jackson are just a few of the all-time greats, the Hall of Famers who have performed in New York City; achieved fame, fortune, and honor; yet remain ever so slightly below the hallowed shrines of Mathewson, Ruth, Seaver, and the rest.

Tom Seaver represents the crux of what makes this book so unique, so compelling, such a nostalgic memory of a town, a team, and a time that is no more. Records still get broken, but somehow the heroes of yesteryear stand above and beyond their successors, untarnished by steroids or, at least in the comparable mind's eye, greed. All that is left is the last of the true New York Sports Icons.

This is a book about not merely their one superstar, but a team that was one big, collective superstar.

Never had any single Yankees, Dodgers, or Giants team captured the imagination of the "city that never sleeps" as did the 1969 Mets. It has never come close to happening in all the years since. Never have the stars been aligned as they were that magical, miraculous summer and fall of 1969 in the greatest city in the world.

At the beginning of 1969 New York City and all it represented was in disarray, fiscally, politically, and on the baseball field: The hallowed shrines of Yankee Stadium and the modern Shea Stadium were both home to cellar dwellers in recent years. "Where have you gone, Joe DiMaggio?" sang Simon and Garfunkel. But then a modern Lancelot in the form of Tom Seaver rode forth to lead the New York Mets to heights above and beyond all glory, before or since. It was the biggest sports story of the 20th century.

This book tells the complete, unvarnished story of the greatest, most improbable tale in the history of American sports: the 1969 "Amazin' Mets" World Championship season. The Mets were led by that rarest of all American heroes, the New York Sports Icon. In a city that produces not mere mortals but sports gods, Tom Seaver represents the last of the breed. His deeds, his times, his town: It was part of a vanishing era, an era of innocence. In 1969, six years after John Kennedy's assassination, Seaver and the Mets were the last grasp at idealism before free agency, Watergate, and cynicism took over. Seaver's great status was that of half rock star, half political figure. Seaver and the Mets were a metaphor for a changing society, the "Age of Aquarius" confluence between blacks and whites during racially divided times, set against a backdrop so perfect it appeared to have been guided by the hand of destiny. Now we can reflect on the political, sociological, and racial views of the 1960s, all imbued by 40 years of experience in America during its most challenging times. It was Seaver and the Mets who stood astride issues such as Vietnam, free agency, and the "new breed" of athletes.

The Mets rode the whirlwind of fame and celebrity after the triumph of 1969, but many teammates were unable to maintain a steady course in their life and career. New York City is a town that builds 'em up to tear 'em down, and many fell victim to that reality. Incredibly, Tom Seaver never was torn down, staying at the top for 20 years, retiring to the broadcaster's booth, where his caramel-rich voice, smooth intellect, and veteran experience made him a popular, admired character to generations beyond his playing days; his teammates and team, however, met less kind fates.

This book is also a nostalgic look back at the hero machine that is New York City. There remain a handful of ultimate sports superstars who stand out in the Big Apple above all others. This book tells the story of how they got there, stayed there, or fell from grace. As times changed, it became virtually impossible for others to follow with Seaver in the footsteps of Babe Ruth, Joe DiMaggio, Mickey Mantle, Joe Namath, and the rest. The true New York Sports Icon may never be seen again.

—Steven Travers

Tom Seaver, here pitching to Johnny Bench in his dominating 1970 All-Star Game start at Riverfront Stadium, may be the greatest of all post-World War II pitchers.

John Rogers Archives

THE 1969 MIRACLE METS

1

"CAN'T ANYBODY HERE PLAY THIS GAME?"

You can play for the Mets. If you want rapid advancement, play for the Mets. We've got the bonus money. We'll even buy you a glove. So join us. Take the bonus money. Play a year or two. Then you can go back to school.

—Casey Stengel

The 1962 Mets were a force of nature. If there is any possible truth to George Burns's statement in *Oh, God!* that the 1969 Mets were his last miracle, then the '62 version was somehow struck by supernatural forces, too. It was a comedy of errors, of flukes, of crazy plays, players, and situations, almost defying logic, therefore lending credence to the notion that the deity got involved. Never has a team played so badly, and never has failure been so loved.

On June 17, 1962 Marv Throneberry was at first base when the Mets caught a Chicago base runner in a rundown between first and second. Throneberry ran into the runner without the ball in his possession and was called for interference. Chicago scored four times after that. When Marv came to bat in the bottom half of the inning, he hit a drive to the right field bullpen, pulling into third with a "triple" just as the umpire called him out at first for having missed the bag. Manager Casey Stengel came out to argue but was rebuffed by news from his own bench that Throneberry also missed second. In July the Mets were 6–23.

Throneberry had some power and four times hit a sign for a clothing company, who awarded him

Casey Stengel went from the most successful manager in baseball with the Yankees to skipper of perhaps baseball's all-time worst team.
Brace Photos

a $6,000 sailboat. Richie Ashburn was also given a boat for winning the team MVP award. Judge Robert Cannon, legal counsel for the Major League Baseball Players Association, told Throneberry not to forget to declare the full value of the boat.

"Declare it?" Throneberry asked. "Who to, the Coast Guard?"

"Taxes," Cannon replied, as in the IRS. "Ashburn's boat was a gift. He was voted it. Yours came the hard way. You hit the sign. You *earned* it. The boat is *earnings*. You pay income tax on it."

At season's end, Jimmy Breslin visited Throneberry in his hometown of Collierville, Tennessee.

"In my whole life I never believed they'd be as rough a year as there was last season," said Throneberry, who believe it or not at one time was considered a prospect with the Yankees. According to most accounts of his career, he was, if not a really good player, not a terrible one; not the "worst player who ever lived," or whatever moniker has been attached to him.

The "worst ball player" never made the majors, or even signed a professional contract. If such a player existed in the big leagues, he lasted one day, one inning, like the 3'7" Eddie Gaedel in 1951. He did not pick up big league paychecks for the better part of a decade, as Marv did. "Terrible" Mets pitchers like Roger Craig (10–24), Al Jackson (8–20), Jay Hook (8–19), and even Craig Anderson (3–17) were not that terrible. Roger Craig was in fact a very good pitcher, Jackson a genuine talent. The truth is, a man cannot last long enough to lose 20 games if he is that bad; he would be drummed out long before given the chance to compile such a record.

Throneberry's home in Collierville was at least 100 miles from anything resembling a sporting waterway, and the man was never going to be part of the "skiff off the Hamptons crowd," wrote Breslin.

"And here I am, I'm still not out of it," said Marv. "I got a boat in a warehouse someplace and the man tell me I got to pay taxes on it and all we got around here is, like, filled-up bathtubs and maybe a crick or two. I think maybe I'll be able to sell it off someplace. I think you could say prospects is all right. But I still don't know what to do about the tax thing."

It was that kind of year.

"We get to the end of the season, and I might need a couple of games to finish higher, and what am I going to get?" Stengel said. "Everybody will be standing up there and going, whoom! Just trying to win theirselves a nice boat while I'm sittin' here hopin' they'll butcher boy the ball onto the ground and get me a run or two. I don't like it at all."

Casey Stengel celebrated his 73rd birthday in a private party room at the Chase Hotel in St. Louis. He ordered a Manhattan.

Marv Throneberry was not the worst player ever, but he was a comedy of errors with the '62 Mets.

Brace Photos

"I've seen these do a lot of things to people," he said of the Manhattan. He smoked cigarettes and let his hair down, so to speak, with Jimmy Breslin. He spoke with trepidation of the Mets' initial visit to the brand-new Dodger Stadium. "We're going into Los Angeles the first time, and, well, I don't want to go in there to see that big new ballpark in front of all them people and have to see the other fellas running around those bases the way they figured to on my own pitchers and my catchers, too. [Maury] Wills and those fellows, they start running in circles and they don't stop and so forth, and it could be embarrassing, which I don't want to be.

"Well, we have Canzoneri [catcher Chris Cannizzaro] at Syracuse, and he catches good and throws real good and he should be able to stop them. I don't want to be embarrassed. So we bring him and he is going to throw out these runners.

"We come in there, and you never seen anything like it in your life. I find I got a defensive catcher, only he can't catch the ball. The pitcher throws. Wild pitch. Throws again. Passed ball. Throws again. Oops! The ball drops out of the glove. And all the time I am dizzy on account of these runners running around in circles on me and so forth.

"Makes a man think. You look up and down the bench and you have to say to yourself, 'Can't anybody here play this game?'"

Hours later, "the bartender was falling asleep and the only sound in the hotel was the whine of the vacuum cleaner in the lobby," wrote Breslin. "Stengel banged his empty glass on the red-tiled bar top and then walked out of the room."

Casey walked to the lobby, stopping to light a smoke.

"I'm shell-shocked," he told the guy working the vacuum cleaner. "I'm not used to gettin' any of these shocks at all, and now they come every three innings. How do you like that."

Roger Craig was a successful pitcher for Brooklyn before he came to the Mets. *Brace Photos*

No answer.

"This is a disaster," he continued. "Do you know who my player of the year is? My player of the year is Choo Choo Coleman, and I have him for only two days. He runs very good."

"This, then, is the way the first year of the New York Mets went," wrote Breslin, an old-time scribe whose clipped style was reminiscent of Ring Lardner (and Mark Twain before that), in *Can't Anybody Here Play This Game?* He went on:

It was a team that featured 23-game losers, an opening day outfield that held the all-time major league record for fathering children [19; "You can look it up," as Casey would say], a defensive catcher who couldn't catch, and an overall collection of strange players who performed strange feats. Yet it was absolutely wonderful. People loved it. The Mets gathered about them a breed of baseball fans who quite possibly will make you forget the characters who once made Brooklyn's Ebbets Field a part of this country's folklore. The Mets' fans are made of the same things. Brooklyn fans, observed Garry Schumacher, once a great baseball writer and now part of the San Francisco Giants management, never would have appreciated Joe DiMaggio on their club.

Bill Veeck announced that the 1962 Mets were "without a doubt the worst team in the history of baseball," claiming that he spoke with authority since his St. Louis Browns were the previous "title holders."

Technically, statistically, and by the record, he was right, but the '62 Mets were not the worst. Veeck's Browns had no name players, nobody worth remembering. The Mets had former big names like Richie Ashburn, Gil Hodges, Craig, Gene Woodling, and Frank Thomas. Over the hill, yes; but there is something not quite right about saying a team with so many onetime stars was the worst ever assembled. Sometimes, not so bad. Ashburn batted .306; Thomas hit 34 homers and drove in 94 runs. Then again, sometimes they sure looked terrible. In June, Sandy Koufax struck out the first three Mets on nine pitches, finishing with 13 Ks and a 5–0 no-hit win.

Certainly no team nearly that bad has been analyzed and talked about so much. Being in New York was part of that. Casey Stengel was part of it. But it went beyond these obvious factors. Sportswriter

Leonard Koppett said it was part of a larger social revolution, embodied by the new, youthful president, John F. Kennedy; the young taking over from the old.

"The times they are a-changin'," sang Bob Dylan.

The players poked fun at each other. There was much self-deprecation in the Mets clubhouse. When Ashburn won the team MVP award, he said, "Most Valuable on the worst team ever? Just how do they mean that?"

Other bits of Stengelese:

- "I don't mind my ballplayers drinking, as long as they don't drink in the same bar as me."
- "We have a great young outfield prospect. He's 22, and with a little luck he might make it to 23."
- "I was the best manager I ever saw."
- "I was fired more times than a cap pistol."
- "I want to thank all these generous owners for giving us those great players they did not want."
- "If I was winning, I'd play five games a day because you tend to keep winning when you are winning. But I had a chance to call this game, so I did. You tend to keep losing when you're losing, you know."
- "Everybody here keeps saying how good I'm looking. Well, maybe I do, but they should see me inside. I look terrible."

First baseman Ed Kranepool, a native of nearby Yonkers, spent most of 1962 in the minor leagues but got called up and hit .167 in his brief stint. He was only 17 years old.

Infielder "Hot Rod" Kanehl, a onetime Yankee prospect, hit .248. Married with four kids, he was one of those "record-breaking" fathers of multiple kids, supposedly something the '62 Mets did better than anything.

"He can't field," club president George Weiss told Casey.

"But he can run the bases," Stengel replied.

"But Weiss always wanted to get rid of me, and now he couldn't because I had become a hero in New York," said Kanehl. "All of New York was asking, 'Who is this guy?' and the front page of the

Ed Kranepool was a New Yorker and original Met.

John Rogers Archives

Daily News had a picture of Stengel pulling me out of a hat like a rabbit."

Kanehl was one of those strange hybrids of baseball: a Yankee farmhand who never made it there but became a household name, still fondly remembered, because he played for the Mets. It did not last long. A few years later he was playing for the Wichita Dreamliners against USC's Tom Seaver, then pitching for the Alaska Goldpanners.

"Even though we lost, we were still upbeat," said Kanehl. "And so was Casey, who was leading the parade down Broadway. A lot of people identified with the Mets—underdog types, not losers—quality people who weren't quite getting it together.

"In May we beat Cincinnati, and we beat the Braves at home, we were playing well, but then we went on the road and lost 17 games in a row. We sure could dream up ways to lose."

When the Mets were mathematically eliminated from the National League pennant the first week of August, Casey called a meeting.

"You guys can relax now," he told them.

The season ended, appropriately enough, with a triple play and a worst-ever 40–120 record. More than 900,000 fans attended Mets games at the Polo Grounds, a significant improvement over the attendance of the New York Giants, a team featuring such stalwarts as Willie Mays, playing at the same park in their last year (1957).

"It's been a helluva year," Casey remarked.

The 1962 New York Mets are still considered the worst team in baseball history. A close second might be the 1963 through 1967 New York Mets. Subsequent Mets teams lacked the hilarity, the lovable frivolity of 1962, but their sheer awfulness did not change very much.

Two years after Rod Kanehl was a "folk hero" of the original Mets, he was playing for the Wichita Dreamliners, facing Tom Seaver of the Alaska Goldpanners. Over beers one night he told Seaver he would be a big-league pitcher. *Brace Photos*

Nevertheless, being in New York had some benefits that by 1968 were beginning to manifest themselves. They were becoming something of a cultural icon. Playwright Neil Simon had a Broadway hit about a slob sportswriter who rooms with a neat freak. It was made into a film, *The Odd Couple,* in 1968. Walter Matthau was Oscar Madison. Jack Lemmon played Felix Unger. In one memorable scene shot in the press box at Shea Stadium, Madison stands between Heywood Hale

Broun and Maury Allen as Bill Mazeroski steps up to bat.

Broun: "Bases loaded. Mazeroski up. Ninth inning. You expect the Mets to hold a one-run lead?"

Oscar: "Whatsa matter? You never heard of a triple play?"

Felix Unger then calls the press box to tell Oscar not to eat any hot dogs at the game because he is planning "franks and beans" for dinner. The call diverts Oscar's attention from the field.

Broun: "A triple play! The Mets did it! The greatest fielding play I ever saw! And you missed it, Oscar. You missed it."

Oscar goes ballistic at Felix for wasting his time over such a thing as that night's dinner menu. It begins a series of tirades over Felix's pesty, neurotic ways.

There was nothing neurotic about the Mets in the 1960s. They were *Hair*, the "summer of love," and the Age of Aquarius all rolled into one—but they would ride to glory on the back of a 20-something ex-Marine from California who approached his job with the efficiency of a Wall Street banker.

2

THE REINCARNATION OF CHRISTY MATHEWSON

Seriously. There isn't a person in the world who hasn't heard of Tom Seaver. He's so good blind people come out to hear him pitch.

—Reggie Jackson

He was the "24-year old reincarnation of Christy Mathewson, Hobey Baker, and Jack Armstrong," according to sportswriter Ray Robinson. He was, according to some, "perfect." They were talking about Tom Seaver, Mets ace and latest All-American Boy. George Thomas Seaver was born on November 17, 1944, in Fresno, California. Everyone called him Tom, except his wife, Nancy, who called him George. Fresno in the 1950s and '60s may well have been the sports capital of America. It was a competitive environment, producing young kids who went on to great success on the diamond. Jim Maloney came out of Fresno to become one of the hardest-throwing strikeout pitchers in baseball, the ace of the Cincinnati Reds. Dick Ellsworth was another hard-throwing chucker who went to the Mets. The 1959 Fresno State Bulldogs made it to the College World Series.

The town did not merely produce baseball stars. Tom Flores was a quarterback hero who would star for the Oakland Raiders, later leading them to two Super Bowl titles as their coach. Daryle Lamonica followed Flores. After Notre Dame he became a two-time American Football League Most Valuable Player, quarterbacking the Raiders into the 1968 Super Bowl.

Seaver had a friend named Dick Selma. He and Selma were rivals throughout Little League, competing for star status, their teams for supremacy. It was an even rivalry until junior high school. Selma continued to grow. As he entered Fresno High School, he was reaching 6' in height with a muscular build. Tom was still 5'6" and 140 pounds as a high school sophomore. On top of this, Tom was by virtue of being born in November younger than most of his classmates, some of whom were born in January and therefore were almost a year older at a time when that year means everything in a kid's development.

"He was the runt of our crowd," Selma recalled.

Selma made the Fresno High varsity as a sophomore, a singular honor that separates a young man from the pack. Tom barely made the junior varsity. While Selma impressed the local prep media and professional scouts, Seaver remained a JV. To still be a JV in one's junior year, as he was, invariably means that one lacks the skills to go beyond high school if indeed he makes the varsity in his last try as a senior. Tom did not throw hard, but he was smart. He learned how to set up hitters, to change speeds, developing a curve and even a knuckler.

Seaver was knocked about in high school, but rarely when he arrived in the big leagues.

John Rogers Archives

"Tom was a hell of a pitcher, as contrasted to a thrower, even when he was on the JVs," Selma recalled when he got to the big leagues. "He knew how to set up hitters, and him just in high school, I'm still learning now."

High school sports success often dictates one's place in the social hierarchy. Being a career JV was a comedown after Little League stardom, but Tom had much more going for him. Despite his lack of size, he was a good-looking kid with an outgoing personality. Tom had easygoing charm and the gift of repartee. He was popular with teachers, with teammates, and most importantly with pretty girls. Above all other things, this is the prized attribute that determines a high school boy's place in the pecking order. He was a good student who decided he wanted to become a dentist.

"He was a real happy-go-lucky guy," Selma said. "He had a lot of friends, and he always dated all the good-looking girls."

In his senior year, Tom went out for basketball, mainly to stay in shape for baseball. He was determined that he would make the most of what looked to be his last year of athletic competition. He was a 5'10", 165-pound guard whose natural athleticism shone through. Surprisingly, he made the all-city team.

The scouts were out in force, but not to see him. Selma was on everybody's radar and would eventually sign with the expansion New York Mets for $20,000. Tom did manage to make it into the starting rotation. Still lacking any heat, he was effective enough, throwing off-speed pitches with control to win six games against five losses and a place on the all-city baseball team, "mostly because there wasn't anyone else to choose," he recalled. "When the professional scouts came around, looking over the local talent, some of the other kids got good offers. I didn't even get a conversation; not one scout approached me."

It was the beginning of the magical "summer of '62," the year depicted by filmmaker George Lucas, who grew up in nearby Modesto and would attend the University of Southern California with Seaver. The world Lucas showed in *American Graffiti* was the only one Tom Seaver knew. It was a unique central California culture of cars and girls. Tom Seaver's Fresno was not quite the Beach Boys' Southland surf magic, nor the brewing, dangerous mix of angry protest, harmful drugs, and unprotected sex that would have such ultimately devastating consequences in the Bay Area.

Tom had his heart set on USC, a private school with steep tuition costs and one of the best dental schools in the nation. He wanted to spare his father from fronting the money. A plan was hatched: instead of college after high school, he would serve in the U.S. Marines. He would save and earn some money, getting some help from the GI Bill. That would only assuage a little bit of the cost. A tiny voice in the back of Tom Seaver's mind would not go away.

What about a baseball scholarship?

This seemed to be a ludicrous proposition. USC had the best baseball program in the nation, led by legendary coach Raoul "Rod" Dedeaux. He had the choice of the best players. If a hot prospect did not wish to go directly into professional baseball, his college choices were basically USC, SC, Southern California, or Southern Cal; at least, it seemed that way. Dedeaux had no more interest in a junk baller from Fresno than the pro scouts who ignored him did.

Seaver graduated from boot camp, joined a Reserve unit, and by the fall of 1963 enrolled at

Fresno City College. For more than a year since high school, he had eaten three squares a day and done countless push-ups, pull-ups, and "up-and-on shoulders." As he got older, he had grown. During this time he had gone from 5'10", 165 pounds to 6'1", 195 pounds. He was a grown man, physically and mentally. He had not picked up a baseball since the summer of 1962, but he had a sneaking suspicion that when he did, he would be able to throw it harder than ever, and if so . . .

The impossible seemed to have occurred. Seaver's 11–2 record at Fresno City College earned the recruiting attention of Rod Dedeaux. He was a legitimate fastball artist. Dedeaux called him the "phee-nom from San Joaquin."

Seaver was sent to the Alaska Goldpanners for seasoning. Dedeaux called Goldpanners manager Red Boucher and inquired of several USC players on the Fairbanks roster. Boucher interrupted him to say that Seaver would be "your best pitcher." Boucher assured him that he would "bet on it," to which Dedeaux replied that the Alaska manager was so high on the kid, "I really don't have any choice."

Seaver had finally assured himself of the scholarship. He arrived at USC during a golden age on campus and in Los Angeles. That fall of 1964, quarterback Craig Fertig led the Trojans to a breathtaking comeback victory over Notre Dame, 20–17. USC's running back, Mike Garrett, would go on to become the first of the school's seven Heisman Trophy winners.

The actor Tom Selleck, a basketball, baseball, and volleyball star out of Van Nuys High School, was on campus. A few years separated them, but Seaver and Bill Lee were in the program at the same time. It was a dominant age, under athletic director Jess Hill the greatest sustained sports run in college history. Aside from Dedeaux's perennial champions, John McKay's football team won two national titles and two Heismans in the decade. The track, swimming, and tennis teams won NCAA titles with regularity.

Cross-town, John Wooden's UCLA basketball dynasty was just heating up that year. Big league baseball was in full swing on the West Coast. The Los Angeles Angels were an expansion team. The Giants and Dodgers had continued their rivalry in California. Sandy Koufax and the Dodgers sold out the beautiful new Dodger Stadium and won the World Series twice in three years.

The USC film school also became world class at that time. Two of its most famous students were in school when Seaver was there. George Lucas would create the blockbuster *Star Wars* series. John Milius wrote the screenplays *Dirty Harry* and *Magnum Force,* then directed *The Wind and the Lion* and *Red Dawn,* among many others.

The USC campus has always been conservative, fraternity-oriented, and traditional, but it was even more so when Seaver arrived. That fall, Republican presidential candidate Barry Goldwater energized a conservative movement based in nearby Orange County, embodied by Republican student politics at USC. Numerous USC (and UCLA) graduates made up the campaign and later administration staffs of Richard Nixon. Among them were Watergate figures H. R. Haldeman, John Erlichman, Dwight Chapin, and Donald Segretti. In the 1976 film *All the President's Men,* the Segretti character tells Dustin Hoffman, playing Carl Bernstein, about the so-called USC Mafia of that era.

Seaver's USC teammate Bill Lee got a taste of the stuck-up nature of social life on campus, which he described in his riotous 1984 autobiography, *The Wrong Stuff.* Lee was dating a beautiful sorority sister until movie star "Alan Ladd's kid snaked her away from me," presumably with a show of wealth.

Seaver enrolled as a predental student, joined a fraternity, and quickly made friends with Dedeaux's son, Justin. His Marine experience immediately separated him from the silly frat boys. He also befriended Garrett. This arrangement came to symbolize all that is righteous about college sports. Here was Seaver, the white middle-class son of an affluent business executive, "prejudiced" while in high school, paired with Garrett, the black inner city son of a single mother. Had they not been teammates at USC, these two never would have found each other. Instead they became the best of friends.

Garrett was an introspective young man determined to make the most of his opportunity. He had been an All-American at Roosevelt High School in Los Angeles and made his name on the football field, winning the Heisman Trophy in 1965 and helping the Kansas City Chiefs win the 1970 Super Bowl. Eventually, he graduated from law school and became USC's athletic director, where he hired the great Pete Carroll in 2000. Garrett was serious about baseball, too. He even took some time off from his NFL career to pursue the game in the Dodgers organization before returning to the San Diego Chargers in 1971.

"Mike was serious about things," said assistant USC football coach Dave Levy. "One time he and I got into a big discussion, and he expressed frustration that he could not rent an apartment in Pasadena because he was black. I just told him he needed to understand there were white folks of good conscience and that you had to let people change. I had discussions with black kids at USC, and I said they needed to take advantage of the educational opportunities that sports provided them. Mike came to agree with me."

"If you'd told me that a black kid from Boyle Heights would win the Heisman Trophy," Garrett said on the *History of USC Football* DVD (2005), "I'd have just said, 'You're crazy.'"

Seaver and Garrett were both intensely dedicated. They worked out together. Justin Dedeaux was amazed that Seaver could keep up with Garrett stride for stride running wind sprints. The Garrett–Seaver relationship also directly marks the beginning of a revolution in sports training, with profound consequences. Baseball players were told not to lift weights; that to do so would "tie up" their muscles, making them unable to throw and swing the bat. But Seaver had seen how much better he had gotten when he got stronger lifting boxes and later doing push-ups, pull-ups, and rifle exercises in the Marines.

Jerry Merz, a friend of Seaver's who studied physical education, recommended that Seaver lift weights to increase his strength. Garrett lifted weights for football, and Seaver asked him to help start a regimen, which he did. Seaver's stocky body responded to weight training, with immediate good results on the field. He would take his weight-training routine with him into professional baseball, influencing a change in the perception of weights in the 1970s. Over time, all baseball players would bulk up on weights, and eventually this led to the rampant use of steroids.

In 1965 Seaver worked hard to make it onto USC's starting rotation. Oddly, it was a down year for the Trojans, who finished 9–11, in fourth place behind conference co-champions Stanford and California, and one game back of cross-town rival UCLA. But Seaver was excellent, winning 10 games against only 2 defeats with a 2.47 earned run average, establishing himself as the undisputed staff ace. He was named to the all-conference team along with Garrett and Justin Dedeaux. A major boost in his confidence came in an alumni game when Seaver got Dodgers first baseman Ron Fairly, a former Trojan, to pop up on a slider. As Fairly ran past Seaver on the mound, he said, "Pretty good pitch, kid." Seaver had retired a big league hitter and allowed himself to dream big league dreams. (Three years later in the major leagues, Fairly connected on a Seaver slider for a home run.)

In June 1965 the very first major league draft was held. Rick Monday, an All-American outfielder for national champion Arizona State, was the number one pick. Because he had not gone into the Marines his first year after high school, the sophomore Seaver's college class was in its third year, making him eligible for the draft. Already, the strategy behind obtaining maximum signing bonuses meant that college juniors would get more, since they had the bargaining leverage of returning for their senior year. A graduated senior had to take whatever was offered him or go home, his eligibility gone.

His favorite team, the Los Angeles Dodgers, drafted Seaver. He and his USC pals regularly went to nearby Dodger Stadium on his uncle's tickets to watch the great Sandy Koufax pitch. Scout Tom Lasorda came around to negotiate. If Seaver had lacked any confidence before, making All-American at the National Baseball Congress, retiring Fairly, and compiling a 10–2 mark for the Trojans took care of that. Lasorda offered $2,000. Seaver came back with $50,000, arguing that Selma had received $20,000 from the Mets out of junior college, and he was a seasoned Trojan star. Lasorda came up to $3,000, but that was that. The tantalizing possibility of Tom Seaver forging a career on the great Dodgers teams of the 1970s would be only that, tantalizing.

"Good luck in your dental career," Lasorda told him.

In January 1966 a winter draft was held. Because of what eventually happened to Tom Seaver, the rules of the winter draft were later changed, but despite being in school, he was selected number one by the Milwaukee Braves, who were that year in the process of moving to Atlanta. Braves' scout Johnny Moore, who had seen 'em all in Fresno, arrived at the Seaver household in a Cadillac. When he left, Tom was $51,500 richer. He was a hot young prospect ticketed for the big leagues, where his teammate would be the great Henry Aaron.

No sooner did he sign with the Braves than he discovered the contract was invalid. USC had played a few early season games. A player could only sign prior to the playing of games on the spring schedule, and the Trojans always got off to an early start. Seaver would have to wait until the June draft, but he was not disappointed. He would pitch for Southern Cal. Then the NCAA declared he was ineligible since he had signed a pro contract. He was like Ko-Ko in *The Mikado,* caught in the middle of a "pretty state of things," wrote his biographer, John Devaney.

Finally, Baseball Commissioner William Eckert got involved. It was decided that a "lottery" would be held. Any team willing to match the Braves' offer could enter it. Three teams—Philadelphia, Cleveland, and the New York Mets—did just that. The Dodgers wanted in, too, but general manager Buzzie Bavasi was so consumed in contract talks with Sandy Koufax and Don Drysdale, both holdouts that spring, that he forgot to get the team's name in. For the second time, the Dodgers passed up a chance to get Tom Seaver.

The Mets were selected, and Seaver reported to Homestead, Florida, where their minor leaguers were well under way for spring training. The experience was extraordinary for him. Four years earlier, he had been less than a "suspect": a warehouse "sweat box" lifter and a lowly Marine recruit with drill instructors screaming in his face. Year by year

Nolan Ryan as a Met. Had he reached his potential in New York, he and Seaver would have been the greatest pitching combination of all time.

John Rogers Archives

things had gotten better for him: junior college ace, proving himself with the Alaska Goldpanners, "big man on campus" at USC; now a bonus baby and, a few months later, married to the beautiful Nancy Lynn McIntyre.

The guy who could not make the Fresno High varsity until his senior year found himself trailed by curious glances and murmurs at Homestead. "That's the guy from USC." "That's Seaver; they paid him over 50 grand." Bud Harrelson, Jerry Koosman, and Nolan Ryan were all in camp, but Seaver was singled out for the special treatment accorded to the most important prospects. It was dizzying, but Seaver had "class," according to Harrelson, who said that despite his place at the top, the bonus baby did not put on airs or try to show anybody up.

Most players start out at class-A ball and have to fight for years to move up the ladder. The combination of Seaver's college record, bonus money, and the team's lack of success meant that he started at triple-A Jacksonville, Florida. Manager Solly Hemus, who had seen a few in his long baseball career, declared him "the best pitching prospect the Mets have ever signed," then paid him the ultimate compliment: "Seaver has a 35-year-old head on top of a 21-year-old body. Usually, we get a 35-year-old arm attached to a 21-year-old head."

Seaver was teammates with Dick Selma at Jacksonville. Immediately he had success and was ticketed as a "can't miss" prospect who would be in the major leagues soon, maybe even in September. He led the team in victories and strikeouts. He was given the nickname "Super Rookie," or "Supe" for short. His future was secure when Hemus said he reminded him of Bob Gibson. When most minor league pitching prospects get hit, they are removed so as to protect their gentle psyches. Hemus realized Seaver had the mental toughness of, well, a 35-year-old. When his rough patches came, as they always do, Hemus kept him in to gain from the experience.

The roughest patch came off the field, when the "wizened" wives and girlfriends of the Jacksonville players set the naive California girl Nancy straight on the notorious sexual habits of ballplayers. Tom assured her of his commitment to her, but her mind was filled with dreadful thoughts.

After a heavy workload at Jacksonville, the Mets decided not to call him up in September. Seaver and his new bride returned to Los Angeles, where he was now just another student at USC. Suddenly Seaver saw a new future in baseball and began to think about broadcasting on the side. He transferred his major from predentistry to public relations. Instead of living near campus, notorious for being near a high crime zone and at that time only a year removed from the nearby Watts riots, Tom and Nancy now lived in upscale Manhattan Beach.

In 1967 Seaver entered spring training amid speculation that he would be a starting pitcher. Had Seaver not been with the lowly Mets, he probably would not have made it to "The Show," as the majors are referred to, as quickly. He would have started out at single-A or double-A ball, then worked his way up. Instead, he did start as a rookie in 1967. In truth, he was as ready as can be. Manager Wes Westrum not only put him in the starting rotation at the beginning of the season, he was talked out of starting him on opening day only out of caution.

The Mets were as bad as ever in 1967, only now they were just terrible, not funny. The old Casey Stengel stories, the wacky "Marvelous Marv" Throneberry antics, were gone. Now they just lost. Seaver was appalled.

"I was not raised on the Met legend," he said. He had no affinity for any of that stuff. Despite being a rookie, he quickly ascended to a position of leadership on the club. When teammates laughed at their ineptitude, he refused to let them get away with it. Once, when Mets players were fooling around in the dugout during a game, Seaver found some spiders nesting in a corner. He scooped them all up and threw them at the offenders, telling them to wake up and pay attention. His attitude would have been taken exception to, except that he was so shockingly good. It earned him immediate respect.

Seaver's work ethic was legendary, his concentration and seriousness unprecedented in Mets history. He was immediately successful. When his brother, Charles Jr., a New York City social worker, visited a client, he saw a poster of his brother hanging in his tenement apartment. It was an era before ESPN, and the lowly Mets were not on national TV very much. Cincinnati's Pete Rose openly wondered who "the kid" was at Gallagher's, a New York steak house, when he saw an out-of-place Seaver sitting at a table by himself. Told who he was, Rose then made the connection. This was the guy who beat his Reds, 7–3, on June 13.

He sure looks young, but the kid's got a helluva fastball.

Against his hero Henry Aaron, Seaver induced the slugger into a double play, but he was almost in admiration of his opponent when Aaron adjusted later and hit the same pitch over the fence. Henry told him he was "throwing hard, kid." He "stalked" Sandy Koufax at the batting cage when the now-retired legend was in town as a broadcaster. When Koufax recognized who he was, Seaver was taken aback but pleased.

Seaver earned a spot on the National League roster for the All-Star Game, played near his college stomping grounds, at Anaheim Stadium. This meant more embarrassed mistaken identity. Cardinal superstar Lou Brock thought he was the clubhouse boy and asked him to fetch a Coke. Seaver dutifully did that, but Brock had to apologize when he was informed who he was.

In the game, Seaver came on in extra innings to retire the American League, saving the National's 2–1 victory. On the season he was 16–13 with a 2.76 ERA, easily garnering Rookie of the Year honors. His 16 victories came with little offensive or defensive support from the 10th place Mets. He easily could have won 20 games in a year in which the great pitching aces of the era—Koufax, Gibson, Don Drysdale, Juan Marichal—were retired, hurt, or slumped. Mike McCormick, a journeyman southpaw with the Giants, won the Cy Young Award, but in truth he did not pitch better than Seaver.

The Tom Seaver of 1967–1968 was still developing. In the beginning, he was considered a sinker/slider pitcher whose fastball was excellent but not nearly at the level of such heaterballers of the time as "Sudden" Sam McDowell or Bob Gibson. But the late maturation process that began when he entered the Marine Corps had not reached fruition. His hard work and weight lifting paid off, and by late 1968 Billy Williams of the Cubs told teammates "he brings it" after being set down by him.

Catcher Jerry Grote was a hard-nosed Texan who whipped the Mets' young pitching staff into form.
John Rogers Archives

Tom and Nancy took to the New York scene feet flying. If ever a "sports couple" was seemingly born for the Big Apple, it was the Seavers.

"Nancy and I love this town," Seaver told sportswriter Maury Allen. "We walk around Manhattan, up Fifth Avenue, past Carnegie Hall, down Broadway. We want to get to the [Metropolitan] Museum of Art and the Museum of Natural History on our next day off."

Seaver felt a natural intellectual curiosity, fueled by his surroundings. The literary nature of New York society did not escape him. He read books by John Steinbeck, who had written of the central California that they both grew up in. Steinbeck's vision of California was much different from Seaver's easy affluence, but Tom had an inquiring mind and absorbed all of it. He read books about politics, satire, and the classic baseball history book *The Glory of Their Times,* which allowed him to realize that he was part of something bigger than himself; that being a New York baseball star was special over and above playing in other cities. He had respect for the game and its traditions, and to Mets fans number 41 began to represent the sort of idol Whitey Ford and Mickey Mantle meant to Yankees supporters. They chanted "Seav-*uh*" as he mowed hitters down at Shea Stadium.

Seaver studied opponents and maintained detailed scouting reports. His dedication was total, but he also smiled and joked around. He was the quintessential "fan" living the fantasy of playing in the major leagues. Almost all big leaguers were high school superstars who took their ability for granted, strutting around like they owned the place. Seaver was still pinching himself. Not only was he privileged to wear the uniform, he was the ace of the staff. On a bad team he was a "stopper" whose victories ended losing streaks.

"There was an aura of defeatism about the team, a feeling of let's get it over with," Seaver recalled. "I noticed that the team seemed to play better when I pitched but . . . that wasn't right, and I said so. I probably got a few people mad, but I went around and told the guys that if they did that for me and not for somebody else, it was wrong."

"When Seaver's pitching, these guys plain work a little harder," noted catcher Jerry Grote.

"You notice his concentration out there on the mound when he's pitching," said Bud Harrelson. "And playing behind him, you try to match it."

His performance in the All-Star Game not only filled him with pride and confidence, but inspired him to try and instill that same attitude in his teammates. He became the undisputed leader of the young Mets. After one dismal game he stood on a stool and stated: "Gentlemen, after watching that performance, I would like to take this opportunity to announce my retirement from the game of baseball." If he pitched well but lost for lack of support, he took the weight of defeat on his own shoulders.

"I just don't feel I'm pitching as well as I can," he lamented. "A mistake here . . . a mistake there . . . they add up. You wonder when you're going to come on and start eliminating the mistakes."

He was a perfectionist, a trait he inherited from his father. It applied to every aspect of his life: the way he dressed, the way he conducted his marriage, his life. He expressed admiration at the art of his brother Charles, who in addition to social work was a sculptor. Tom admired the sense of perfection in the work that seemed impossible to obtain in the messy, up-and-down competition of baseball. Still, each game he came out hoping for a perfect game, something Sandy Koufax had done. Koufax once said that he wanted a perfect game until the first man reached base; a no-hitter until the first hit; a shutout until the first run . . .

He made no excuses just because he was a rookie. He handled every aspect of his business, not just pitching well but fielding his position, showing some pop with the bat, and cheerleading on days he did not pitch. The older Mets were replaced more

Tom Seaver's first pitching coach was Harvey Haddix, who once pitched a perfect game into the 12th inning for Pittsburgh. *Brace Photos*

and more by youngsters who emulated Seaver's professionalism.

"For the first time maybe," Seaver told a *Sport* magazine reporter years later, "we realized that we had guys who cared deeply whether we achieved, that we had pitchers who could hit occasionally and who wanted to win so desperately. Looking back I think it was the first time in my experience with the Mets that we believed in each other, the first time I felt that that I wasn't here to lose."

Pitching coach Harvey Haddix marveled that Seaver absorbed his lessons, did not need to be told something twice, and analyzed his performances thoroughly. On road trips, he sat with Mets broadcasters Lindsey Nelson and Ralph Kiner, figuring he someday would be doing that, too. He never tailed off, as so many young hotshots do when the league figures them out, or they lose the psychological edge. In fact, Seaver in 1967 established a trait he maintained throughout his career: a strong finish. After winning the Rookie of the Year award, he said it was "nice," but added the unthinkable: "I want to pitch on a Mets' pennant winner and I want to pitch the first game in the World Series. I want to change things . . . the Mets have been a joke long enough. It's time to start winning, to change the attitude, to move ahead to better things. I don't want the Mets to be laughed at anymore."

Announcer Ralph Kiner was a former slugger known for his malapropisms. *Brace Photos*

In 1968 Gil Hodges took over as manager, and the complexion of the Mets began to change. Some of those youngsters who Seaver first met during spring training in 1966 were breaking into the big leagues. Jerry Koosman, Tug McGraw, Bud Harrelson, and Nolan Ryan were the face of the "new Mets." An incredible amount of optimism surrounded the club throughout the winter and then spring training. Considering how bad they had been, it seems to have been misplaced. Considering what they did just a year later, maybe not so much. The ultimate optimist was Seaver, but Hodges was a winner as a Brooklyn Dodgers star, a fan favorite and one of those guys who were not so far from earning status in the true New York Sports Icon fraternity. He expected to win, too.

For Tom Seaver, 1968 was another year of great success matched by frustration. Outside of the superhuman Gibson, he pitched as well as anybody else in the league, but if the 1967 Mets had failed to support him, they looked like the "Murderers' Row"

Yankees compared to the 1968 version. Seaver said they owed the rest of the staff as much as they had given him but did not mean that they metaphorically skip town on his day to pitch.

He again appeared in the All-Star Game. In August his desire for perfection almost came to fruition when the Cardinals' Orlando Cepeda broke up his bid for a perfect game in the seventh inning. It served to whet his appetite for one. He won 16 against 12 losses, with a 2.20 ERA and 205 strikeouts. There was a distinct improvement in his velocity as his body grew in strength. Seaver dominated the opposition and could have won 20 or even 24 games in 1968, but the Mets were abysmal behind him.

They hit .228 as a team but gave Seaver even less. Over one 11-game stretch, his ERA was 1.91, but opposing pitchers were 1.72 against New York bats, when they scored a mere 19 runs overall. Seaver's record during that period was 2–5.

Off the field, Seaver visited Vietnam vets in the hospitable. Nancy was a self-confessed "liberal," opposed to the war. Seaver still had the Marine experience drummed into his being, but he questioned America's involvement. He read enough and understood history, so he realized that appeasement fails. The true horrors of Communism had not been fully revealed, either. But for now, Seaver was aghast at the loss of American life, the suffering of the wounded.

He gave his time to crippled kids, leaving the hospital with tears streaming down his face. Seaver was a Christian, but he kept his religious views private. He had a deep social conscience, understood that he was a role model, and knew from having admired hero-ballplayers himself what an impact he had on their young lives. Over the years, as he saw how those he thought were his friends really just wanted to get something from him, he would shut down somewhat, become wary, but in 1968 he was still a wide-eyed idealist who thought he could change the world.

Seaver's good looks and charm; his adorable wife; his college pedigree and athletic talents were by the end of the 1968 season reminding some old-timers of another New York mound icon, Christy Mathewson. Mathewson had come off the Bucknell campus and electrified baseball in the early part

Bob Gibson and Tom Seaver were the two preeminent pitchers of their era, and as division rivals they engaged in fierce battles with many brushback pitches. *Brace Photos*

of the century. The similarities between Matty and "Tom Terrific," as he was being referred to, were striking.

Despite the Mets' batting woes, there were hopeful signs. Rookie of the Year Jerry Koosman got the support Seaver did not. He also made the All-Star Game, winning 19 against 12 losses with a 2.08 ERA. The southpaw from Minnesota threw almost as hard as Seaver. Jerry Grote also made the All-Star team. With good young pitching, New York finally lifted themselves from 10th to 9th place with a 73–89 record, which, despite a second half slump, was reason for celebration among their supporters. But Seaver, Hodges, and the young team found no reason to jump for joy over a below .500 season. They had their hopes set on bigger and much better things. However, Hodges suffered a late-season heart attack in 1968. His availability was in doubt when the season ended. Somebody wished Seaver luck the next year; hopefully more run support.

"So much depends on number 14," Seaver said of 1969. Fourteen was Hodges's number.

3

HIGH HOPES

I have a dream.

—Dr. Martin Luther King Jr.

High Hopes" was Frank Sinatra's campaign song for John F. Kennedy in 1960. Indeed, JFK's high hopes came true, but so much had occurred in the star-crossed decade that followed; no pundit, no prophet, no political scientist could possibly have painted a picture describing the changed, topsy-turvy, tragically beautiful world that followed. The cataclysmic differences between 1960 and 1969 mark the great social upheaval in American, and possibly world, history. Perhaps only wars have brought about such change, but even that is arguable.

The year 1969 dawned, and with it high hopes that change was in the air. So much had gone wrong that it seemed there was no place to go but up. Richard Nixon was sworn in on January 20. He was a Californian but, like so many of New York's greatest sports stars over the years, was also a bona fide New Yorker. He had taken a job with a "silk stocking" Wall Street law firm in 1963 and lived in a fancy East Side building that also housed Nelson Rockefeller. His New York connections paid off when the Empire State gave him the electoral votes he needed to win the presidency.

Now America looked to him to extricate the country from Vietnam. The Right wanted him to turn up the heat militarily, forcing the Communists to capitulate. The Left knew that Nixon had established diplomatic ties with Soviet leaders like Nikita Khrushchev. They hoped he could arrange a deal with the Russians that would benefit everybody, the result being American withdrawal with honor.

New York had particularly high sports hopes for 1969. Something was in the air. Aside from having a quasi-New Yorker in the White House, the city was enthralled with the Jets. On January 12 "Broadway Joe" Namath engineered the seminal event in NFL history, a 16–7 upset of Baltimore. Mayor John Lindsay attached himself to the team, leading the over-the-top celebration when they returned from Miami. It had been such an upset, such a miracle, and was so full of magical serendipity, that all things seemed possible. Namath and the Jets embodied the very essence of change, in sports and in society. So influential were the key players in the Jets' saga that there was a sense, unrealistic as it may have been, that they could do anything. In this regard, it went beyond the playing field. They could affect society. They could help *end the war.*

Ex-New York Giant Wes Westrum managed the Mets before Gil Hodges was hired prior to the 1968 season. *Brace Photos*

Despite Seaver's Rookie of the Year performance in 1967, it had been a year of reversal, a 10th place finish after ending up 9th the previous season. Wes Westrum was fired. During the World Series between the Boston Red Sox and St. Louis Cardinals, a plan was hatched to attract Gil Hodges, then managing the Washington Senators, to the Mets. When approached, Hodges expressed an interest, and why not? He had done a good job in Washington, but the Senators were not threatening to become contenders any time soon. Hodges was, of course, a Brooklyn icon, and it was the Dodgers whose memories were most closely associated with the early Mets. He had married a Brooklyn girl, lived in the borough during his playing days, shopped in the stores, sent his children to the schools, and worshipped in the local church. After accompanying the Dodgers to L.A., he had returned to New York with the Mets in 1962 and 1963. Despite having lost all his skills, he was a fan favorite. Gil was one of the game's all-time gentlemen and good guys, but as a manager he was no pushover. He seemed to be just right for the times, the kind of man who could handle the modern player. A deal was worked out with New York sending a prospect who never panned out and $100,000 to the cash-strapped Senators. Hodges was the Mets manager for 1968.

"The ownership, Donald Grant, Herbert Walker, and Luke Lockwood, quickly came to me and said, 'We want you to do whatever you want to do, but we would like you to take a long look and think about Gil Hodges,'" recalled Bing Devine of

Whitey Herzog took all the credit for the Mets' success before becoming manager of the Cardinals. *Brace Photos*

his last move with the Mets before going back to St. Louis.

The deal was effectuated in large measure because Devine's assistant, Johnny Murphy, and Washington GM George Selkirk were old Yankees teammates. Murphy took over as the Mets GM. According to Whitey Herzog, a member of the Mets front office at the time, *he* was the man who got things done.

"When [Devine] left the Mets, they made John Murphy the general manager," said Herzog. "John was a fine man, but his nickname was 'Grandma'—he just couldn't make a decision. That was fine with me, since I moved in to make all the tough ones for him. . . . He let me run the organization pretty much as I wanted."

The outspoken Herzog told writer Peter Golenbock that M. Donald Grant "was a stockbroker who didn't know beans about baseball but thought he did. I've run into guys like Donald Grant a lot in my career, and everywhere they show up, they're trouble."

"All of us knew Gil, knew who he was and what kind of ballplayer he had been," said Bud Harrelson. "He brought credibility to the team as soon as he arrived. Because he had come from the American League, he kind of just let us play in 1968 and didn't presume he knew everything about the league and the Mets. But you always knew he was in charge. Gil was a big, strong man, and I don't think anyone wanted to find out how strong."

Ed Kranepool symbolized the "old Mets." He had been there since the beginning. A high school wunderkind and local product, Kranepool had gone through the motions for six years before Hodges arrived. He had little incentive to do much more than that. The team was bad, if not outright comical. Little was expected of anybody. Hodges inspired him that maybe he could experience true excellence before hanging up his spikes. He also sensed that the fans were ready to close an old chapter and start a new one.

"I always felt that New York fans were and are the greatest in the world," he said. "They were always knowledgeable, and by 1967 last place wasn't fun anymore." When Hodges came on the scene, "it wasn't a matter of just showing up anymore . . . so many guys were so used to losing that they had negative habits. It's contagious."

Ed Kranepool, who symbolized the "old Mets," was a casual guy who some said did not take his career seriously enough. *John Rogers Archives*

Longtime American League journeyman Ed Charles had a last chance to win with the '69 Mets.
John Rogers Archives

Ed Charles was a veteran of the American League, where he had seen Hodges operate. He had just a few good years left and had never been with a winner.

"Hodges changed the losing mindset," Charles said in *Miracle Year: 1969 Amazing Mets and Super Jets* by Bill Gutman. "He was an upfront type of manager, very knowledgeable about the game, very firm in what he expected from the players. He told us when we were out there he expected 100 percent effort. If we couldn't give it because of a physical reason, he wanted us to tell him, because he wouldn't put us on the field."

This required a level of trust and team sacrifice that was unusual for ballplayers. Seaver, for instance, told his manager when he was tired instead of fibbing so he could stay in the game past the point of effectiveness. It was a fine line that some could perceive as a lack of guts, but Hodges knew Seaver left it all out on the mound. His drop-and-drive pitching style required a level of fitness, strength, and endurance like few others. The two developed a rapport that quickly became mutual respect.

The young 1968 Mets drew well but were totally overshadowed by the Jets. Young players Bud Harrelson, Jerry Grote, and Ron Swoboda improved. Young pitchers Nolan Ryan, Dick

Selma, and Jim McAndrew showed promise. Veterans Phil Linz, Al Weis, Art Shamsky, Don Cardwell, Ron Taylor, and J. C. Martin gave the team stability. Cleon Jones looked to be on the verge of stardom. His childhood pal from Mobile, Alabama, Tommie Agee, came over from Chicago. Agee hit .273 with 22 home runs and 86 RBIs in 1967, swiping 44 bases for manager Eddie Stanky's "Go Go White Sox" as they battled for the pennant until the last week. But in the "Year of the Pitcher" (1968), Agee was overwhelmed. His .217 batting average, 5 homers, 13 stolen bases, and 17 runs batted in were pathetic.

Seaver and Koosman dominated on the mound. Koosman, a native of Minnesota, had signed in 1964. Without the college polish of Seaver, he took longer to develop but had come up at the end of the 1967 campaign. Nobody could have predicted his 19-win, 2.08 ERA performance in 1968. Despite winning three more games, Koosman said, "I probably wasn't on the same level as Seaver." There was no sense of rivalry between the right-handed Seaver and the southpaw Koosman, other than healthy one-upmanship. Koosman was happy to let Seaver take the lead as the "face" of the team. He was not the kind personality who needed extra attention.

Bud Harrelson specialized in "little ball."

National Baseball Hall of Fame Library

Hodges had played for Casey Stengel with the Mets, and even though the Dodgers teams he starred on had a "set in stone" lineup, he became a disciple of Stengel's platoon system. It was a matter of necessity, especially in the offensive doldrums of 1968. Swoboda clashed with the manager, but most saw its benefits.

"When Gil got there, I was coming off my best year in 1967, thought I had arrived as a major leaguer, and probably thought I was a little more important than I should have," Ron Swoboda recalled. The young outfielder was headstrong but introspective. He rubbed some people the wrong way and was irritated by others, but he had the ability of discernment: to study things, learn from his faults, and admit his mistakes. "I was never cool with the platooning," he said, "but in the end Gil proved that he knew what he was doing."

Smooth southpaw Jerry Koosman appeared to be Cooperstown-bound in 1968–69.
National Baseball Hall of Fame Library

The Mets finished in ninth place with a 73–89 mark, one game better than Houston in 1968. It was a tremendous improvement over all previous Mets teams, but the high hopes of individual players still looked unrealistic entering 1969. The lack of offense seemed to be impossible to overcome. After Seaver and Koosman, the only pitcher with a winning record was Cal Koonce. Tug McGraw had seemingly lost ground. Nolan Ryan was a project like the pyramids or the Tennessee Valley Authority. However, on September 24, 1968, Hodges suffered a heart attack on a hot day in Atlanta. It was mild. The consensus was that he could return in 1969.

Ron Swoboda held out but reported to St. Petersburg and signed by March 1. Swoboda had tried to entertain the writers at the New York Baseball Writers banquet by allowing a straitjacket to be placed on him, which he would then wiggle out of, Harry Houdini style. Swoboda never got out of the straightjacket and had to be extricated backstage.

Swoboda, known as "Rocky," was brash, outspoken, and articulate. His honesty got him in trouble on more than a few occasions. He and Seaver clashed.

"Seaver had Hall of Fame written on him when he walked into camp and pitched his first game in '67," Swoboda said. "He was a finished product when he came there. I don't ever recall the sense of him being a rookie. He came out of the box a big league pitcher, and there was this golden glow about him. This was clearly *big* talent, intelligent, capable, controlled, and awesome stuff."

But they were not "tight." Swoboda admitted he said some things he should not, that he would have been "smart had I hung around Seaver." Seaver and Harrelson were "California guys," and Seaver came from "a different socioeconomic level," which apparently rankled the blue-collar Swoboda. Plus Seaver was "a younger, more aware person" than he was.

Swoboda debuted with the 1965 Mets, as did Tug McGraw and Bud Harrelson. He found himself on the roster after Paul Blair, a major prospect, was left unprotected, snatched up by Baltimore. Casey Stengel first saw Swoboda when he was at the University of Maryland in 1964. He hit a ball over the center field fence at Miller Huggins Field in St. Petersburg, a feat never previously accomplished by a Met.

Swoboda *was* blue collar as a player with a blue-collar background. Perhaps he was not a baby boomer statistically (having been born in 1944 in Baltimore), but he was one in reality. In the past, a guy like Swoboda might have been a boxer, a heavy on the docks, but in the new postwar sensibilities, he found himself in college. He was bright and observant yet headstrong.

His dad—"my hero," Swoboda called him—was a World War II waist gunner on a B-29 at Tinian, a hot spot in the South Pacific theater. After the war the elder Swoboda went into the automobile business. He had done some boxing and passed on the toughness to Ron, who admitted that there were times it was necessary to "go out there to bust somebody's head."

Swoboda's story is emblematic of why so many players come from the West, where the weather is good and the programs are excellent. In Maryland, he played a total of eight games his senior year at Towson High School. When he floundered at some curve balls, he figured that was it; he did not have the stuff.

Rough-hewn Ron Swoboda was something of a "bull in a China shop." *John Rogers Archives*

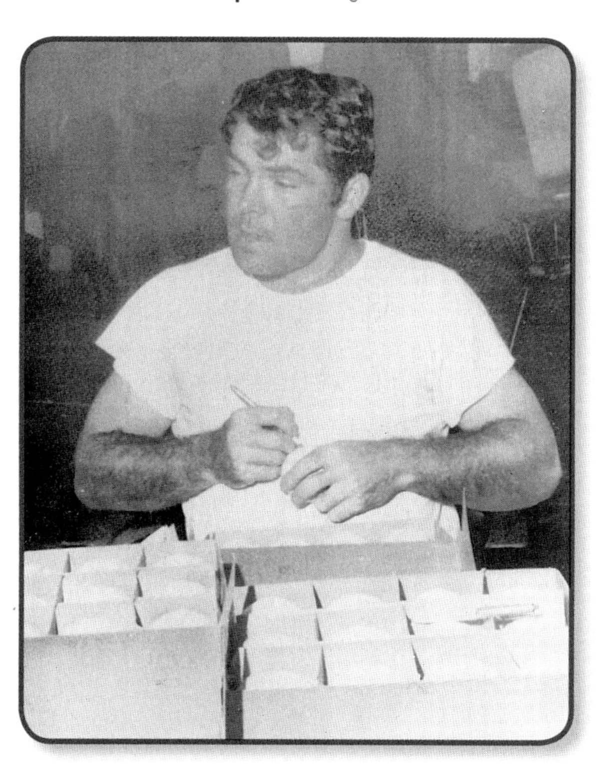

He went to the University of Maryland and was given some baseball money, but mainly he had to work his way through. He met his future wife, Cecilia, and in the summers played for a legendary Baltimore semipro outfit called the Leone Boys Club, sponsored by an Italian restaurant called Mama Leone's. Featured years later in *Sports Illustrated,* it was run by a local man named Walter Youse and offered the kind of organized baseball that Tom Seaver was playing with the Alaska Goldpanners. Reggie Jackson was another of the many top players who emerged from the program, which was so good college coaches sent prospects from all over.

It was with the Leone's club that Swoboda improved and was scouted, becoming a bonus prospect. The Mets offered him $35,000. Swoboda was savvy enough to realize he could shop around and get more, but this was around the time that Casey Stengel was inviting the "youth of America" to come play for the Mets. It was well known that players could get to the major leagues faster with this organization than any other. It was the reason Swoboda signed with New York and played no small role in the club's eventual success.

While still a minor leaguer, Swoboda hit a home run in an exhibition game in which the catcher was Gus Triandos, a big name in his hometown of Baltimore. Triandos had worked at a car dealership in the off-season and gotten to know Swoboda's father, who had invited him to be a dinner guest at the Swoboda home.

"This was pretty heady, pretty awesome," Swoboda said of the experience.

Swoboda impressed people and quickly moved up to triple-A Buffalo, where the team played at War Memorial Stadium. It was "the most depressing place I have ever walked into," Swoboda recalled. "It looked like a prison. . . . The only thing missing from the clubhouse was bars." This was two decades before it was chosen for its decrepit appearance in *The Natural,* starring Robert Redford. It also became the site of some of O. J. Simpson's greatest exploits with the Bills.

During a road trip to Richmond, Virgina, Swoboda observed "the black guys and the dark-skinned Latinos"—Pumpsie Green, Choo Choo Coleman, Elio Chacon, and others—get off at another motel. It opened Swoboda's eyes. He had grown up in Baltimore, a "border city" just a half hour from Washington, D.C. Baltimore

Choo Choo Coleman was one of those early Mets who for some reason seemed comical. *Brace Photos*

was notorious for its Confederate sympathies during the Civil War. The motel incident reminded him that Baltimore was de facto segregated, but he had "never thought to ask why." Occasionally, white teams played black teams. On the sandlots there was mixing, with no trouble; but there were schools for whites, schools for blacks. A white section, a black section. It was not like Alabama, with "white only" drinking fountains. It was subtle, almost subversive. Now Swoboda had minorities who were teammates, friends, and it hit him hard that "this was 1964," the year President Lyndon Johnson got the Civil Rights Act going, yet here this was happening.

As a kid, Swoboda had been saved from a beating by three white kids when some blacks intervened, for reasons he never figured out. He was taught "you have no right to look down on anybody. You respect everybody." Before becoming the big, tough "Rocky" of big league fame, he had been a sensitive kid, picked on at school, and felt a kinship with the downtrodden.

He did not make a big deal of the segregated motel incident, but he filed it away in his memory. If he would ever have the chance, he wanted to effectuate change. The "youth of America" Casey Stengel called for would include a number of these kinds of fellows: young, race-neutral whites, enlightened beyond the previous generation. The Mets of the 1960s, run by blue bloods—Yalies like George Weiss running the front office and Herbert Walker a minority owner—saw the future.

Just as the Yankees and Brooklyn Dodgers featured star players from California who gave their teams a certain personality, so too did the Mets. Seaver was the star from USC, and his best friend was the skinny guy from Hayward, California, Buddy

Tug McGraw was half Dennis Hopper, half Hank Williams, and all Northern California. *Brace Photos*

Harrelson. But neither of these guys had "California personalities," at least not in the goofy, "hey, dude" beach boy stereotype. Seaver was all business, like a Wall Street executive. Harrelson was less corporate, but he was quiet and serious. But another stereotype had long existed: the flaky southpaw.

In this case it was Frank "Tug" McGraw. He broke into the big leagues with a splash, beating Sandy Koufax in a head-to-head match up at a time when Seaver was fighting to make the starting rotation at Southern Cal. McGraw was the next big thing before Ryan or Koosman, but in the spring of 1969, he had fallen behind all those guys. Even rookie Gary Gentry was ahead of him. McGraw had been a starter but not gotten it done, so now he was in the bullpen. In 1969 the best pitchers were starters. The castoffs were relievers. Oakland's Rollie Fingers was a tremendous prospect as a starter. It was years before young stars were brought up as closers.

McGraw was from Vallejo, California, just across the Carquinez Straits from Rodeo, where another flaky southpaw, Lefty "El Goofy" Gomez, had been born. Vallejo is 25 miles north of San Francisco and just a short drive east of Marin County, a place that in the swingin' '60s was the swingin'est. Marin was, at least according to mythology, the home of hot tubs, peacock feathers, key parties, swingers, cults, alternative sex styles, classic porn, drugs, infidelity, and the nouveau riche. Both San Francisco and Marin, which looked across the northernmost part of the bay at Vallejo, were close geographically yet light years away psychologically, financially, socially, and aesthetically.

It was as if the "planners" of the Bay Area, one of the most beautiful natural locations, as well as architecturally with its bridges, skyline, and unique, diverse communities, found the most desultory place and said, "Put Vallejo there." The hills were bare, the few trees lacked the splendor of the rest of the area, the bay was marshy there, and the wind blew cold.

The Buckner brothers came out of Vallejo. Bill was a star with the Dodgers, star-crossed in Boston. His sibling, Jim, was a career minor leaguer. McGraw also had a brother, Hank, who was good but not as good as Tug. McGraw and Buckner were the odd mixture of laid-back West Coast types, yet kind of from the wrong side of the tracks. They both liked to party and loved the ladies, had the looks, but were just a little lawless. McGraw enjoyed a good bar fight. He was just crazy enough to get after guys bigger than he was.

Every guy who ever played minor league baseball played with Tug McGraw. Every guy who ever served in the Marines served with Tug McGraw. He was a type. You remembered this type. He got the chicks, was usually adept at pool, drank a lotta beer, and was crazy. He probably rode a chopper. You did not mess with him, but he was cool. He was not serious enough to succeed, and you later found out he returned home and now tended bar, worked construction, or maybe even moved to Vegas to become a male gigolo. Only *this* Tug McGraw, against all odds, it sometimes seemed, was destined to make it.

"He was California all the way, man, full of these different expressions about things," said Swoboda. "He had about four or five different words for [breasts], you know, very much a California personality." Swoboda simply thought the guy had spent too much time in the sun, a typical put-down of the California player over the decades. McGraw simply *had fun*. Seaver, in contrast, loved baseball, but it was a job, a career.

"I'm going to work now," he would tell his wife, Nancy, as he left the Greenwich, Connecticut, spread he eventually bought.

McGraw's nickname came from his mother, who called him her "little Tugger" when she was breast-feeding him. His old man was a firefighter, apropos in that the son became the baseball version of one. After Tug's father hurt himself, he took a nightshift job with the water department so he could watch his kids play ball.

McGraw went to St. Patrick (now called St. Patrick-St. Vincent) High School, where he drove the nuns crazy. He was 4'11" as a freshman, weighing in at 98 pounds, but if somebody tried to take him on, he was all fists. He was mainly a showboat, though, who sought attention, trying to impress the girls, cracking wiseacre jokes, and being a general brat. Because the pitcher's mound was the center of attention, that was where Tug wanted to be. The coach, Father Feehan, put him in center field. It was not quite the same dynamic as the famed Brother Matthias–George Ruth relationship at St. Mary's Industrial School for Boys, but it was what it was in Northern California of the late 1950s and early 1960s. Father Feehan was virtually blind and did not notice when Tug and teammate Bobby Hay, a pitcher who wanted to play the outfield, switched jerseys. Tug became a regular starter as a junior, while the scouts turned their attention on his talented older brother Hank, a catcher.

In 1961 Hank signed with the expansion Mets for $15,000 and paid off the old man's debts. Tug finished up at St. Vincent's and moved on to Vallejo Junior College. He had no business playing football at his size, but this guy was Evel Knievel in cleats until he suffered a cracked vertebra and a concussion. He no doubt had never heard of the German philosopher Friedrich Nietzsche, who famously said, "What does not kill me makes me stronger," but the crazy Tug lived by that creed. Recovered from the football injury, he tried to do a flip onto a hayloft, missed, and was out the first five weeks of the baseball season. He was the anti-Seaver, the controlled guy who had a careful plan and stuck to it at another J.C. about 200 miles south of where McGraw was at that time.

Finally, McGraw returned to the mound and found his body had matured, and with it his fastball. The St. Louis Cardinals wanted to see him play against fast competition, so they asked him to go to a collegiate summer team in Canada, not unlike the one Seaver played on in Alaska. His coach was Ray Young, who ran Stanford's program. McGraw received $300 for some nonexistent job and was made fun of by sophisticated college teammates when he asked what "prime rib" was. Strong Canadian beer and Canuck farm girls occupied his attention more than pitching, which was not enough to impress St. Louis into signing him at the end of the summer.

As a sophomore at Vallejo J.C., he led the team to the state championships but was knocked around in the finals. St. Louis lost interest. Tug McGraw was not exactly four-year college material, so it was time to "fish or cut smelt." He called up Mets scout Roy Partee, who had signed Hank, and told him he wanted to be part of the team's "youth of America" movement. After a tryout, he was given $7,000. Over the next year, something happened not unlike what was going in with young Seaver. No longer 4'11", 98 pounds, McGraw filled out, put some hop on his heat, and impressed the right people in the New York organization. With any other team, he would have languished in the bushes for years, but under Casey Stengel's plan, opportunity came aknockin'. By 1965 he was pitching at Shea Stadium. For Casey Stengel.

"He was talking and jabbering away, to nobody or anybody or everybody, even to me, and it was a blast just meeting him," McGraw said of his first impression of the "Ol' Perfesser."

Beating Sandy Koufax in his rookie year (1965) got him attention, but over three years he was spotty. It was obvious he was not ready for major league competition and could easily have lost confidence in himself. In 1966 he pitched poorly at Jacksonville. Seaver, Koosman, and Ryan were all in the organization, stealing his thunder. But in instructional league, he developed the out pitch that saved his career. Ralph Terry, a onetime 20-game winner for the Yankees, taught him how to throw a screwball. Even though Carl Hubbell and Christy Mathewson had been Hall of Famers using the "fadeaway," as it was called in Matty's time, Mets coach Warren "Sheriff" Robinson told him to concentrate on his curve and control.

In 1967 he had a poor spring. Desperate, like Gaylord Perry when he went to the "spitter" against the Mets in the famed 23-inning game of 1964, McGraw made a last-ditch effort to master the scroogie, resulting in a 10–9 record with a 1.99 ERA. In a call-up to New York, however, McGraw and Wes Westrum did not react well to each other, and he did not get the chance to shine.

Westrum was an old school baseball man, cut out of the Leo Durocher cloth; a Giant on the 1951 team who could not relate to the young player, circa late 1960s. McGraw was a hayseed, a Hank Williams song, but nevertheless he was definitely of the "new breed."

Thinking he could be released and out of baseball at any time, McGraw looked for other career opportunities. He apprenticed at a barber shop in the Bowery, cutting the hair of bums and the homeless. Despite the smell, he got something out of it. He certainly was no aristocrat. Seaver, for all his hoary phraseology about not judging another man who seemed to be below him in societal rank, never would have cut dirty hair. Seaver's friends were people he perceived as working hard to get where they were, like Mike Garrett at USC. But despite the obvious differences, Seaver found something to admire in McGraw; the little guy who learned an out pitch, a screwball, and used it to get back to the big leagues.

But in 1968 McGraw got into it with longtime Mets coach and organization man Sheriff Robinson. Older brother Hank did the same thing, ending his career. Entering 1969, Tug was an unknown quantity. The team was still not convinced his screwball was a big league out pitch. He had more arm problems, but would stick.

Some years ago, I was an assistant baseball coach at the University of California. We went to Wichita, Kansas, for the NCAA regionals and played Baylor in the first game. During batting practice, fellow assistant Bob Ralston and I approached Baylor coach Mickey Sullivan, an old-timer, and introduced ourselves. In the course of that conversation, Coach Sullivan said he had scouted Nolan Ryan as a Texas prep. We expressed that Nolan must have been a Lone Star State legend like Ken Hall, the famed "Sugar Land Express," who garnered a huge retrospective in *Sports Illustrated,* which anointed him the "greatest high school football player of all time." Not so, said Coach Sullivan.

"He threw about 86 miles an hour," he said to our surprise.

The Mets were a team of disparate characters and personalities: the "golden boy" (Seaver); the rough edged "Rocky" (Swoboda); the hybrid surfer/gun rack dude (McGraw); the quiet gentleman (Nolan Ryan), among others.

Ryan hailed from a small town called Alvin, Texas (which teammates said was so tiny it did not have a "last name"). If he threw only 86 miles an hour there, after signing with the Mets, he was seemingly touched by the hand of God. In the entire history of the game, before or since, nobody has ever thrown as hard as Nolan Ryan. His speed was miraculous, going from average in Alvin to marvelous in Marion (1965) within a matter of weeks; then great in Greenville (1966), where he was 17–2 with an astounding 272 strikeouts in 183 innings. His spectacular heat elevated him all the

Southpaw fireballer Jerry Koosman took a roundabout way to New York, but by 1969 was one of the most promising young stars in the game.

John Rogers Archives

way to New York's Shea Stadium at the end of the 1966 campaign.

In 1967 and 1968, however, Ryan exasperated the Mets, resulting in minor league demotions or down time resulting from inconsistency, military service, or injury. His teammates called him "the phantom" because his mound appearances were so few and far between, but when he did take the hill, he could throw a baseball through a car wash without getting it wet.

"He just blew everybody away," said Rich Wolfe, who roomed with Ryan's minor league teammate Shaun Fitzmaurice at Notre Dame. Wolfe followed Ryan closely in September 1966, when his friend Fitzmaurice and Ryan were called up to the big club together. They went to games at Shea Stadium. Ryan started against the Braves. Superstar third baseman Eddie Mathews stepped into the box and saw the first pitch whiz past him. He looked at catcher Jerry Grote, uttering a swear word in reaction to it.

Ryan had a big, high kick, long stride, and straight-over-the-top delivery. Eventually, he modified it, apparently influenced by Seaver. He developed a hesitation/tuck of his knee to his chest, dropped to get full use of his legs, and went to more of a three-quarter-arm deliver. His control eventually improved. But with the Mets he was wiry and wild as a March hare.

Even though he had a good attitude, Ryan did not have great work habits. Apparently, nobody had really emphasized physical conditioning to him. He was lazy less out of a lack of desire and more because he did not seem to know better. Some thought he was "too nice." It was a mean era. Books such as *Ball Four, North Dallas Forty,* and *Semi-Tough* portrayed rough 'n' tumble athletes who liked to drink, swear, chase women, and disdain authority. Ryan was quiet, reserved, religious, and on a team of young studs let loose among the fleshpots of Manhattan, happily married to his lovely childhood sweetheart with the biblical name of Ruth. In this respect he had more in common with the family man Seaver than the wildman McGraw.

Swoboda first saw him pitch a bullpen session in an empty Astrodome. He said the sound of Ryan's fastball smacking into the catcher's glove sounded like "shooting skeet." Apparently the Astrodome had pigeons, and a maintenance man would clear them out with a shotgun. It sounded like that.

Catcher John Stephenson once took a Ryan fastball directly on the chest protector, which was designed to withstand high-velocity baseballs. He was out three weeks. Ryan was a highball pitcher, though, and the National League was still considered a low-ball strike zone.

Ruth Ryan could not handle New York. Nolan was equally intimidated. They never socialized, which for the most part meant drinking; not their gig. He had the respect of teammates because he was real. His ways were his, and Ruth's. They did not look down on others who liked to get out and about. The Seavers, while not party animals, were more social, visiting museums, the opera, and other highlights of the Big Apple. The Ryans were not up to that.

As the Mets prepared for the 1969 season, many felt it was a "make or break" year for Ryan. His incredible fastball was already being compared to the likes of Walter Johnson, Bob Feller, and Sandy Koufax. Not even Seaver and Koosman, who threw heat, were in his league. If this guy could reach his potential . . .

Jerry Koosman was another country boy who had escaped the kind of attention that Dick Selma and Tom Seaver got in scout-heavy Fresno, or Nolan Ryan in talent-laden Texas. The weather was so cold in Minnesota that by the time kids really got out on the field, school was almost out. Koosman's high school did not even have a baseball team. If a community did not have a big time American Legion program, local players could be overlooked. It was hockey country.

Koosman came out of Appleton, where he was born in 1942 to a farming family. When not tending to livestock, he played some semipro baseball before going to college to study engineering prior to getting drafted in 1962. Stationed in nondescript places that did not feature baseball teams, he came home on leave. What happened next was perfect timing for Koosman and eventually the Mets.

He went for his annual dental exam. Koosman's dentist was Bob Miller, who just so happened to be the commanding major general of the Minnesota National Guard (he was neither of the Bob Millers who pitched for Casey Stengel, one of who whom answered to Nelson). Koosman asked him if he could help transfer him to a unit that had a baseball team. In order to effect the transfer, Koosman

Jerry Grote, along with Tom Seaver and Jerry Koosman, had made the 1968 National League All-Star team. *John Rogers Archives*

Owner Joan Whitney Payson with manager Gil Hodges. *John Rogers Archives*

needed to test for Officer Candidate School because the base Miller had the power to transfer him to was part of the Fifth Army out of Texas. It was a helicopter unit with the best baseball team in the Southwest. Koosman would need to be a warrant officer in order to train to be a helicopter pilot. As an engineering student, he had the aptitude.

At some point, Koosman's pitching skills became apparent, and he claims his orders were changed from helicopter training to "play baseball down there," which he did for 17 months. He later told Peter Golenbock that Bob Miller saved him from flying choppers. Those guys all went to Vietnam with a poor rate of survival, since they had to hover in sight of the Viet Cong, shooting at them while boarding wounded and evacuees.

The serendipity did not end there. His catcher on the Army team was the son of a Shea Stadium usher. Through that connection, scout Red Murff was sent to see him pitch. With the draft and a war brewing, so many young men were in the Army that it was worthwhile to scout the military teams looking for nuggets . . . like Koosman.

He signed on August 28, 1964, in anticipation of an October discharge. Koosman went to college that fall and reported to Homestead, Florida, in 1965, but impressed nobody. Pitching in the Army was not the kind of pedigree that made a guy stand out. But Frank Lary, the famed "Yankees killer" of the Detroit Tigers who always seemed to have the Bronx Bombers' number, was the Mets minor league pitching instructor. He taught Koosman a slider. Like McGraw's screwball, it would make him a major leaguer.

At Auburn of the New York–Penn League, he had a startling 1.38 ERA. Suddenly, he was a prospect instead of a suspect. His teammate was Steve Chilcott, a catcher who was the number one pick in the entire 1966 draft. According to Reggie Jackson, a collegiate superstar at Arizona State, the Mets chose the white Chilcott because Reggie "dated a white girl," which Reggie found amusing since she was actually Mexican, and he was half-Spanish himself. Chilcott threw his arm out at Auburn and never made it. Jackson as a lifelong Met conjures numerous enticing scenarios. Another hot prospect on that club who never panned out was 6'5" pitcher Les Rohr.

After a brief big league debut in 1967, Koosman was sent back to Jacksonville for more seasoning. He pitched well and earned a return to New York during the September roster expansion. Wes Westrum liked Koosman but was fired shortly after his arrival. Gil Hodges took over in 1968.

"Looking back, he was feeling the club out and learning the organization," said Koosman. Koosman's first start in 1968 at San Francisco was postponed because of Martin Luther King Jr.'s assassination. Instead, he debuted with a 4–0 shutout of Los Angeles at Dodger Stadium. The series in L.A. symbolized a subtle change; the Dodgers were no longer dominant, and in 1968 they were little better than New York.

Rookie pitcher Gary Gentry came out of the same program at Arizona State that produced Reggie Jackson, Sal Bando, and Rick Monday of the A's.
John Rogers Archives

In Houston, Hodges used the entire staff in a 24-inning loss to the Astros, 1–0, when a ground ball to Al Weis took a bad hop. The next game at Shea Stadium, Koosman was for all practical purposes the only available pitcher. When he loaded the bases against San Francisco in the first inning, it looked like a long afternoon. Koosman simply overpowered Willie Mays, Jim Ray Hart, and Jack Hiatt, all dangerous hitters. Ron Swoboda's mouth just dropped seeing it. A star was born.

Koosman ran his scoreless innings streak to 21 against Houston in a 3–1 win. Largely because of his tremendous mound work, the press started to think unthinkable things early in 1968, although the club's offense was so dismal that it could not be overcome.

Koosman befriended Ryan, "a farm boy from Texas, and I'm a farm boy from Minnesota, and neither one of us was comfortable in New York," said Koosman. "It was way out of our realm of upbringing. Neither one of us was used to the lifestyle. Going from the farm to New York City, I don't know of any other extreme a person could have as a young person. Look at the change in the pace of life. You go from the farm to the tension and the crowd, something neither one of us was used to."

Seaver was "a friend." Younger than Koosman, Seaver's worldliness always made him seem older. "He was a college graduate [actually, Seaver went to USC every off-season for years and did not get his degree until well into the 1970s], well spoken, well read, a man who handled himself real well with the press."

Koosman's description of Jerry Grote was the same as Ron Swoboda's: "red ass," but "he'd fight tooth and nail 'til death to win a ball game."

Grote controlled the pitching staff like a Marine drill instructor. The staff seemed more concerned with earning his respect than anything else. If Grote respected you, everything else was in order anyway.

The Mets played above their heads until the 1968 All-Star break. Seaver, Koosman, and Grote were all selected for the game in Houston, and they returned riding high. But the Mets slumped in the second half of the season.

Koosman pitched the day Hodges had his late-season heart attack, almost blaming himself for getting knocked out in the sixth inning, as if that caused the seizure. Koosman, who did not play in high school or college, had experienced real success for the first time under Hodges and was very concerned that "Number 14," as they called him, would not be back in 1969.

Koosman's 19–12 record with a 2.08 ERA was even more spectacular than Seaver's support-deprived 16–12 with a 2.20 ERA. However, he did not repeat as a Rookie of the Year winner, as Seaver had been in 1967. Cincinnati's Johnny Bench earned the award, apparently when a writer in Chicago named Enright split the decision, giving it to Bench by half a vote.

Gary Gentry brought a 150-pound St. Bernard with him to spring training.

"Mrs. Payson [Joan Whitney Payson, majority owner and president of the Mets] doesn't have enough dough to feed that thing," Johnny Murphy said kiddingly.

Gentry was a rookie trying to make the staff. Spring camp was his chance to prove himself. When the players struck at the beginning, it was a real shock to the system, and to the fans, who had never fathomed such a crazy notion. Gentry needed the whole spring to make his impression. But while other young pitchers sweated out the strike, costing a couple weeks of preparation, he never seemed to worry.

Gentry was tall, thin, and threw heat. He was a high school phenom, but his father, a schoolteacher, wanted him to go to college before signing a professional contract. After turning down suitors from Baltimore, Houston, and San Francisco, Gentry went to Phoenix Junior College, and from there a scholarship to baseball powerhouse Arizona State. He played for coach Bobby Winkles right after the Sun Devils won the 1965 College World Series behind Sal Bando and Rick Monday. Gentry was right behind Reggie Jackson, who was a year behind Bando and Monday. In 1969 ASU would win their second national championship.

Gentry was 17–1 with two victories in the College World Series. His gaudy record, however, was an indication of something amiss in the Arizona State program. Over the years, a number of Sun Devil hurlers have compiled big records like Gentry's: 17–0, 19–1, and the like. Winkles and later coach Jim Brock tended to overpitch their aces. Many promising Sun Devils experienced arm troubles and did not enjoy as much big league success. Gentry, who did not use his legs as Seaver and Koosman did, would experience arm problems later, but in 1969 he was young, strong, and seemingly carefree.

Gentry had been given a nice bonus by the Mets in 1967, progressed nicely through the minor leagues, and at 22 was seen as the 1969 version of Seaver and Koosman. The press took to calling him "the new Tom Seaver." It was a big expectation, and he had competition, namely from Ryan, but Gentry was loosey-goosey about it.

Jim McAndrew was a bundle of nerves, but not Gentry. A code of machismo, established by Seaver, ruled the Mets' pitching ethos. Seaver was

Gentry, like many of his teammates, looked too young to compete in the rough 'n' tumble world of the major leagues. *John Rogers Archives*

no gentleman on the hill. In a league without designated hitters, he was willing to go after batters, incurring the wrath of such opposing "head hunters" as Don Drysdale and Bob Gibson. In one legendary encounter, Gibson and Seaver retaliated against each other with wicked fastballs that, if landed in the wrong place, could kill a man. Seaver threw a 99 mile an hour fastball that seemingly split the difference between Gibson's skull and his batting helmet.

"I know you got better control than that, Tommie," Gibson said to the glaring, unsmiling Seaver. Respect had been earned.

McAndrew was called "Moms" because he lacked the fire of Seaver, Koosman, and now Gentry. Ryan was still working on this part of his makeup. He would not achieve his potential until embracing it.

Being tough was "an important thing," Swoboda said. Pitchers often are at either one end of the spectrum or the other. If they are good, they are the most respected players on the team. Good pitching stops good hitting, it is 90 percent of the game, and if a team has it, they are given the opportunity to win. On the other hand, bad pitching can ruin the best efforts of an otherwise good team. The blame game is an easy one to play in a clubhouse. A pitcher needs to display a "gunslinger" mentality, like a quarterback in the huddle during a two-minute drive. Gentry was a cowboy, and it came naturally to him.

"His stuff was every bit as good as Seaver's," said Swoboda. This was quite a statement. "He had just as live an arm."

Swoboda, in order to keep his reflexes sharp, would go to the bullpen and spell the bullpen catcher. When he caught Gentry's fastball, it simply exploded with a wide variance of movement. Plus, "Gary was this western guy who just wasn't afraid of anything," said Swoboda. "He was a cowboy, a skinny kid with a tremendous arm. He was great."

On the mound, Gentry challenged hitters inside, or up and out over the plate, daring them with his great movement and tremendous velocity. He came straight over the top, his ball exploding on the home plate zone, resulting in broken bats, "blue hammers" (jarring pain to the hand and fingers when the ball makes contact with the low end of the stick), and checked-swing strikes.

Fans often do not understand the true nature of the big league hurler, the kind of stuff a talented young pitching ace possesses. Television does not accurately depict it. Most seats in the ballpark do not reveal it. Only those right behind home plate, or behind the dugout near home plate, see the real thing. It can be awe-inspiring, leaving the fan in admiration of anybody who has the courage to stand in against it without fear, much less *hit it.* Of all athletes—dunking forwards and majestic passing quarterbacks, among them—the hard-throwing pitcher may be the most magnificent figure in sports.

Here Gentry is seen clicking his heels, an act that mocked the Cubs' Ron Santo, who made it a practice after Chicago victories. *John Rogers Archives*

The Mets had four of the best: Seaver, Koosman, Gentry, and Ryan. Now, to harness all that talent.

While few things are given less notice than big league exhibition games, the Mets did beat the defending World Champion Detroit Tigers, 12–0, and the defending National League pennant winning Cardinals, 16–6. The thing most people watched that spring, however, was Hodges. He appeared to have made a complete recovery from his September heart attack, writing an open letter to sportswriter Red Foley stating, "I've never felt better."

"Most of the guys had a philosophy similar to mine," Tom Seaver wrote of the mindset going into 1969, in *The Perfect Game.* "Maybe they didn't articulate it, but deep down they shared my attitude. I wanted to be the best ballplayer, the best pitcher Tom Seaver could possibly be. Jerry Grote wanted to be the best catcher Jerry Grote could be, and Cleon Jones wanted to be the best outfielder Cleon Jones could be, and Bud Harrelson wanted to be the best shortstop Bud Harrelson could be.

"If each of us achieved his goals—a reachable, realistic goal—individually, then we could all reach our team goal, no matter how unrealistic, no matter how impossible it seems to outsiders. . . ."

That spring, Seaver, Grote, Harrelson, and Ryan bonded on regular fishing trips under Bayway Bridge in St. Petersburg, a retirement community and longtime home of spring training teams. Occasionally, they were joined by Hodges, who had

Spring training for the Mets in 1969, as with all teams every year, was about fundamentals.
John Rogers Archives

been advised by doctors to lose weight and get more exercise, which he endeavored to do by trying to stop smoking and making the trek down to Bayway Bridge with a pole and some shrimp bait.

Sipping coffee or beer, the young Mets philosophized and predicted. There was bravado, perhaps unrealistic expectations of their own chances, and some put-downs of the competition. Pittsburgh, a perennial contender, had problems. Philadelphia was not strong. The Expos were the "old Mets," as far as they were concerned. Durocher's Cubs were seen as the main competition . . . for second place. St. Louis was the prohibitive favorite.

"You know, we could win our division if we play up to our potential," Seaver dared to say.

It was the first time such a thought was uttered. That spring, Seaver continued to analyze the Cardinals, comparing players and pitchers, noting the Cardinals' loss of Roger Maris to retirement and Orlando Cepeda to the Braves. He logically assumed that there was no way Bob Gibson could be as good as he had been in 1968. Gibby was the reason the mound had been lowered.

Agee had to avoid major batting slumps, such as the brutal 30 at bats without a hit he endured early in 1968, sending him on a downward spiral. "This is a guy who hit .270 as a rookie," Seaver assessed. "He showed he can hit 20 home runs and better."

Jones was coming off a .297 campaign, but Seaver noted that he batted .360 in the second half. Jones would need to be the anchor for Agee, his pal from Mobile. The other guys needed to be on: draw walks, bunt, get hit by pitches, steal bases, and generally make things happen.

Hodges began to talk about 85 wins. Seaver called himself "The Supreme Optimist with that touch of reality," almost an Age of Aquarius kind of attitude. "The Supreme Optimist thinks we'll finish second in the Eastern Division of the league," Seaver told Joe Durso of the *New York Times,* not wanting to overdo Hodges. "Maybe third, but more likely second. The only team we can't catch is St. Louis. The only team we have to fight off is Chicago. But we can beat Pittsburgh, Philadelphia, and Montreal."

This no doubt resulted in a few guffaws in Pittsburgh and Philly. In the final game of spring training, the Mets drove Cardinals pitcher Ray Washburn, a longtime nemesis, off the mound early to win a game the Cardinals probably could care less about. It was treated enthusiastically by New York. Seaver gave up two hits in seven innings, looking like a world beater.

Hodges had a coaching staff made up of veteran baseball men.

Rube Walker "was one of the best pitching coaches," Art Shamsky wrote in *The Magnificent Seasons.* "He was a player's friend, too."

Walker had been Roy Campanella's backup in Brooklyn, unfortunately behind the plate when Bobby Thomson hit the "shot heard 'round the world."

Eddie Yost had been known for scratching out bases on balls with the Washington Senators. Yost was a collegian from New York University, a thinking man's baseball player. Yogi Berra was "dumb like a fox," according to Shamsky, who realized he had arrived because "Yogi now knew my name."

The best news as spring training broke was Hodges's health. He had rested four weeks after

Mets pitching coach Rube Walker.

John Rogers Archives

Coach Eddie Yost (right) was called "the walking man" when he played for Washington.
John Rogers Archives

his heart attack before resuming his duties in the warmth of Florida, where the Mets had an Instructional League squad. He gave up smoking and dropped from 225 to 201 pounds.

Computers had been around at least since the 1930s. By the 1960s, they were popularized in science-fiction magazines, in movies like *Dr. Strangelove,* and by NASA. A computer was used to analyze data and predict the outcome of the 1969 baseball season. Among its findings was one surprise. The Mets were rated second best in the National League defensively, Seaver and Koosman virtually at the top on the mound; and, according to the computer analysis, if New York scored 100 additional runs, they would win 100 games and the Eastern Division. The "wild card" was their 36 one-run losses of 1968, a fact already analyzed by Gil Hodges.

As the 1969 season was about to get under way, two distressing reminders of the year that was 1968 reared their ugly heads. In a Los Angeles courtroom, Sirhan Sirhan admitted killing Robert Kennedy. James Earl Ray pleaded guilty to assassinating Dr. Martin Luther King Jr., then retracted his plea, opening up myriad conspiracy theories.

But optimism and "high hopes" were the order of the day with the New York Mets.

"We knew that our best days were in front of us," said Seaver.

Gil Hodges and coach Yogi Berra were winners all their lives. *John Rogers Archives*

4

IN THE "BIG INNING"

In the big inning, Gil created the 1969 New York Mets, and it was not so good. At first.

—1969 Miracle Mets, 4:1

Out of the darkness that was the New York Mets of 1962–1968, the Spirit of Gil moved upon the face of Shea Stadium.

And Gil said, let there be Tom Seaver, and it came to pass that George Thomas Seaver of the Fresno Seavers, the University of Southern California, and Bayside, Queens, stepped forth in the manner of a Knights Templar to do battle with the heathens from Quebec, Canada, the Montreal Expos, on the cold, blustery afternoon of April 8, 1969, at Shea Stadium.

In looking back from the perspective of time, the "big inning" of the 1969 season was the last possible result that, given how the season would play out, might have been expected. It was Goliath running roughshod over the Israelites, the Americans taking a licking "their first time at bat against the Germans," to quote General Omar Bradley in *Patton* after the debacle at Kasserine Pass.

The high hopes of spring training were at full peak when the Mets broke north. Hodges was recovered from his heart attack. New York played excellent ball in Florida, knocked off the Cardinals, and had Seaver primed. Even the most pessimistic Mets fan, convinced that they were the same old losers, only no longer lovable, felt that finally someone had been *invented* for them to beat. Despite optimistic fishing trips under the Bayshore Bridge in St. Pete, neither their 1968 record nor 1969 spring convinced everybody that New York could finish ahead of Chicago, Pittsburgh, or Philadelphia. St. Louis was an impossible goal. But Montreal (as well as West Division expansion club San Diego) represented something so mediocre even the Mets lorded over them.

Tom Seaver fires away.
National Baseball Hall of Fame Library

Or so it seemed. At first.

The 1969 Expos were an oddity. Minor league baseball had been played in Canada for years (Jackie Robinson broke the "color barrier" with the Montreal Royals in 1946), so it was not a given that Seaver would defeat the Expos in the expansion club's inaugural major league baseball game of 1969. Stranger things had happened. But the nature of that game was so out of character with everything that could have been expected—New York's 1968 hitting woes, Seaver's overpowering stuff, supposed Met defensive prowess—as to make people just scratch their heads.

The contrast from the Florida sun to wintry conditions had its effect on Seaver, whose high 90s heat, exploding and moving, came in flat at around 88 miles an hour, perfect batting practice fodder for Montreal. The Expos went after the two-time All-Star like they were the 1961 Yankees. Hodges stuck with his ace, thinking each inning that the guy would settle down.

It was not all Tom's fault. When he needed a break to get out of a jam, he did not get it. Liners were misjudged in the windy sky, grounders booted by clunky gloves. "I think I've seen all this before," said veteran sportswriter Maury Allen. "Another bad ball club."

Then there were the Mets bats, last in the league the previous year (.228), only today they made Shea look like a pinball arcade. It remains one of the ugliest games in New York Mets history, the antithesis of tight, taut baseball rhapsodized over by the likes of Roger Angell.

There is an expression: all's well that ends well. Or a win's a win. In baseball, in all sports, coaches and managers take it any way they can get it. Despite the ugliness, they could have been winners anyway. Seaver was ordinary, giving up two runs in the first inning. New York came back. Seaver struggled, throwing 105 pitches, told Hodges he was done (as if it was not obvious), and departed with a 6–4 lead. He still could have gotten credit for the lackluster victory.

Al Jackson and Ron Taylor were roughed up. Rusty Staub went deep, and Montreal forged an 11–6 lead. The Mets still could have pulled it out, finally giving their fans an opening day win, and gotten 1969 off to a decent, even exciting start. Alas, they fell just short after Duffy Dyer's three-run pinch homer in the ninth, losing 11–10.

"My God, wasn't that awful?" Seaver said to the writers afterward. They agreed, and the next day's columns were negative, expressing little confidence that the high hopes of St. Pete would translate into a winning spring start, not to mention summer or fall. The most frustrating thing was to finally get real run support and waste it.

"You know Seaver is a better pitcher than that," Gil Hodges told the press. "The next time we get 10 runs when he's pitching, I think we'll win."

On April 25 the Chicago Cubs entered Shea Stadium. For the first time in years, in decades, since 1908, the Cubs had *swagger*. Their manager, Leo Durocher, was *not* a sympathetic figure. This was a guy who said he would knock down his own mother to win a game. Babe Ruth beat him up when, as his roommate, Durocher stole his watch. He was a gambler, a hard drinker, a womanizer who cheated on his wives. He ordered his pitchers to throw at the opponents, often to outright hit them. He wanted spikes flying, did not mind if the other guy got hurt. He probably used a spy in the scoreboard to flash signals to the Giants, giving them an edge in 1951. He went for every advantage, legal, illegal, or immoral.

Chicago manager Leo Durocher was the "man you love to hate." *Brace Photos*

He was a backstabber, a "table for one" guy who played politics, went after the other fella's job, position, wife, girlfriend, sister, friend. He spent years in L.A. lobbying for Walter Alston's job, making fun of the hayseed from Ohio behind his back, to the writers, with players. Durocher had an exclusive Hollywood Hills tailor, a mansion in Trousdale Estates, and drove a Caddy. Alston lived modestly, went back to Darrtown in the winter, and wore clothes off the rack. Leo had guys in the press do his dirty work. He made fun of people on a lower pay scale ("My dry cleaning bills are bigger than his salary"). His endorsements were for cigarettes and beer. He smoked, got in guys' faces, and reeked of tobacco. The umpires felt his spittle on their faces, his shoes "accidentally" kicking them during arguments. He had a deal with Schlitz beer, an appropriately ugly name for an ugly man. Durocher was no matinee idol, but he could "dirty talk" a woman into bed.

"Always try to get her in the sack the first five minutes of a date," he advised. "That way if she says no you've got time to score another broad. You'd be surprised, there's a helluva lot of famous broads who say yes quick."

Durocher bragged of his sexual conquests, mostly lying, not caring if he spread rumors or impugned the reputation of an actress in the tabloids. He was from Massachusetts, seemed like he was from the Bowery, but thought of himself as Beverly Hills or Park Avenue. He cultivated big-shot friends like Frank Sinatra, George Raft, New York Mob boys, gang hitters. It was always "Frank called" and "Frank's comin' by," and most everybody looked at each other, rolled their eyes. B.S.

Branch Rickey fired him for immoralities, using the cover of his gambling suspension of 1947. What an odd couple those two made. Leo and Walter O'Malley got along. Not surprising. Strangely, the word that most appropriately suits Leo is not immoral, but amoral. He was not evil. If the right thing was convenient, that was okay by him. If anything good can be said of Leo, it was that he was not a racist. Maybe an anti-Semite, probably used the N-word, but for effect more than anything. He gave Willie Mays his chance, stuck with him when Willie needed a friend. It was a shining moment for "Mista Leo," and he deserves credit. Mel Durslag wrote there was a "good Leo" and a "bad Leo," which was better than just a "bad Leo." It's worth noting that Leo publicly appealed to God for salvation in an interview later in life.

Giants superstar Willie Mays had reached greatness under Leo Durocher in New York and in 1969 was in the twilight of his great career. *Brace Photos*

But beyond all other considerations, Leo Durocher was a winning baseball man. He was a Yankee in their heyday, a member of the St. Louis "Gashouse Gang"—winners—and resurrected losers into winning outfits in Brooklyn, New York, Chicago, later even in Houston, for a while at least. He was Billy Martin before Martin, cut out of the same cloth. He always wore out his welcome but left his mark wherever he went.

If Hodges was a new wave manager, platooning, using a five-man rotation, employing advance scouts, Durocher was old school, brother. His starters went every fourth day, and they went nine innings. His regulars did not beg out, take days off, sit out the nightcap of a twin bill, a day game after a night game, or with hangovers, hangnails, or hangdog attitudes. They played through injuries and pain. Durocher played to win. If the season was lost, he would dog it, not care, let his work ethic slide, but he did not tolerate it in others. If the pennant was still on the line, he was relentless. He did not care about second-place money, which some players and coaches needed in those days. He had his, probably got dough from his actress ex-wife, keeping him in style. Maybe he did a little gigolo work on the side.

Chicago's All-Star shortstop Don Kessinger.
Brace Photos

Durocher took over a yery young, very talented team in 1966. They played well below their potential. The Cubs probably took a year to get used to the tyrant. Second baseman Glenn Beckert, shortstop Don Kessinger, and catcher Randy Hundley were All-Star quality young players, now in their prime. Left fielder Billy Williams was, like Ernie Banks, headed for Cooperstown, but he was still at the top of his game. He played *every day.* He had a big consecutive game streak going, although he still had a ways to go to catch Lou Gehrig.

They had an outfielder named Jim Hickman, an ex-Met. Leo prodded Hickman, made fun of his old team, using that to motivate him. In the first half of 1969, it was working. The Cubs had let a promising center fielder named Adolfo Phillips go. He could not adjust to the "bad Leo," who had no empathy for him. Whatever soft spot he had in 1951 for Willie Mays was lost. His young players did not get any leeway. Besides, Leo was smart enough to know he had *Willie Mays,* and Phillips was no "Say Hey Kid." Phillips's replacement was Don Young, a rookie who supposedly had defensive skills but was a jittery mess around "Leo the Lip." Durocher openly criticized him in the press.

In 1969 Cubs center fielder Billy Williams was in the middle of a consecutive-game playing streak en route to the Hall of Fame. *Brace Photos*

But what the Cubs had, and boy did they ever have it, was pitching. Gold star, gold plate pitching. The mother's milk of winning baseball; 90 percent of the game. The right stuff that stopped good hitting. As the season shaped up, it was apparent that Cub pitching was at least as good as Cardinals pitching, Tigers pitching . . . and Mets pitching.

Their ace was a country hardballer named Ferguson Jenkins. If baseball had modernized since the days of Denton True "Cy" Young and "Iron Joe" McGinnity, this guy was a throwback. He pitched nine innings every time out, or so it seemed. Pitch counts? Fergie didn't need no *stinkin' pitch counts.* Hitters knew what was comin'. High heat, brush back, in, in, in; bust the hands, break the bat, numb the fingers, blue hammers all day . . . then a nasty slider for *strike three!* His pitching motion was utilitarian, he worked real fast, probably cheated a little, had a temper, and nobody wanted to screw with him. He was Gibson's equal as a competitor. In Chicago, they were just glad he was on their side. It was like being with Patton or MacArthur. You did not want to be against those guys.

Next was right-hander Billy Hands. An up-and-coming star, now experienced, he would pitch 300 innings, win 20; a day laborer in Chicago's summer sun. Hands could win a Cy Young some day, maybe be more than that.

Then there was Ken Holtzman. He was tall, skinny, and Jewish. Later in Oakland they called him "Jew." In Oakland Kenny was a huge success on a fighting, scrambling team of varying ethnicities and backgrounds, all fitting together seemingly because of their disparities; a crazy club in crazy uniforms, everybody an oddball, their ethnic differences somehow an advantage, and winners all. But in Chicago it was a mean environment akin to *Lord of the Flies.* As long as Kenny won, he and Leo were all right, but if he did not, then it got ugly. Whether Kenny was in Leo's doghouse because he was Jewish was really just speculation, but it seemed that way. Perception is half the environment. Early in 1969 Holtzman was unhittable. He had been an All-American in college, but his competitiveness was a question. Even Red Boucher sensed that in Alaska, when he picked Seaver over the more-heralded southpaw to pitch in the National Baseball Congress at Wichita. Now he seemed to have found his place in this tough baseball world, like Koufax finally had. Holtzman threw gas and had pinpoint control. Like Jenkins he did not fool you. Eighty, 90 percent fastballs, up and in, down and away, a little changeup, a wrinkle curve, and talent from the left side. He was golden. But Kenny was a business major in school, read the *Wall Street Journal* in the clubhouse, put business plans together on the plane. No chew. Light drinker. Leo tolerated it as long as he won, but if that train stopped rolling, there would be trouble down the line.

It did not end there. Leo had more arms. Rich Nye was a talented lefty out of the University of California. His potential was like that of Holtzman, but he was a college boy, from Berkeley, so that made him suspect in Leo's eyes. Hey, *Frank* never went to college, dropped out of school in Hoboken . . .

Phil Regan was one of the toughest relief pitchers in baseball, kind of the last of the old school bullpen aces before Rollie Fingers and Goose Gossage redefined a closer's role. Dick Selma, Seaver's boyhood pal, was very effective in whatever way he was used. Ted Abernathy had a *nasty* submarine pitch delivered from below his knees.

Seaver had gotten the best Montreal could muster on opening day, Bob Gibson twice, and now Ferguson Jenkins when Fergie was probably at

Tom Seaver's delivery has been described as the most perfect ever. *John Rogers Archives*

Cubs bats could not be stopped in 8–6 and 9–3 wins. Chicago was the hottest team in the National League. Leo talked it up with his boys in the New York press corps. The Mets? They was nothin'. No respect. Ron Santo was outspoken. Nobody gave the Mets any respect except for Ernie Banks, who could find something nice to say about the Grand Wizard of the KKK. But before Chicago could depart, having raped and pillaged the Big Apple to their satisfaction, Tug McGraw stepped up big time with a 3–0 "stopper" win in the series finale. New York was 7–11.

On May 2 and 3 Chicago defeated New York, 6–4 and 3–2 before wild cheering at Wrigley Field. The Cubbies were the toast of the North Side. The whole, early shaky Mets season was seemingly always on the line, and Seaver would be asked to respond each time. On May 4 he came through with a 3–2 win over Billy Hands. In the second game of the doubleheader, the Mets made a statement, winning 3–2 again to split the series.

Seaver's game was key. It was a Sunday, the crowd loud and boisterous, drinking beer, the "bleacher bums" in full force, May weather starting to break the Chicago winter. Durocher was in the other dugout. The Mets were the baseball image of *nice guys*, and everybody knew what Leo predicted for that. Hodges was a churchgoing fellow, quiet, unassuming. Another Walter Alston guy, who

the absolute apex of his career. It was just a rumor that New York City paramedics were called to the clubhouse after the game for removal-of-bats-from-anal-cavities after Jenkins used nasty inside heat to shove them up there all day. Tom was effective but got touched, losing 3–1.

probably wore suits off the rack and was faithful to his wife.

Chump, thought Leo. Gil had a bunch of college guys, frat boys. Seaver, the preppie. Softies from California, surfer dudes like McGraw; Harrelson, who was scrawny and could be taken out by a spikes-flying slide into second, breaking up two. Koosman, an engineering student. So was Jay Hook. That's impressive. Ryan, who threw hard but was scared of his own shadow. He did not have the guts to come inside. Kranepool playing out the string as usual. Agee in center, pretty good with the South Side White Sox, but a bust in the Big Apple.

All-Star third baseman Ron Santo was a Windy City fan favorite then and now. *Brace Photos*

Ron Santo faced Seaver. He was the face of the Cubs, the Italian guy, outspoken, a hard-ass. The time had come. No provocation really, other than Leo's *presence* in the home dugout. Seaver let one fly right at Santo's batting helmet. It flipped him. Santo stared out at Tommy Tom Tom.

So that's how it's gonna be, eh?

It was a baseball code, the way the game is played. The Cubs star brushed himself off, the crowd booing. Did Leo scream obscenities at Seaver, the home plate umpire, turn to Billy Hands and tell him to "stick it in his ear"? No. He sat in stony silence. This situation required no words.

When Seaver stepped in against Hands, he got nicked on the arm. It was on. Hands got one in the leg. The benches looked to clear, players on the steps, ready to rumble. The umpire stepped halfway out to the mound. He warned Seaver, a $50 fine. Seaver knew he had reached the tolerance limit and could not afford another one lest he be thrown out. He needed to stay in to win.

It was the baseball version of Tataglia trying to take down The Don: "business, not personal." Both clubs were on edge, verbalizing, squaring off against each other. A rivalry was brewing. Seaver kept dropping, and driving, dropping, and driving . . .

Pitch after pitch. Cheese. Hard, hard sinkers, the kind that wore out Grote's hand, left him black and blue, broke bats, made the ball hit wood like shot puts, induced grounders struck by noodles. Good old country hard ball. Tom accepted the $50 fine as a small price to pay for victory and respect.

"That was my first really satisfying game," he told the media afterwards. He could enjoy the second game, sit around half-clothed, taking his time, savoring the fact that he was *a big leaguer*. He was an

All-Star, his potential and reputation sky high, and Tom Seaver knew how to play it. He was central casting's typecast Star, but underneath all of it he was packing crates in 100-degree Fresno heat, rooting for "Dandy Sandy" at Dodger Stadium, using guile to get high school hitters out. He was a fan living a fantasy, not going mano a mano with Leo and Ron Santo at Wrigley Field. He drank some beer, iced, showered, and rooted his team to victory in the nightcap. A great day in the Windy City.

"I tried to brush him back in New York, but I didn't do much of a job," Tom told Larry Merchant of the *New York Post* when asked about the Santo brushback. "He was hitting me well. Possibly he's taking the bread out of my mouth."

This was Leo's philosophy, one of the reasons he did not want college boys. Ken Holtzman could go into businesss. He did not need baseball. Seaver's old man was an executive. Where's the hunger? He wanted gutter guys who felt that if they failed in baseball, they were destined for the streets. Like Carl Furillo forced to work construction, bitter. But Seaver was the "new breed." He had served in the Marines; he had a "war face."

Santo had a habit after wins of jumping up in the air and clicking his heels. The "bleacher bums" loved it, opponents stewed. "I had to make sure he respects me," Seaver continued. "You can't let hitters dominate or intimidate you. The hitter shouldn't intimidate the pitcher, and the pitcher shouldn't intimidate the hitter, but there has to be respect. I had to let Santo know I knew what he was doing to me. Then Leo had Hands hit me. What do I do, throw a bat at Leo? I had to do what I did. It's a part of baseball. It's a good hard game."

Seaver fought like the CIA, not the infantry. There was a method to his madness. A time for an intellectual approach, mind games, deception, and a time to demonstrate to the enemy that if they went too far, they faced "mutual assured destruction." Seaver had a reputation as a control pitcher, but his fastball in his prime years—and he was on the cusp of it now—were close to 100 miles an hour. He was *dangerous.*

"This is the code," wrote Merchant. "But the thing is someone can get hurt or maimed with a baseball. . . . The man who shoots back and kills may not know the first man was just issuing a warning. They are fooling with bullets."

"You would have thought it foolish to throw at us when we had Tom and myself and the other guys, who could throw hard, but we weren't that well known yet," Koosman recalled. "But they helped get the fire going. They generated a lot of energy. That was one club you loved to beat."

Seaver saw no ethical quandaries. "There's a fine dividing line between throwing at someone or brushing him back. It's the difference between good hard baseball and dirty baseball."

But the Mets would face Chicago again down the road, and Leo Durocher played "dirty baseball." When the Mets reached the .500 mark at 18–18, it was celebrated as a major accomplishment in the New York press. Seaver had the perfect reaction to it: ".500 is nothing to celebrate," he said. The tone was set.

5

MEET THE METS

The "new breed" is here, baby.

—Tommie Agee

As the 1969 season began to develop, the New York Mets began to demonstrate a distinct personality. They were part of the changing times, on and off the field. That spring, the great Mickey Mantle tearfully announced his retirement from baseball. The New York Yankees got off to a mediocre start. Their famed stadium was empty. Press attention was focused on the Mets. The Yankees were yesterday and had been for five years at least.

The Mets were becoming as popular as the "Super Jets." *John Rogers Archives*

Shea was the place to be, just as it had been during the football season. Off the field, Mets players reflected the new sensibilities. They wore mod clothes, turtlenecks, a little jewelry maybe, sideburns, and flared bellbottoms. They spoke in the new dialect. It was a groovy time, man. They were with it. As for the war, there were divisions. They were mostly small town guys, and the old values that especially make up the athlete's creed led them to support their country, the president, and the troops. Most voted Republican, but it was a far less conservative bunch than any average big league team of five years before. Truth be told, they probably were a little more to the left than the average sports team, circa 1969–1970.

Black players on the Mets were distinctly of the "new breed." This was New York during a time of change. Their hairstyles, clothing, jewelry, and attitudes were reflective of the times. They felt free to flirt with white girls, to meet them in the Manhattan hot spots or on the road without fear of the old-time recriminations about "their place" in the hierarchy.

The Mets were popular, young, and attractive, and unlike the 1962 "all-time record for fatherhood" team, had their share of swingin' bachelors. The sexual revolution was up and running, and they were in the right time and place. Joe Namath had made it perfectly acceptable to kiss 'n' tell. After Namath, there was little debauchery the Mets could engage in that was going to shock anybody. *Ball Four* was still a year away from publication. Its revelations were shocking not so much because it told truths that people already suspected or knew about sex, pep pills, and other aspects of the game, but rather because it tended to name some names, some pretty important names. But hey, after Namath said he went to bed the night before the Super Bowl with a "blonde and a bottle of Johnnie Walker Red," the fantasy life of pro athletes was open for all to live vicariously by.

But an interesting dynamic was already in play by 1969. It really had started two years earlier and would continue to be a dominant, eventually divisive aspect of the Mets. Resentment would rear its ugly head, and not just from players but from writers, too.

Tom Seaver did not cheat on his wife.

This really does not sound like much, but left as an open statement the unsaid words, which every married Met and his wife thought of if not verbalized, was that it meant the other guys did. Now, nobody really, other than Tom Seaver, truly, actually knows that Tom Seaver did not cheat on his wife, Nancy. But it was his reputation, then and now. Every team he played on, every teammate; the word was that Seaver did not cheat.

The 1969 Mets were a baseball version of *The Mod Squad*. *John Rogers Archives*

Baseball players and pretty girls go together like peanut butter and jelly. *John Rogers Archives*

Did all his teammates cheat? Of course not. But the fact that pro athletes cheat on their wives is such a given and always has been that it is simply accepted common knowledge that those who do not are exceptions to the rule. It is the price paid by the wife of a pro athlete; in accepting the money, the fame, the travel, and the excitement of the life, you accepted the fooling around. Most just held to the rule that it be confined to the road during the season. No girlfriends of wives. Not in their hometown. Keep it away from the kids. Boys will be boys.

The ballplayers often tended to marry high school sweethearts. The conservative, family-support nature of teenage sports meant that the guys more often came from a tight-knit background and married "a girl just like the one who married dear old Dad." But there were exceptions.

Namath did a motorcycle movie, and a PR photo showed him playing "tonsil hockey" with sexpot Ann-Margret. Namath was shirtless, Ann in a bikini. The photo made it look like they were both naked as jaybirds, her ample breasts squeezed against Joe's hairy chest, and God knows what was going on down below.

The single guys, some divorced men, plenty of married fellows, went after the "groupies," the "Baseball Annies" who could be found in every nightclub and hotel bar, outside the stadium, down by the dugout. They "dressed for *sex*cess," in tight miniskirts, big hair, low-cut tops, bare midriffs, high heels, "red lips and painted *finger*tips." It was a "Girls, Girls, Girls" world, and these guys were welcome to it. That was the style. Sexy hippie chicks. Horny airline stewardesses, whose attire in those days pretty much said, "Coffee, tea, or me."

But the sexy girls were no less likely to be faithful to some ballplayer they were having a fling with than vice versa. Some of these groupies became wives. Stories and rumors about how Jim met Jane were rampant. A girl would be passed around, sometimes by several guys in the same night in the same room. This was and always has been the scene. Two weeks later, she is exclusive?

There is no evidence that Tom Seaver was ever a monk. Dick Selma said he dated the best-looking girls at Fresno High. Use your imagination beyond that. After he met Nancy, he dated beautiful sorority girls at USC. But Seaver knew this world, the world of infidelity. Not up close, but he was savvy enough to know the things that matter—family, children, trust, faith—get eaten alive by cheating hearts.

In 1969 they began to call him "perfect."

"I'm not perfect, because I drink beer and I swear," he said. "There's only one perfect man, and he lived 2,000 years ago." He was not a guy who went around asking guys if he could talk to them about Jesus Christ, but he wore a St. Christopher's medal and seemed to walk the walk.

While still in college, Seaver decided he wanted to marry Nancy. He was apparently able to discontinue whatever it was he might have done with those USC coeds, which as Matt Leinart demonstrated years later, could be a free-for-all. As a minor leaguer at Jacksonville, a town with Southern belles, honky tonks, and strip clubs, he sat in his hotel room, lonely. Nancy came out, and they were married in a small ceremony. He could not wait out the season.

All work and no play can make for boring Mets.
John Rogers Archives

So by 1969 the word was out: Seaver did not cheat. There was never any indication that Seaver called guys out who did. Years later in Cincinnati he was good friends with Johnny Bench, a notorious chick hound. One of Bench's favorite ways to relax his ace pitcher with the bases loaded would be to saunter out to the mound and ask Tom to "check out the blonde behind home plate."

"How do you think I got into this trouble in the first place?" Seaver laughingly replied before invariably striking out the batter to end the threat.

Seaver, whose politics were probably moderately Republican, maybe libertarian, was a "live and let live" type. He enjoyed a good joke, laughed like a hyena, and probably enjoyed hearing ribald stories of teammate escapades.

But there was still a tension. A look, a remark, a shared knowledge. *He knows what I did. He can hold that over me now.*

Over the years, Seaver had a reputation that was truly unusual. There were others who were faithful, but Seaver was said to be so admired, so influential, such a leader by example on and off the field, that *other guys would not cheat.* A goody-goody might be made fun of. Seaver was no goody-goody. He was a leader, a Marine. He threw heat, made Ron Santo eat dirt, and traded aspirin tablets at the noggin with Gibby.

So there were divisions forming. There were those who admired the Seaver credo, following it even when it was hard. Then there were those who *wanted the man to cheat on Nancy!* Go ahead; everyone does it, man. She'll never know.

The Mets had attractive wives and girlfriends. Just being in New York, this upped the "attractiveness factor" a few notches, like a team in L.A. or Texas. Gary Gentry's wife was similar to Nancy Seaver: pretty, blonde, and poised. Her husband was said to be "the next" Seaver. Nancy Seaver was a doll. A classic California blonde, she dressed like a fashion model: tam-o'-shanters, shawls, pretty dresses. An Irish lass.

Cleon Jones, like teammate Tommie Agee, San Francisco's Willie McCovey, and the Braves' Hank and Tommie Aaron, was from Mobile, Alabama.
John Rogers Archives

Seaver and Nancy were "Ken and Barbie dolls." His teammates loved Seaver, they admired him, and, man, he was "our savior," but there were a few mutterings here and there.

Jesus, are you kidding me?
Who do they think they are?

Cleon Jones was the anti-Seaver. The fact that Cleon Jones and Tom Seaver could be teammates, colleagues . . . *friends?* . . . well, that was the story of America, too. A few years later, Jones was arrested in a van parked outside Shea Stadium for possession of drugs. The newspaper reported, "Jones was found nude, in the company of a young lady, not his wife." He and Seaver eventually had a falling out, on account of Jonesie's indiscretions. Seaver only cared when he thought it started to hurt the ballclub . . . and his win-loss record.

Jones needed to be motivated. Hodges knew that. Cleon came from Mobile, and *everybody* moves at a different pace down yonder. He was 6' tall, a muscular 195 pounds. He grew up in a racially hostile environment. The year he made his big league debut, Birmingham police chief Bull Connor sicced dogs and ordered rubber truncheons on blacks marching for their rights. He tried college at one of the traditional black universities but never made it through. Had he not been a baseball player, he would have been subject to the vagaries of life in the "Redneck Riviera," which was what Alabama quarterback Ken Stabler called the Gulf coast of Alabama. Jones was a rarity who threw left but batted right-handed. As a youth in Mobile, he played sandlot ball with a right field fence so close that balls over it counted as outs, so he switched from left- to right-handed. Cleon grew up "hard,"

Jones, like Rickey Henderson in later years, was a rarity: a left-handed thrower and right-handed hitter.
John Rogers Archives

according to Ron Swoboda. He and Tommie Agee played baseball and football on the same high school team.

He led the International League in errors in 1965, and on this Mets team, defense was imperative. But he could wake up at midnight on Christmas Eve swatting a line drive. He had almost hit .300 in 1968, a year in which almost nobody sniffed that magic number. He got hot in 1969 and was embarking on stardom.

His teammate, Tommie Agee, was a more sensitive soul, but like Cleon hailed from Mobile. Mobile was the home of many a great athlete. Alabama quarterback Scott Hunter (later Bart Starr's successor in Green Bay) was from there. Satchel Paige was originally from there. Willie McCovey and the Aaron brothers, Hank and Tommy, had grown up playing on the Mobile sandlots. Agee, the American League Rookie of the Year in 1966, was a grizzled veteran by 1969 because he had experienced so many ups and downs. The Mets got him for Brooklyn-born Tommy Davis, thought to be over the hill with injuries (he still had a few hits left in him with Baltimore down the road).

"I was a year ahead of Cleon in school," Agee recalled.

Told that Cleon was five days older, Agee responded, "He's older, but I'm smarter."

Lou Brock said Jerry Grote was the toughest catcher he ever ran up against. Brock squared off for years against Johnny Bench. 'Nuf said. He blamed others for his poor performances in the beginning, especially an anemic bat, but he learned to protect the plate. He called a great game, and the pitchers swore by him, even if they did not really dig the guy.

Bench would embarrass Jack Billingham by catching one of his "fast" balls barehanded. Grote would fire the ball back to Jim McAndrew harder than McAndrew pitched it, right at the belt buckle, literally "buckling" him. He tried it with Koosman, who told him if he ever did it again, he would "kill" him. He never did it to Seaver. Ex-catcher Wes Westrum tried to take Jerry under his wing.

"If Grote ever learns to control himself, he might become the best catcher in the game," he said.

One of Harrelson's specialties was the hard-to-catch pop-up. *John Rogers Archives*

Buddy Harrelson had speed and agility. He was not as great in the field as Luis Aparicio or Davey Concepcion. Cal Ripken, Nomar Garciaparra, Derek Jeter, and Alex Rodriguez were not on the scene yet. He was what a shortstop looks like. After hitting .108 in a 19-game 1965 call-up, Buddy became a creditable switch-hitter. He stole home twice in 1966 and became a Gold Glove winner. He was consistent and a fan favorite.

Born in Niles, California, on June 6, 1944, a day in which America was preoccupied with events on the French coastline, he grew up in Hayward. Today, Hayward is part of the urban sprawl of Oakland and the gritty East Bay, but back then it was the country. There were no A's games to go to when he was growing up. He was 5'10" and a half, maybe, and weighed all of 155 pounds soaking wet. He and Seaver became pals. They liked to drink beer and golf.

Whether Harrelson and Seaver were close because Buddy did not cheat either is just speculation. Who really knows such things? But he was quiet, studious, and dedicated. Seaver loved those qualities in a teammate. Unlike Seaver, Harrelson slogged through the minors. He may have been part of the "youth of America," called to opportunity with the Metsies, but his road was a two-year slog at Salinas, just down the road from his Hayward roots, then Buffalo and Jacksonville. His build and appearance were made for jokes and put-downs from grizzled vets, but he just played through it. He hit .219 in 1968 but was learning how to swing from the left side.

Seaver met Harrelson at Jacksonville in 1966 and thought he was "a skinny runt of a kid who never said a word." They broke into the big leagues with lasting results in 1967. In Seaver's third career start, he led 1–0 in the seventh inning at Chicago. Harrelson's error allowed the tying run to score, but Seaver won 2–1 in 10 innings to improve his record to 2–0.

Lindsay Nelson carried on the tradition of Southern announcers of New York teams, in addition to his work with Notre Dame football.

National Baseball Hall of Fame Library

"I felt just great," Seaver recalled. But Buddy was sitting in front of his locker holding his head in his hands, miserable because he cost Seaver a shutout. "Forget it, Buddy," Seaver told him. "We won. There'll be lots of shutouts."

Despite the error that cost Seaver the shutout, Harrelson was a player who possessed some very useful talents. He was very adept at racing to catch pop-ups in foul territory. Like Seaver, he had tried college at San Francisco State, but unlike Seaver he did not finish up. He missed two weeks doing his Army duty in 1968 and was slated to miss parts of June and July in 1969 doing the same thing.

Johnny Murphy was a Yankee pitcher, a durable right-hander saddled with the enigmatic nickname "Grandma Murphy" when he toiled for Joe McCarthy's champions of the 1930s. He played a dozen years at Yankee Stadium and was one of the first "relief specialists" as bullpen roles evolved.

Murphy posted 12 wins out of the bullpen in 1937 and 1943 and had 107 career saves and 73 lifetime victories. He was very effective in World Series play, compiling a 1.10 ERA in six separate Series. He finished with Boston in 1947 and went into player development with the Red Sox.

While George Weiss, Bing Devine, and others helped develop the Mets (their "college philosophy" after going with veterans early), Murphy is the man who ultimately built the 1969 Mets (with great help from assistant Whitey Herzog, who never missed the chance to tell anybody who wanted to listen how great that help was).

The ownership wanted Gil Hodges, but he was under contract with Washington, and it was easier said than done. It was Murphy, friends with Washington GM George Selkirk from their Yankees days, who made it happen. Officially, Devine was still the general manager when it occurred, but it was Murphy (who replaced him shortly thereafter when Devine when to St. Louis) who arranged a "trade" for Hodges, a rare but not unheard of event for managers. Hodges came back to New York for $100,000 and pitcher Bill Denehy. The Mets had been rumored to be after Hodges since Casey Stengel's 1965 retirement.

Murphy also made one of the biggest trades in all of Mets history, the acquisition of Tommie Agee and utility man Al Weis from the Chicago White Sox after the 1967 campaign.

Some of the most famous baseball announcers over the years have included Vin Scully and Red Barber of the Dodgers; Mel Allen of the Yankees; Lon Simmons, Russ Hodges, and Jon Miller of the Giants; Harry Caray of the Cubs; Harry Callas of the Phillies; Bob Prince of the Pirates; Bob Elson of the White Sox; Bill King of the A's; Dick Enberg of the Angels; and Ernie Harwell of the Tigers. Add to that list the name of Lindsey Nelson, who eventually won the Ford C. Frick award and a place in the Hall of Fame.

Nelson is one of the "giants of baseball broadcasting," wrote Peter Bjarkman in *The New York Mets Encyclopedia.* He saw it all, beginning with the

Bob Murphy was part of a trio of Mets announcers with the team since its 1962 inception. His brother, Jack, had San Diego's stadium named after him.

National Baseball Hall of Fame Library

1962 campaign. Just being able to keep an audience through so many long, losing games was an art.

Nelson started after World War II in his native Tennessee. He re-created baseball for the Liberty Broadcasting System and became popular when night games came into being on a regular basis, which had a big effect on the listening audience size. He honed his skills with NBC and became adept at all sports.

Nationally, Nelson was well known as a college football announcer, especially as Notre Dame's game announcer and for many years their Saturday (and Sunday) man, when Irish games were aired across the country.

"Purdue failed to sustain a drive, so after punting we pick up action with the Irish taking over at their own 45," Nelson always seemed to be intoning in a staccato-yet-smooth, very-distinctive-yet-not-quite-Southern accent. For years, Nelson's voice was synonymous with the Cotton Bowl.

Nelson came on board with the expansion Mets in 1962 and gave them imprimatur. The hiring of Southern broadcasters was a long tradition in New York that included the likes of Allen and Barber. Nelson's voice could not be pinpointed. To many he even sounded like a native New Yorker. It was a somewhat nasal accent, but lively and knowledgeable. His colorful, checkered sport jackets were his trademark.

Nelson's partner from the beginning was Bob Murphy, another Hall of Famer. He became Boston's play-by-play man in 1954, covering the great Ted Williams in his twilight years along with Curt Gowdy. Like Nelson, he was adept at college football. His older brother, Jack Murphy, was a renowned San Diego sports columnist whose efforts brought big league ball to that city. The stadium was named after him.

The third Mets broadcaster in 1969 was also a Hall of Famer, which had to be a record. Like Nelson, Ralph Kiner wore snazzy sportcoats. In 1951 Kiner hit 51 home runs for Pittsburgh. He led the National League in homers for five straight seasons. Only Babe Ruth and Mark McGwire surpass his lifetime ratio of 1.0 home run per every 14.1 trips to the plate.

Kiner was a minor league general manager in the Pacific Coast League before entering the broadcast booth with the Chicago White Sox. He, Nelson, and Murphy had been intact since the 1962 inception. He was by 1969 a mainstay on Mets TV and radio broadcasts, hosting the well-known *Kiner's Corner.* His "Kinerisms" and malapropos, sometimes unfit for print, included "We'll be right back after this word from Manufacturer's Hangover."

6

THE LEAPING CORPSE

Pastime, National, 99; after a lingering illness.
Remains on display at Cooperstown, N.Y.

—*Roger Angell,* The Summer Game

On May 28 Jerry Koosman struck out 15 in 10 innings of an 0–0 game with San Diego. McGraw came on in relief and held the line, and Harrelson hit a homer to win it, 1–0. Over Memorial Day weekend, New York swept San Francisco four straight at home. They then beat Los Angeles three in a row at Shea, followed by a three-game sweep at San Diego. After beating the Giants, 9–4, at Candlestick Park on June 10, they completed an 11-game winning streak. Gaylord Perry beat Gary Gentry, 7–2, the next day to end it.

The 11-game winning streak was the first defining moment for the 1969 New York Mets. First, crowds at Shea were out of control for the Giants and Dodgers. There was no vestige of old Brooklyn and Polo Grounds rooters there for the Californians. It was all Mets: foot stomping, chanting, placard waving, noise making. It was kids and grandparents, stockbrokers and schoolteachers. All sense of old Yankee Stadium decorum, like bored

In late May and early June, baseball became just plain fun for the Mets. *John Rogers Archives*

operagoers, was out the window. It was a rock concert; the Fillmore East, Woodstock, Hendrix going electric. It was "Seav-*uh*, Seav-*uh*," and "Let's go *Mets*; let's go *Mets!*" With a lead late in the game, they let loose with the old football plea for "*DE-fense, DE-fense.*" Girls danced, some even threatened to do a little more than that. Male fans did not object. Couples kissed, parents approved. It was a carnival, Mardi Gras.

Hard-throwing rookie Gary Gentry helped bring the Mets into contention. *John Rogers Archives*

But it was the Giants and the Dodgers. It was the old ghosts being exorcised after pasting some 170 defeats on the Mets over the previous seven seasons. For the very first time, the two great National League traditions had come to New York only to play a decided second fiddle to the Mets. It was not like these were bad clubs, either. Both would battle for the Western Division crown until the end. Los Angeles had been down in 1967 and 1968, rebuilt, and featured a young, talented club that would form the great champions of the next decade. They made New York look like the veterans.

On May 30 Seaver won his seventh game, 4–3, over San Francisco, the second win of the 11-game streak. Gentry won the next day, 4–2. The sweep was completed in the next game, 5–4. Koosman stopped L.A. cold, 2–1. On June 3 Seaver fired a three-hitter to beat the team he rooted for as a kid, 5–2. Ed Kranepool hit a home run in the fifth, then another in the sixth. It was the first time the Mets had ever been above .500 in June.

On June 4 all bets were off. Los Angeles and New York went at it for 15 innings. As in the long, losing doubleheaders against the Mets and Dodgers of the Polo Grounds era, Mets fans stayed put, loud and exuberant. Only this time it was not just joy over "lovable losers." In 15 innings New York held the line in an incredible 1–0 win to complete the sweep. Los Angeles had men on base all game but could not score them.

In what may have been the best play of the regular season, at least, Al Weis reversed gears to grab a ball deflected off the pitcher's glove, then threw the Dodgers runner out at home plate on a bang-bang tag play. All the luck seemed to have swung toward the Mets. For the first time, people started thinking about contention. St. Louis was struggling so far, and what was going on at Shea Stadium appeared to many to have a divine touch to it. Flying to the West Coast afterwards, Seaver realized that the talk in St. Petersburg was for real.

In San Diego, Gentry stopped the Padres, 5–3. Koosman struck out 11 in a victory. Seaver won his 10th game of the season at Candlestick Park, 3–2, in 10 innings over the dangerous Giants. Ron Taylor picked up the save. Tommie Agee was hot. It was New York's 11th straight win. After San Francisco finally ended the streak, the Mets (29–23) were solidly in second behind Chicago and six ahead of the Cardinals.

The Cubs got off to a 35–16 (.868) start and were all getting endorsement deals. Leo Durocher had his own radio show, leading him to say little to the writers he considered beneath him. *Sports Illustrated* did a feature on their helmet-wearing "bleacher bums."

"Pitching is still the name of the game, and the Mets have it," said Montreal's Rusty Staub, not quite ready to hand the division to Chicago. "In the old days of the Mets it wouldn't have happened. They weren't blood and guts, like these guys. Now I think they can win."

"The Mets are always in the game with Seaver and Koosman," said Ron Taylor.

Others still needed to be convinced. Seaver knew Pete Rose from All-Star Games and casually mentioned that they might see each other in the play-offs. Rose looked at him like he was nuts, but Seaver told him, "Pete, we've got some guys who can get the ball over the plate."

On Sunday, June 22, 55,862 came out for a doubleheader with St. Louis. Baseball was on fire, in no small part because of the Mets. That day, the 394,008 fans who attended games broke the all-time single-day record. The Mets looked "cool, loose, rich—like the old Yanks," according to Roger Angell, who may have been overdoing it a bit by this point, so enthused was he. (It was during this time that Angell's dispatches for *The New Yorker*, later captured in his classic book *The Summer Game*, were being written. Angell's writing, particularly his partisan, fan-friendly descriptions of the 1969 Mets—Angell usually sat in the stands with his daughter instead of in the press box—remain some of the finest baseball prose ever committed to paper.) With Koosman mowing 'em down in the second game, Rod Gaspar threw Lou Brock out at home plate to save a 1–0 win.

"Brilliant baseball," wrote Angell. "Day to remember."

"The Mets have grown up," said Los Angeles manager Walter Alston. "They no longer beat themselves. They hold onto one-run leads, and they make the big plays."

Sportswriter Joe Trimble called them the "best expansion team in major league history, beyond a doubt." It had taken "eight years and much patience," but the whole roster aside from Agee and Grote was produced by their farm system.

Harrelson recalled that the West Coast series "was the biggest turnaround. Up to then, we had never played well against West Coast teams, especially the Dodgers and Giants. They always kicked our butts. This time they came in and we beat them in New York, then went out to the coast and beat them again. And that's when we began to say, 'Hey, we're competitive. Things are different.'"

In San Francisco, the Mets held a team meeting to address the issue of brushback pitches. Seaver and Koosman stepped up and responded when the other team tried to pitch New York tight, and "that sent a message that the Mets wouldn't be intimidated," recalled Ed Charles.

"Koosman would throw a baseball right through you," recalled Swoboda. "Seaver would hit you, and Gentry was fearless."

Fielding support became the cornerstone of the club's success. Jerry Koosman (left) congratulates his supporting cast after a win. *John Rogers Archives*

As the season played out, Ron Swoboda dealt with the frustration of platooning with Art Shamsky, while Rod Gaspar would come in as a defensive replacement. He felt the best way to deal with the situation was through action, not words. Rather than complain to Hodges, he asked Eddie Yost to hit him countless balls in the outfield in an effort to improve defensively. Yost would tire of hitting liners, sinkers, wall-bangers, stinging grounders, and high pops to Swoboda, who worked on positioning, dealing with sunglasses, and setting up for throws.

It was an example of true professionalism on Swoboda's part. He was willing to work hard in order to improve. Yet somehow in the strange, cliquish world of big league baseball, Hodges and his coaching staff did not see it that way. They thought Swoboda was trying to show them up, that his willingness to pay the price was like telling them what to do, to force their hand. It was a "Joe College" move. "High school Harry." *Attaboy, attaboy.* The code of conduct on big league teams has seen some changes over the years, mainly because so many players are now collegians, but in 1969 there was still some of the same rough "tobacco juice" world John McGraw once defined.

On the other hand, Hodges went against the grain when he found out Don Cardwell threw a spitball, ordering the veteran to cease and desist. Most managers awarded cheating, in all its varied forms: the spitter, the "phantom swipe" of second on a double play, stealing signs, picking up on what pitch was coming. Leo Durocher treated cheating like a religion.

Amos Otis, a hotshot prospect who had been forced out of position—to third base—was sent back to Tidewater in June. According to Ron Swoboda, Otis "never got a chance." Also in June, the Mets pulled off a very important trade, acquiring power-hitting first baseman Donn Clendenon, 33. Clendenon had been a staple in Pittsburgh but was recently dealt to Montreal as part of the expansion shake-up, then to Houston. It was the culmination of a long process that originally ticketed

The June trade acquiring Donn Clendenon was the key moment in the team's surge to contention. *John Rogers Archives*

Atlanta third baseman Joe Torre for New York. Murphy went after Richie Allen of the Phillies, but Philly wanted too much in return. Montreal then offered Clendenon for Gentry and McAndrew, but Murphy declined. Atlanta offered Torre, a native New Yorker, who would have been a natural Met. Braves GM Paul Richards wanted Kranepool and Grote, but New York refused to let them go.

Torre would have solved the "third base problem" of 39 players at the "hot corner" since 1962. Many youngsters had been tried at third base without success, including a prospect named Danny Napoleon.

"Danny was no better at third than the real Napoleon was at Waterloo," wrote Jack Lang of the *Long Island Press* (also *The Sporting News'* Mets beat writer).

Clendenon was considered a malcontent in Houston, where as a black man he did not feel comfortable. On the June 15 trading deadline, Houston all but dumped him to New York for Kevin Collins and three minor leaguers (one of whom, Steve Renko, had a creditable career).

"With one swing of the bat he could put us in the game or put us ahead," said Koosman.

He was "loud and boisterous," and it "didn't take long for him to be a team leader," acknowledged the man who now had to platoon with him, Kranepool.

"He became the first legitimate guy who could turn the game around for us with one swing," said Bud Harrelson.

Clendenon knew Hodges. Prior to an exhibition game a few years earlier between his Pirates and

Hodges's Washington Senators, Clendenon sought out Hodges for advice because "he's the best guy for any right-handed first baseman to copy . . . he will give you all the help he can. I had 'stiff hands' and was always told to use both hands when taking throws. Gil said it wasn't necessary and showed me how to relax my hand and catch the ball with the glove."

"Donn was not only a clubhouse lawyer, he was a [real] lawyer," said Swoboda. "He was a member of the bar, an off-season lawyer for Scripto. Donn was a very educated guy. And he had a big mouth; he was always talking, always giving you [crap] about something, but it was wonderful, all good [stuff]."

With Clendenon hitting from the right side, it allowed Hodges to platoon Kranepool against right-handed pitching. Clendenon was a clutch RBI man and seemed to be the missing piece on a club already coming together. His addition to the team also seemed to provide social cohesion. Agee and Jones felt slightly isolated as black players. Clendenon seamlessly straddled the white and black worlds, and through him players mixed. Swoboda started to invite the three of them to his home. His wife would cook, and they would "drink beer, eat crabs, and tell stories." Seaver and his wife welcomed Donn to the Mets family.

Relief pitcher Ron Taylor was an electrical engineer who went on to become a doctor. Koosman had studied engineering. It was an educated group, and they found kinship with Clendenon. The more educated Mets had the ability to communicate without flaunting their book smarts at those with less schooling.

Seaver, like many Mets, went to a mostly white high school, but met black teammates in Alaska and at USC. "On the Mets, I saw no racial friction at all, never a slur, never an insult," Seaver recalled. "During the 1969 season, Cleon Jones, Tommie Agee, Ed Charles, and Donn Clendenon each made significant contributions to our pennant drive. I didn't think of them as *black* Mets. Just plain Mets."

Clendenon took to Seaver immediately. When he saw him arrive in the clubhouse on game days, he called him "the chubby right-hander." Seaver would laugh and reply that he was still "growing" and the veteran Clendenon was just "jealous."

Nancy Seaver reached out to the 6'4" first baseman, too. "I know who you are," she told him when she first saw him at Shea Stadium. Clendenon was wearing a Jamaican shirt and vest. Clendenon pretended to put the moves on her. On another team, in another year, not long before that, it could have been big trouble; but Tom and Nancy thought he was the coolest dude they had ever seen.

Life was good, and it was great to be a Met.

This was a group of guys who symbolized the new era, what with a war going on and people thinking in different ways. "God, it was exciting, stimulating," recalled Swoboda.

7

THE FIRST CRUCIAL DAY

For the New York Mets in 1962, the first year of their existence, their finest days were rainouts.
—Paul D. Zimmerman and Dick Schaap, The Year the Mets Lost Last Place

On July 8, 1962, the New York Mets made three throwing errors in one inning, allowed five unearned runs in an inning, lost to St. Louis by 14 runs, and in the process allowed 41-year-old Stan Musial to hit no less than three home runs against them. They were 25–59 (.280).

Precisely seven years later, on July 8, 1969, the Mets woke up with a 54–34 record, five games back of the Chicago Cubs. The rest of the National League East was effectively out of it, in small measure because in head-to-head games with New York, they had fared poorly. St. Louis, the preseason favorite, suddenly looked old at 40–44, seven and a half back of the Mets. The Mets had knocked Pittsburgh off. The Pirates were floundering at 38–43. The Phillies and Expos were playing out the string.

Mrs. Joan Payson paid for the Mets game to be transmitted by a special radio broadcast to her temporary vacation home in Maine, where she was staying. What she heard was a pitchers' duel, with Fergie Jenkins and Jerry Koosman working fast and furious, a flurry of strikeouts in an 0–0 game until Ed Kranepool, booed each time his name was announced, lofted one over the right field fence to give New York a 1–0 lead.

Ernie Banks answered with a solo shot of his own, and it was 1–1. In the seventh, Koosman walked Jenkins, of all people. Durocher manufactured a run via a sacrifice bunt and Glenn Beckert's single to make it 2–1.

In the stands, a fan named Joe Delberti displayed a sign reading UNBELIEVABLE. Two attractive brunettes paraded a placard asking WHATEVER HAPPENED TO MARV THRONEBERRY?

In the eighth, Jim Hickman took Koosman deep, something he sure did not do much of in his

Mets owner Joan Whitney Payson had the crucial Chicago series transmitted by a special radio broadcast to her Maine vacation home. *National Baseball Hall of Fame Library*

New York days. With the score 3–1 and Jenkins still firing seeds, Mets fans began to resign themselves to the fact that they were going to be six back.

When the Cubs took the field holding a two-run lead in the ninth, Mets third base coach Yogi Berra passed Banks and said, "We're gonna get three in the ninth and beat you." This time Ernie, normally full of chatter and good cheer, remained silent.

As this was happening, a man in the Ridgewood section of Queens named Frank Graddock, who had been drinking and watching the game all afternoon, observed his wife, Margaret, casually flip the station to her favorite daytime serial, *Dark Shadows.* On that day viewers would learn whether Quentin, who carried the curse of the werewolf, would be able to keep the mummy's hand he had been pursuing through the last few episodes. Frank was uninterested in Quentin, the curse, or the mummy's hand.

In the ninth inning, Hodges pinch hit .245-hitting Ken Boswell for Koosman. Boswell was a pull hitter with some power. Cubs center fielder Don Young played him in right-center, a little too deep. Boswell had a bad hand. After working Jenkins to two and two, he hit a fly ball to straightaway center. If his hand did not hurt, he may have hit it right to Young. If the Cubs advance scouts

Second baseman Ken Boswell, considered a defensive liability, in 1970 set a record for errorless games. *Brace Photos*

Don Young's mishandling of a fly ball was the first chink in the Chicago armor. *Brace Photos*

had known, Young would have been stationed right where the ball was hit. Instead, Young froze like a deer caught in the headlights. Supposedly a defensive specialist—Young's bat was certainly not exceptional—he lost the baseball for a crucial split second in the midsummer haze and background of white shirts in the crowd.

Don Kessinger and Beckert saw Young's fatal hesitation and tried to make up for it, but Boswell's lazy pop was, as they say, a line drive double in the scorebook. Suddenly, more than 50,000 Mets fans made mental note that Chicago had committed the kind of faux pas previously reserved for their guys. Reservedly watching the fast-paced pitchers' battle, their guys striking out, popping up, and weakly grounding out against a future Hall of Famer in his prime, now they came to their feet; imploring, hoping, desperately shouting.

In Queens, Frank Graddock was watching Quentin try to decide whether to keep the mummy's paw or return it in exchange for advice from the witch Angelique, since she was an expert on how to shake the werewolf's curse. Before this information could be made known to Margaret, Graddock switched the station back to Shea Stadium. The tying run was coming to the plate.

Nobody got up in the Cubs bullpen. Durocher's creed was *finish what you start.* Out in the midsummer sun, Jenkins, perspiring and toiling, missed with two balls. Randy Hundley went out to chat with him. Durocher watched stoically. Tommie Agee then popped up to Banks for the first out.

Donn Clendenon came in to pinch hit for light-swinging Bobby Pfeil, who was playing in Bud Harrelson's place while he did his two-week military training stint. Clendenon tended to strike out a lot and at the time actually held the National League record for a season, a mark Bobby Bonds would break. Even though a home run would have tied the game, Clendenon did not feel he could handle Jenkins' still formidable stuff, so he choked up on the bat, hitting a liner to the warning track. Maybe, had he not choked up, he would have cleared the wall, but then again, maybe he would have swung and missed.

Young raced after it, this time without hesitancy. Ball, glove, and fence met at the same time. The ball landed in Young's glove for a tantalizing millisecond but immediately popped out. The crowd held its breath, the "snow coned" white baseball held precariously in the webbing of Young's mitt, then let out a roar that could be heard in West Islip, Long Island, when it plopped to the ground.

Or was that gentle Leo cursing out Young?

Boswell had to hold at second and only made it to third, but his run was not the material thing. Clendenon reached second with one out, and Shea was a madhouse. So was the Graddock household. Frank hit Margaret when, just as the Mets threatened with two on and one out, she tried to switch back to *Dark Shadows,* hoping to observe Angelique explaining how she, too, had once been bitten by a vampire.

Ed Kranepool, who was regularly booed and considered a waste of potential, became a hero on July 8, 1969. *John Rogers Archives*

Cleon Jones came to the plate, hitless all day, but Jenkins was withering. He smoked a line drive double over Ron Santo's head, scoring Boswell and Clendenon to tie it. The Cubs bullpen was up by now as Durocher went out to talk it over with Jenkins. He kept him in the game. Shea throbbed with emotion. The noise, the fevered passions, were unlike anything ever felt at Yankee Stadium. It was Ebbets with Duke at the plate, Jackie dancing off third; "Broadway Joe" eyeing the Raiders' secondary with a minute or so left, the goal post within his sights; it was all of it all rolled into one.

The Jets, in fact, were gathering for the 1969 training camp at Hofstra University on Long Island. According to sportswriter Dick Schaap, they were watching, cheering for the Mets on a television set in assistant coach Walt Michaels's room.

Durocher ordered Art Shamsky to be walked. Wayne Garrett grounded to Beckert as hoped for, but it was not hard enough to turn two. Beckert threw Garrett out at first while Jones went to third, Shamsky to second.

Ed Kranepool, the symbol of all those bad Mets teams (of Casey Stengel asking, "Can't anybody here play this game?"), the bonus baby from James Monroe High who never became the hometown hero, the man who just played out the string, stepped to the plate. No time for the usual boos. Cheers resounded as his name was called.

With J. C. Martin on deck, the percentage play would have been to walk him, but Durocher was not playing percentages. He stuck with the laboring Jenkins and showed disdain for Kranepool by ordering his man to pitch to him.

In Queens, Frank Graddock punched his wife so hard she had to crawl into her room. He switched from *Dark Shadows* back to the game. Margaret's injuries were fatal. The next day Graddock would be charged with first-degree murder.

Jenkins missed high on the first pitch. Then he came back low and outside. Kranepool normally would have taken it, but he was guessing that way and wanted to punch an opposite-field hit between Kessinger, playing toward the middle, and Santo. But the pitch was farther out of his hitting zone than he thought, and his efforts were weak. The bat almost left his hand, but contact was made, resulting in a lazy pop that eluded Kessinger, landing in the outfield grass. Jones romped home.

The Mets raced out of their dugout. Koosman was the unlikely winning pitcher. The celebration had all the earmarks of a World Series victory, and the roar of the crowd was mind-boggling.

It was 4:14 p.m. on the afternoon of Tuesday, July 8, and at that precise instant, the Mets became the official passion of New York City, *the team* relegating the mediocre Yankees to backpage status; and the miraculous nature of the 1969 baseball season manifested itself as self-evident truth.

The 11-game winning streak of May and June; beating the Dodgers and Giants: all of that had been important, but now the ghosts of "Willie, Mickey, and the Duke," as the song goes, were replaced by a new generation, a "new breed." It was like John Kennedy's "new frontier" come to life. It was the "great beginnings" from the opening of Stanley Kubrick's *2001: A Space Odyssey,* embodied by Richard Strauss's *Also Sprach Zarathustra.*

No metaphor, no description is too hyperbolic to describe what was happening. It was that huge. In a city that had seen everything, it was, if not new, so different, so refreshing and wonderful as to be a . . . *miracle.*

8

THE BIRTH OF A TRUE NEW YORK SPORTS ICON

That perfect game, captured once as a boy, eluded him as a man.

—John Devaney, reflecting on Tom Seaver's perfect game as a 12-year-old Little Leaguer, Tom Seaver: An Intimate Portrait

On July 9, 1965, the Houston Astros defeated the New York Mets for the seventh straight time that season, 6–2, behind a sensational teenager named Larry Dierker. Houston scored five runs in the second inning when Mets second baseman Chuck Hiller and shortstop Roy McMillan made errors.

Four years later (and 45 minutes after Lindsey Nelson announced, "It's absolute bedlam. You could not believe it. It's absolute bedlam," when Ed Kranepool drove in Cleon Jones to beat Chicago 4–3) another event occurred that utterly eclipsed that one. It was at 9:55 p.m. on Wednesday, July 9, 1969. In the pantheon of greatness reserved only for that most heroic of all heroes—"in the Arena," as Theodore Roosevelt liked to call it, the bright lights of Broadway, the Great White Way, and Shea Stadium illuminating him in all his splendor—the next New York Sports Icon emerged.

By 5:45 p.m., Shea Stadium's parking lot was full, and the stands were mostly full. The excitement and air of anticipation was at a fever pitch. It was a World Series atmosphere. Leo Durocher, who saw it all long before this night, was nonplussed, playing gin rummy in his office with old friend Barney Kremenko of the *New York Journal-American.* With a mass of writers and TV people on hand,

Joe Reichler, an assistant to new Commissioner of Baseball Bowie Kuhn, entered to ask if, maybe, possibly, could he, uh, come out and say a few words? Durocher gave Reichler the "bum's rush" in favor of his gun rummy match. Reichler asked if Durocher would sign on to a postseason tour of Vietnam. Durocher ignored him.

Jimmy Qualls was a 22-year-old rookie who had just been called up from Tacoma of the Pacific Coast League. He was only now starting to get his swing down, having missed two weeks to serve with his Reserve unit in Stockton, California. In the Mets clubhouse, Qualls' surprise start left Seaver, Grote, and pitching coach Rube Walker looking for a scouting report. Without any computer databases or Internet searches yet available, they had to rely on Bobby Pfeil, the only one to have seen him hit. Pfeil recommended "hard stuff"—fastballs and sliders—as opposed to curves and changeups.

"He can get his bat on the ball," he told Seaver.

At 7:48, Seaver began to get loose, but he was experiencing trouble. There was a twitch in his shoulder. He went through 103 pitches, trying to get the kinks out. "It still feels a little stiff," he told Rube Walker as he made his way to the dugout.

"Do the best you can," Walker replied.

Outside the stadium, a group of about 50 kids, described by one police officer as a "raving mob," managed to sneak into the park when Jerry Koosman's wife, Lavonne, arrived and the gate was opened for her. It was a portent of future events. The game was a sellout—59,083—with standing room only packed shoulder to shoulder, some fans having waited since 7:30 in the morning. Outside the stadium, hundreds of fans stood in fruitless lines, hope against hope that they would catch a break, an extra ticket; scalpers, some just soaking up the atmosphere, listened to transistor radios. The excitement was as high as for any conceivable sporting event: a USC–Notre Dame game at South Bend with the national championship on the line, a Final Four in basketball, or a pro football contest at Shea Stadium. The tension was as so thick it could be cut with a knife.

Baseball was back!

Finally, Tom Seaver, now stiffness-free and throwing easily, took the mound. His fastball simply exploded. The Cubs hitters stared at it, or at what they *heard* of it, since they could not actually see the thing.

New York then faced Ken Holtzman. Holtzman had gone 9–0 in 1967 but was 11–14 in 1968. With Chicago sprinting out to an early lead in 1969, Holtzman was their best pitcher, at least as effective as the redoubtable Ferguson Jenkins. He won nine straight again, but entering the game he had lost three straight.

Holtzman was a streaky pitcher. There was no mystery to him. He threw real hard with little else in his repertoire. He relied on location, in many ways the baseball version of the Green Bay Packers' sweep.

When Holtzman won nine straight, all was right. If his velocity was off, his fastball straighter than usual, his pitches out over the plate, trouble found him, and it did this night. Tommie Agee lined the first pitch like he knew what was coming, down the right field line for a triple. Shea was awash in sound, and out of that a thunderous chant arose: "Let's go *Mets!*"

Bobby Pfeil, who Ron Santo did not think could hit his way out of a paper bag, did his best imitation of Rogers Hornsby: first pitch, double in the left field corner, 1–0. Seaver's pre-game admonition for a 9–0 first inning lead so he could "finesse" the rest of the way looked possible at this point. They were teeing off on the Cubs southpaw.

Durocher, who sat cross-legged while Jenkins battled nine complete innings the previous day, immediately called for submariner Ted Abernathy to get loose quickly down in the bullpen. With Cleon Jones coming to the plate, fans began to climb over the fence. Park police cleared some away from the "batter's eye," the black background behind center field so hitters did not have fans blurring the pitch.

"I have been to every ball game here, and I have never seen anything like this," broadcaster Lindsey Nelson told the hundreds of thousands tuned into the television broadcast. "People are everywhere."

Then, just like that, Holtzman settled down, striking out Jones and Donn Clendenon in the process of pitching out of the jam. But he had no time to gather himself on the bench. Seaver retired Chicago one-two-three in the second inning, causing Rube Walker to tell Gil Hodges that he had "no-hit" stuff. Indeed, Mets fans were seeing something very, very rare.

Many a well-pitched game marks an average baseball season, but Seaver was out of his shoes, above and beyond even his best games over the course of his first two and a half years. He was bringing it in the high 90s, maybe breaking 100 miles an hour, with perfect control and rhythm. What these fans were seeing was Koufax on his best night; Gibson in full domination mode, or any of the all-time legends, whether it be Walter Johnson, Lefty Grove, or Bob Feller. They say "good pitching beats good hitting." It does, but it has to be exceptional. Seaver was beyond exceptional. He was simply unhittable. His stuff could not be touched, merely waved at, gawked at, stunned by.

Poor Kenny Holtzman, a mere mortal in fruitless opposition to a god, took the mound in the second. With one out, he induced Grote to hit a sharp bounder to Santo, who chested it to the ground with his customary grit but for some reason could not pick it up. Grote reached. Then Al Weis's perfect double-play ground ball skimmed through Kessinger's glove. The "god" Seaver now stepped in against his onetime Alaska Goldpanners teammate. As if to demonstrate it was no fluke that Seaver had gotten the final roster spot in 1964, he tomahawked a line drive between first and second base, scoring Grote. Then Agee doubled off the right field fence, scoring Weis and moving Seaver to third. Chicago's Rube Walker (Verlon, the brother of Mets pitching coach Al—they shared a nickname) went to the mound to remove Holtzman, who was not a rube. Durocher sat in the dugout, disgusted.

Shea was frantic. With Seaver knocking the eyelashes off flies from 60 feet, 6 inches, plus swinging the bat like he was Bobby Clemente, the outcome of the game was utterly without doubt. It was full throttle momentum, and Chicago was as done as an overcooked Thanksgiving turkey.

"Break up the Mets!" began to be heard. It was a strange plea that fans occasionally chanted in Seaver's rookie year, when he for the first time demonstrated such unaccustomed excellence that the people conceived in jest that he had made them too good for the rest of the league. In past years, fans and writers had legitimately asked for the Yankees dynasty, or Connie Mack's greatest A's teams, to be "broken up." In Mack's case they were, mainly when the Great Depression made it impossible for him to keep paying his high-salaried stars. But no such luck with the Bronx Bombers, at least until now. What was going on up at Yankee Stadium was attrition, a decaying empire.

Abernathy was effective and held New York without further scoring, but that was immaterial, especially when Seaver mowed through Chicago in the third, one-two-three. In the stands, Dick Schaap and Paul Zimmerman, two experienced journalists, were roaming about. They sensed history in the making and, because they were working on a book called *The Year the Mets Lost Last Place*, they paid particular attention to the fans' reactions, trying to figure out what made these special, lively baseball fans tick. They approached George Hubela, in his early 20s from Brooklyn, sitting in the loge section back of home plate with his brothers, Louis (14), John (13), and friend Ralph Vilardi (14). Hubela displayed a Mets banner.

On the night of July 9, Tom Seaver became forever immortalized. This sequence shows him in top form.
John Rogers Archive

"The Mets are the greatest," said Hubela. "They're the team that's happening, baby. This is it—the 'new breed.' Jets and Mets, Mets and Jets. That's it. No other teams. The Mets have already gone all the way. They're here. They're going to the moon, the next flight to the moon." He managed to sound like a famous TV Brooklynite, Jackie Gleason's *Honeymooners* character, Ralph Cramden.

Hubela had already mailed in for World Series tickets. "Just wait," he said. "I'll be here." Hubela was typical of the Mets fans. Indeed, the team itself was not the only thing that was "new breed." Hubela and the other fans, none of whom sat on their hands like Yankees fans always had, were decidedly different.

In the fourth inning, Seaver faced the top of the Cubs' order—Kessinger, Beckert, and Williams—for the second time. A strikeout and two easy grounders to Ed Charles made quick work of them. In the fifth, Santo, Banks, and Al Spangler went down—a fly ball, a grounder to shortstop, and Seaver's eighth strikeout. In the sixth, as he went through the Cubs order for the second time, Ed Kranepool said it: "He's got a perfect game." The tradition in the dugout of a pitcher with a no-hitter, much less a perfect game, is to say nothing, but it was obvious to every player and fan in Shea Stadium that evening.

At the offices of the Associated Press in Midtown Manhattan, baseball writer Ed Schuyler was dispatched to Shea Stadium in case Seaver pitched a perfect game. Schuyler had done the same thing in 1968, arriving just as Orlando Cepeda of St. Louis broke it up.

On Long Island, Nelson Burbrink, the scout who signed Tom Seaver off the USC campus a mere three years earlier, got in his car after scouting a prospect. As the car eased onto the Long Island Expressway, he heard Lindsey Nelson on WJRZ say, "Tom Seaver will get quite a hand when he comes up to bat here. He's faced 18 Cubs and retired them all."

Sitting in a box seat near first base, Nancy Seaver began to cry. Seaver glanced at her and saw the emotions start to spill out. The atmosphere was utterly electric, almost indescribable, a buzz of sound and anticipation bubbling to the surface, threatening to swallow up a stadium, a whole city.

Kessinger led off the seventh, the top of the order for the third time. Seaver had been pounding fastballs on Chicago all night, but thinking that he should give them a little wrinkle, he curved the Cubs shortstop, who sliced a liner to left field. At first Seaver thought it was their first hit, but the ball hung, and Jones grabbed it easily. Beckert popped to Swoboda, sweating bullets of nerves in right. Williams bounced to Charles. Shea exploded.

With one out in the top of the seventh, Jones lined a homer, an "insurance" run on a night Tom Seaver did not need it. The score was 4–0. In the bottom half of the inning, Hodges sent Rod Gaspar to right field in place of Swoboda, Wayne Garrett to second, and Bobby Pfeil to third, replacing Charles.

"You go into a game like this, cold and everything, and you're just hoping you can do the job if the ball is hit to you," Gaspar was quoted saying in *The Year the Mets Lost Last Place.* "It's a perfect game. We're going for first place. All the people in the park. It's frightening."

In the eighth, Seaver induced Santo to fly to Agee. Then, facing Banks and Spangler, he seemed to jet it up a half notch. The middle innings were over, his pitch count low, the game in hand. There was no holding anything back. Incredibly, he started throwing harder. The Mets fans watched; loud, crazy, boisterous, yes, but by now in awe. They were observing a baseball Michelangelo, a sculptor of the mound. Seaver, who admired his brother the sculptor, and wanted to somehow duplicate in baseball what he could do with clay, was now accomplishing this task.

Old-timers, who had seen it all over the past 50 years of baseball in the golden age of New York, knew instinctively that the 24-year-old Californian was a new Koufax, a Ford, a Newcombe; maybe better than any of those guys. A "new breed." After Seaver rocketed a heater past Spangler to end the eighth, he walked off the mound to insane cheering. Announcer Bob Murphy then stated, "LADIES AND GENTLEMEN, AFTER EIGHT INNINGS, TOM SEAVER IS WALKING INTO THE DUGOUT WITH A PERFECT BALL GAME."

Grote grounded out, but Weis singled. Seaver donned a batting helmet, undid the donut from his bat, and gave his warm-up jacket to the batboy. It was 9:55 p.m., Wednesday, July 9, 1969, the seminal moment in which George Thomas Seaver entered the pantheon.

The crowd rose; they had been continuously cheering all through Seaver's dominant eighth inning, building to a crescendo that rocked the five-year-old stadium to its very core. It was the sound Marilyn Monroe *wished* she heard when she gyrated before the boys in Korea; the sound Joe DiMaggio *had* heard when he was at his heroic best at Yankee Stadium, the knowledge of which he so contemptuously informed the breathless Marilyn when she tried to tell him, "Joe, Joe, you never *heard* such cheering."

It was what Namath heard less than a year earlier, but according to all the pundits, all the experts and futurists during this age in which Alvin Toffler's *Future Shock* was being taught in schools, it would never be heard again at a *baseball game.* That was yesterday, passé, old school. But here it was. Tom's official entrance and acceptance into the pantheon of the rarest of the rare: the true New York Sports Icon.

Packers fans treated Bart Starr and Vince Lombardi like pagan idols. In Los Angeles, Sandy Koufax was given the star treatment. Many cities had their heroes, and of course they cheered wildly, they were loud, and it was electric.

But this was New York.

This was the biggest of the big time, the ultimate stage, the winning over with the most impressive of all bravura performances the most cynical, loud-mouthed, hardcore, hard-to-please sports aficionados on the face of the earth. In this we get to the heart of what made this different, what made this a *miracle.* The winning over of the crowd, the total, childlike exuberance of the hard-bitten seen-it-alls, had a Pentecostal touch to it. They were *children,* all of them. The middle-aged men, who toiled for big bucks on Wall Street or union wages in a delivery truck; the grandmothers wondering what was happening to kids these days—all the drugs and sex and lack of respect—yet it all came together here, with Seaver a Pied Piper who did not quite know what was happening himself, so magical and mystical was it. The young man who old folks related to, the sex symbol who was faithful to his wife, the sports hero who seven years earlier was 6–5 pitching for the Fresno High varsity was now a New York hometown hero.

So the sound washed over Tom Seaver. The stadium clock ticked 9:55, then 9:56. Above the stadium, Christy Mathewson, John McGraw, Babe Ruth, Lou Gehrig, Branch Rickey, and Mel Ott formed a ghostly Hall of Fame, granting approval, imprimatur to the newest member. Ruth called Seaver "Keed." Matty told McGraw, "He reminds me of me." Rickey saw the perfect harmony of black and white teammates, the stands a diverse mix of New Yorkers, and nodded approval over that which he had wrought.

In the Mets dugout, Yogi Berra understood that a new guy was joining that exclusive fraternity, the one that included Joe D. and Mick. In the Cubs dugout, Durocher looked enviously at the 24-year-old, knowing this mere child was ascending to a place where the "Say Hey Kid" was; a place where diamond gods resided in regal splendor; a club he was barred from entering into no matter how expensive his silk suit, or how stylish the dame on his arms. It was like Frank and Dean entering the room, turning and saying, "Sorry, Leo, not tonight," just as a giant bouncer stood between him and the entrance to the hallowed palace they were in and he was not.

Somewhere in America, Joe Louis and Rocky Marciano knew that Tom Seaver felt that special sense of recognition they had worked so hard to attain during all those nights at the Garden. Somewhere in Manhattan, probably at the center of a social whirl that had stopped itself in its tracks to watch the Mets game on television, Frank Gifford was smiling at the TV image of another Trojan entering the pantheon he had forged in the previous decade. Out in California, a Glendale banker named Casey Stengel was most likely asleep when it happened, but upon his awakening and perusal of the *Los Angeles Times* the next morning, the "Ol' Perfesser" surely knew that a Met was in the most exclusive of clubs. Somewhere else, in temporary retirement after Pete Rozelle told him it was Bachelors III or football, not both, was Joe Willie Namath. He had a blonde on one arm, a brunette on another, and a bottle of Johnnie Walker Red in the middle. His sense of inclusion, his egalitarianism forged in a tough Pennsylvania upbringing, honed in segregated Birmingham where he walked the streets of the "colored section" like Huey Long, made Joe Willie smile.

Sure, New York's big enough for the two of us. Welcome to the club, Tom.

So be it. So it was. The latest true New York Sports Icon, the *savior,* then laid down a perfect sacrifice bunt. The runner moved to second as he jogged off the field, cheered as if he had just moved a mountain.

An estimated two and a half million New Yorkers were now watching Seaver trot off the field. Over the past innings, phones rang, doors were knocked on, people left all forms of human endeavor to rush home: to a bar, to a car radio, anywhere, to hear or see this *happening.* It was like Orson Welles's recreation of *The War of the Worlds.*

"Housewives not the least interested in baseball have been dragged to the set by their husbands to watch history," wrote Dick Schaap and Paul Zimmerman. Little kids, boys and girls, foreigners, people of all stripe who call themselves "New Yorkers," found a common bond in Seaver and the Mets at this instant. Schaap and Zimmerman informed readers that a Chrysler commercial played in between the bottom of the eighth and the top of the ninth, urging car buyers to "dream the impossible dream." The song "The Impossible Dream" from *Man of La Mancha* was popular at that time in part because it was associated with Boston's "Impossible Dream" pennant chase of 1967. Now it applied to the Mets.

Nancy Seaver wept as she watched her husband take the mound for the ninth. Next to her was Tom's father, Charles, a former Walker Cup golf champion in his own right. Tom's body was floating with pure adrenaline. He had thrown a perfect game as a Little Leaguer, then had all his hopes and dreams for a baseball future seemingly dashed when he made the move to the "big diamond," then high school, where the likes of Dick Selma—now a spectator sitting in the opposing team's dugout—had surpassed him by leaps and bounds.

Some 59,000 fans chanted "Seav-*uh*, Seav-*uh*." It was beyond incredible, beyond heady. He later said his arm was light, as if detached from his body. He was in touch with his feelings. His heart pounded furiously, but the crowd noise was somehow so great as to be silent. He was in a zone. Few ever reach such a zenith. It is the rarest of air, the highest peak in the mountain range.

But with all of this going on, Seaver still had a job to do, and it required concentration. Amid all of the furor, he dropped, drove, and delivered furious heat to Randy Hundley. Hundley, as if acknowledging that to actually swing and hit Seaver was by now beyond conception, tried to bunt his way on. The ball came right back to Seaver, the easiest play in the world, except that under such intense pressure some people stiffen right up. Grote told him he had plenty of time, and Seaver threw out Hundley as if he did not have a care in the world.

Bud Harrelson, his best friend on the ball club, was watching the game at a restaurant called Giovanni's in Watertown, New York, where he was stationed for two weeks of summer training. Nobody knew who he was. Now he was a fan like everybody else.

At seven minutes after 10 o'clock, Jimmy Qualls strode to the plate. Qualls was the only Cub to get decent wood on a Seaver pitch all night, hitting a sharp line drive caught at the warning track, then a liner to first base. A left-handed batter, he had 47 major league at bats prior to his stepping in against Tom Seaver. Agee in center field was not sure where to play him. Seaver was throwing so hard that it seemed implausible that Qualls would pull him, but he seemed to be on Tom's pitches in a way no other Cub was that night.

Bobby Pfeil's "scouting report"—hard stuff—was all Grote and Seaver had to go by. Seaver had dominated with the best fastball in the game, and that was what he and Grote agreed on. As he nodded yes to the sign, Ed Schuyler of the Associated Press arrived in the Shea Stadium press box.

Tom Seaver went into his windup, dropped, and delivered. Instead of sinking action, down and away, the pitch came in waist high. All night, Seaver was perfect with his location, but his heat was so great that he could get away with a mistake. The Cubs simply could not hit what they could not see. Major league hitters feast on fastballs, much preferring it over curves and off-speed stuff. Their reflexes are the best in the world. They are the most skilled of athletes, those who engage in what Ted Williams called the "single most difficult act in sports," the hitting of a "round ball against a round bat at 95 miles per hour," as Pete Rose described it.

In Little League, high school, and college, the overwhelming fastball artist dominates with speed alone. His competition cannot touch it. At some point, usually in the minor leagues and especially when he reaches The Show, he discovers, sometimes alarmingly, that he is now facing the only 400 or 500 men on the face of the planet who *are* capable of dealing with his heat. An adjustment, an accommodation, must be made. This decides whether he will continue with a successful big league career or become a coach, a scout, a salesman . . . a writer?

Seaver was throwing *so hard* that the best-hitting team in baseball during the first half of the 1969 season was stopped cold, unable to get around on it. That rarest of feats, the fastball they knew was coming, could not be hit. It was like an overwhelming army that blasts past all defensive positions but cannot be stopped by tricks, decoy, or espionage.

But Seaver, dropping and driving, dropping and driving all night, over and over, expending all that energy; now, in the ninth, he was just a quarter-inch off with his fastball. Qualls was the one Cub who seemingly felt no pressure. Little was expected of him. He had not been around all season, subject to Leo Durocher's demands and psychological games. Suddenly, he was Ted Williams or Duke Snider, seeing the ball and reacting to it.

Bat connected, solidly, and the ball carried on a fly to deep left-center field. Agee broke after the ball but quickly snuck a look at Jones, as if to say, "Hey, man, you better get to it 'cause I ain't got it."

Jones just shook his head.

More than 59,000 people groaned as the ball dropped in for a single. Nelson Burbrink and Bud Harrelson swore. A few boos for Jimmy Qualls were replaced by a cheer, louder than ever, for Seaver, now a solitary figure on a mound of dirt surrounded by green grass. Another prolonged standing ovation. Seaver later called it the biggest disappointment of his life, "within my grasp," knowing he might not, probably would not, ever get another chance at something this close to perfection.

With a 4–0 lead, Seaver straightened up, took the mound, and worked to the next two Cubs hitters, retiring them easily. The celebration on the field was muted, but the crowd let forth still more outpourings of adulation. A star was born, that was for sure; manifested, more like it. Seaver disappeared into the clubhouse. Later the crowd, not wanting to leave, chanted, "We want Seaver," but he was gone. The 59,000 made their way into the parking lot, the subways, the bars of Queens and Manhattan, to celebrate and talk it over. What a night!

Seaver was immediately met by Nancy, still battling tears. "I guess a one-hit shutout is better than nothing," she told him. Tom Seaver's greatest triumph was a melancholy moment. Despite the incredible flow of electrical energy, despite now being a mere three games out of first place, the New York clubhouse had a subdued quality to it, but it was nothing compared to Chicago's.

"Nobody was going to beat Seaver tonight," Durocher told the writers. "I never saw him throw so hard. If he keeps throwing that hard, nobody's going to beat him. But I don't think he will.

"We're still three games ahead. And from now on the Mets are going to find the going rougher. They're going to see the best pitchers in the league."

Gentle Leo refrained from predicting "100,000 suicides" if the Mets let their fans down after such a big buildup. He had made his suicide remark in 1952 when the Giants threatened a repeat of their 1951 "shot heard 'round the world" comeback. Then he smiled. "That Qualls ruined you guys," he said. "He made you rewrite your stories."

"There was no pressure on me at all," Qualls told reporters. "All I wanted to do was get a base hit and get something started."

"Dear Diary, last night I sat in, with 60,000 other rabid believers, on the birth of a folk hero," wrote sportswriter Ray Robinson. "The folk hero . . . was Tom Seaver, a right-hander, possessing the virtues of Prince Valiant."

9

THE WRATH OF GIL

Because all those men which have seen my glory, and my miracles, which I did in Egypt and in the wilderness, and have tempted me now these ten times, and have not hearkened to my voice; Surely they shall not see the land which I sware unto their fathers, neither shall any of them that provoked me see it.

—Numbers 14: 22–23

Many said that Tom Seaver was the Mets' "savior," and that his "birth" was July 9, 1969. Indeed, that entire evening at Shea Stadium had a Pentecostal feel to it. Like the Chosen People who preceded the real savior, this team could see the baseball version of the Promised Land. It was so close they could touch it, almost tasting the "land of milk and honey." But like the biblical Chosen People, they would not simply enter it. They would have to fight for it. And they would face his wrath first: the wrath of Gil Hodges.

While the Apollo astronauts were preparing to ascend to the moon, New York traveled to Chicago, where skinny Al Weis hit home runs on consecutive days to spur two wins in the three-game series. Soon after that, though, the "Pentecost" ended and the sky high Mets finally returned to normalcy. The team traveled to Montreal, where they took on the first-year expansion Expos. Montreal under manager Gene Mauch was not as bad as the 1962 Mets, but they were close: 52–110. Yet somehow, they played the Mets fairly even in 1969, at least in the first half of the season. They had knocked Seaver around on opening day, before he was a superstar. They took a game at Shea Stadium sandwiched in between the crucial Cubs series, but neither of those two wins came easily for New York.

Gil Hodges was mild-mannered and friendly, but nobody wanted to get on his bad side. *Brace Photos*

Then the Mets rode into Montreal so high they did not need an airplane. At first it seemed to be more of the same, with Koosman gliding to a 5–2 win. But the next day the great Tom Seaver, the unhittable master, was terribly distressed by severe stiffness, which became actual pain in his throwing shoulder. He lost a pedestrian 5–4 game to Bill Stoneman, a pretty good pitcher who threw a no-hitter in 1969. The next day Gary Gentry pitched well, but not well enough in a 3–2 loss. They lost a series to *the Expos.*

After that came the All-Star break, a needed and necessary three days off for most ball clubs, but curiously not of value to the Mets. Regardless of the Montreal series, the Mets were the hot team in the National League and were better off playing other not-so-hot teams.

Nevertheless, the break came. Some of the Mets coaches went up to the Catskills. They were notorious cheapskates, complaining about the cost of everything; gotta tip this guy, gotta tip that guy. Then again, this was an era in which the minimum big league salary was around $7,000 a year. These guys were working men, not retired millionaires from their playing days who coached out of a sense of noblesse oblige. Seaver, Koosman, and Jones were all selected to the National League team for the All-

Gary Gentry gets a little bad feedback.
John Rogers Archives

Coach Joe Pignatano, like many "organization men," tended to watch his pennies. *Brace Photos*

Star Game, which was a blowout National League win at Washinton's Robert F. Kennedy Stadium.

The summer of 1969 was a momentous period in this nation's history, for good and most definitely also for bad. On the good side was that American astronauts successfully landed on the moon on July 20. It was a spectacular achievement, a response to President Kennedy's vision of "landing a man on the Moon and returning him safely to the Earth." It was an outlandish proposal, yet both the Soviets and the United States entered into a fierce "space race," with the moon being the ultimate prize of the victor.

By 1969 the Soviets were, to paraphrase the late astronaut Gus Grissom, "in our shadow." After having to abort a 1968 trip within sight of the moon's rocky terrain, *Apollo 11* took off in July 1969. On July 20 Neil Armstrong and Buzz Aldrin (with Michael Collins circling anxiously overhead) stepped out on its surface, with Armstrong announcing, "That's one small step for man, one giant leap for mankind." (Ironically, the Mets observed the moon landing from an airport in Montreal, where they were stuck because *their plane did not work.*)

On a decidedly bad note in August 1969, the Manson killings rocked Los Angeles. Charles Manson, a would-be songwriter and career criminal who had spent the majority of his life behind bars, sent his commune-like "family" on a killing spree, using the victims' blood to spell words like *PIG* and *WAR* on the walls of the sites of this mad crusade. Neighbors heard screams, but this being Hollywood, they figured it to be an orgy, a cult meeting, a witch's coven, or any number of "ordinary" happenings of this time and place.

"It seemed like the world was going insane," Art Shamsky recalled.

The other seminal nonsports event of 1969 was Woodstock. Whether this was good or bad depends on one's point of view. For some, it was a free demonstration of peace, love, joy, and harmony. For others, it was a dirty, filthy event that emphasized drugs and fueled the sexual revolution.

On August 17 Hurricane Camille, a category 5 storm, hit the Gulf Coast. Huge hurricanes had pounded Florida in the 1930s but subsided somewhat over the decades. The lessons from the earlier storms were lost. In the 1930s there was a small population in the area, so the weather mainly just hit beaches with little damage to property. There was no cable TV warning or 24-hour news cycle sensationalizing them. When word of Camille came, people in Miami and other locations in its path held "hurricane parties," in some cases with tragic results when the storm came through. All in all, 248 died, and billions of dollars were lost in damages.

John Wayne's *The Green Berets* was a box office hit. Its theme song, "The Ballad of the Green Berets," was a popular tune, belying the idea that everybody in America opposed the war or supported the protesters.

"We were all aware of what was going on in the country," Jerry Koosman recalled. "I remember watching the moon landing on television in a Montreal airport. So much was happening then, with Vietnam and all the demonstrations and protests at home. Yet as a team, I don't recall us talking much about politics."

Outfielder Art Shamsky had a way of keeping things in perspective. *Brace Photos*

In August, with the Mets having lost the momentum of early July, Tom Seaver contacted USC and told them to expect him to start classes in early October, as the Mets would not be in the postseason after all. Down by nine and a half games, however, Gil Hodges still demanded professionalism.

On July 30 the Mets faced old nemesis Houston. Like the Mets, for the very first time the Astros were in contention, in the "wild, wild West" with Atlanta, San Francisco, Cincinnati, and Los Angeles, all neck and neck. Houston featured Larry Dierker and Don Wilson, two of the hardest-throwing pitchers in baseball. They set records for strikeouts of opposing hitters. Wilson managed a no-hitter in 1969. Their plush indoor facility, the Astrodome (known as the "eighth wonder of the world"), was built for pitching and defense, their specialties. The Astros were a loose group.

Joe Morgan was still with Houston that season. Center fielder Jim "the Toy Cannon" Wynn was a power threat. The 1969 Astros, like that season's expansion Seattle Pilots, were immortalized by Jim Bouton's *Ball Four.* Bouton, who was traded to Houston in the second half of the year, revealed a bawdy drinking song the team recited after wins. Catcher Johhny Edwards would "drink too much and call some long home runs." The team's ability to exasperate old-school manager Harry Walker with their penchant to "drink and fight and [perform other acts] 'til curfew comes around" was glorified.

In the ninth inning of the first game of a doubleheader at Shea Stadium, Houston scored 11 runs, including two grand slams, to win, 16–3. "Using the word *played* is somewhat of a misnomer—we were massacred in both contests," was the way Art Shamsky described it. The second game was "even uglier."

In the third inning of game 2, Houston scored 10 runs after two men were out to complete the sweep, 11–5. "This was the worst day I've seen as a Met," said Seaver. "It was like it must have been seven years ago."

An incident in this game has long been called the "turning point" of the season, although that is debatable on several levels. Johnny Edwards hit a slicing ball down into the left field corner. Cleon Jones barely jogged after it, picked it up, and lobbed it back into the infield. The home fans booed his obvious lack of hustle.

Hodges headed out to the mound. He was superstitious about not stepping on the first base line, but this time he paid no attention. He was furious. Instead of stopping at the mound to remove a hapless pitcher, he continued on. Bud Harrelson saw him coming and thought maybe he had done something wrong, but the seething Hodges continued into the outfield grass. Hodges confronted Jones. After a few words, Hodges headed back to the dugout, a contrite left fielder a few steps behind him. Years later, Jones explained the incident to Art Shamsky for Shamsky's book *The Magnificent Seasons*:

Nobody knows what really happened except Gil and me. All anybody knows is that he came out on the field and pulled me out of the ball game. But, this is what happened. The ball was hit down the left field line, and there was no way you were going to stop him from getting a double. So I ran after the ball the best way I could. It was soaking wet in the outfield that day, and I had a bad ankle. When Gil walked out to me, I was surprised as everyone else. First, I thought he was going to take out the pitcher. Then, I thought he was going to say something to Harrelson. But, then, when he walked past Buddy, I looked back. I thought something had happened behind me. When I turned around, he was coming right toward me. He got to me and said, "What's wrong?" I said, "What do you mean, what's wrong?" He replied, "I don't like the way you went after that last ball." I said, "Gil, we talked about this in Montreal. You know I have a bad ankle, and as long as I wasn't going to hurt the team, I would continue to play." And then I said, "Look down." And he did. His feet were in water. He said, "It is bad out here. I didn't know it was that bad. You probably need to come out of the game." So I said, "Fine," and we walked in together. A few days later we had a conversation, and he said, "You know I wouldn't embarrass you like that, but I look at you as a leader on this club. Everybody seemed like they were comfortable getting their tails kicked, and I didn't like that. . . ."

Everybody misinterpreted what happened. But in a way it proved a point and woke us up. That was his way of trying to shape up the ball club.

When Hodges came home that evening, his wife, Joan, told him that he should not have embarrassed Jones the way he did. "You want to know something?" Hodges told Joan. "I didn't even realize I was doing it until I was past the pitcher."

"Hodges and Jonesy had a rocky relationship," Swoboda recalled, because "Cleon wouldn't go out there for outfield practice, or sometimes Cleon wouldn't take batting practice."

Swoboda's assertion that Hodges and Jones had a "rocky relationship," in part because of Jones's failure to practice his defensive skills, brings up a conundrum of sorts, since Swoboda also claimed that *he* and the manager were on uneven terms because Swoboda practiced defense *too much.*

"Houston was the toughest club we faced," said Koosman. "They had a great pitching staff with Larry Dierker and Don Wilson. We had a heck of a time beating them.

"But I didn't see what Gil saw. I didn't see that Cleon didn't hustle after the ball." Still, Koosman added, "you don't slough off when you play for Gil Hodges. You give him 100 percent all the time. It sends a message to the rest of the ball club."

Whether the "wrath of Gil" was planned or not, the event is viewed through the prism of history as a catalyst, but in reality the team sank further into the abyss after that.

10

RESURRECTION

Believe in miracles.

—Karl Ehrhardt, the "Sign Man of Shea"

"Journalistically, it's conventional to want to look for turning points," said Ron Swoboda. "In a 162-game season there's no single turning point. There are a collection of things that turn you in another direction, and for us the collection was Cardwell, Koosman, Gentry, and even McAndrew getting physically well. . . . They all had little things bothering them, and they didn't pitch very well in the first half of the year. Everyone but Seaver. Seaver was the same; dead steady."

On August 16 Seaver started against San Diego, the worst team in the league. He told Grote if the Mets could not get happy against the Padres, they did not deserve a pennant. Warming up, Seaver was overjoyed to discover the stiffness had disappeared as mysteriously as it came. The San Diego series was a real ordeal: back-to-back doubleheaders. With Seaver's arm seemingly touched by an unseen hand and suddenly as strong as it had been on July 9, the first-year expansion club was helpless in a 2–0 Mets win. In the second game, and in both of the next day's twin bill, New York pitching held up in tense one-run victories: 2–1, 3–2, and 3–2.

Hodges benched Jones. Swoboda took his place and had a chance to face right-handers over the next few games, collecting a substantial portion of runs batted in.

"As late as August 19, we were still nine and a half games back, but then we started to make our move," Koosman said. "Seaver and I won our last 15 starts."

Over the course of mid-August to the last game of the regular season on October 2, Seaver and Koosman were as "lights out" a pitching combination as has ever been known over a similar stretch. This is not an exaggeration, as it takes into account such stalwart duos as Christy Mathewson and Joe McGinnity (New York Giants, 1900s), Christy Mathewson and Rube Marquard (Giants, 1910s), Chief Bender and Ed Plank (Philadelphia A's, 1910s), Waite Hoyt and Herb Pennock (New York Yankees, 1920s), Lefty Gomez and Red Ruffing (Yankees, 1930s), Bob Feller and Bob Lemon (Cleveland Indians, 1940s), Sandy Koufax and Don Drysdale (Los Angeles Dodgers, 1960s), Juan Marichal and Gaylord Perry (San Francisco Giants, 1960s), Bob Gibson and Steve Carlton (St. Louis Cardinals, 1960s–1970s), Catfish Hunter and Ken Holtzman (Oakland A's, 1970s), and the staffs at Atlanta (Greg Maddux, Tom Glavine, John Smoltz) and Oakland (Barry Zito, Mark Mulder, Tim Hudson) in the past two decades.

As for "hot" pitchers over a single year or partial season, Seaver in 1969—and in particular after August 5 (his last defeat, 8–5, at Cincinnati)—is matched only by a handful. Old-timers such as Mathewson, Cy Young, Grover Alexander, Walter Johnson; "one-year wonders" like Jack Chesbro (1904), "Big Ed" Walsh (1906), and "Smoky" Joe Wood (1912) must have their statistics viewed in the context of the "dead ball era." More recent hotshots such as Dean Chance (1964), Denny McLain (1968), even Gibson (1968) and Drysdale (during his 58 straight scoreless innings in 1968), plus Ron Guidry (1978), Steve Stone (1980), and Orel Hershiser (1988), are among the few who might match up with "Tom Terrific's" dominance. So, with that in mind, it must also be stated that as good as Seaver was, Koosman was just as good.

The "Tom and Jerry Show" was off the charts. Their confidence was at such a high level that they simply determined to do things, then willed it true, as if pitching baseballs to big league hitters was the easiest act in the world. In many ways, both pitchers ruined it for the rest of their careers. Seaver's record, of course, speaks for itself: a first-ballot Hall of Famer with the highest percentage of votes in Cooperstown history. Yet even in his best subsequent years, it was always hard work for him. Koosman was an effective big leaguer who never really repeated his 1968–1969 dominance. Certainly he did not sniff what he did in late August, September, and October of that year.

Both were hard workers, and their careers reflected success based on that ethic, their talent and competitiveness, but the pure ease with which they mowed down all comers was so spectacular, and so rare, really, that it gives off the unique, unseen, unexplainable whiff of a miracle. Was it just good pitching and some luck? Maybe.

Koosman and Seaver challenged each other, acknowledging their one-upsmanship with gestures from mound to dugout: 10 strikeouts would have to be matched with 11; a hitter sawed off after predicting the count in which it would happen; "making little bets as to who could get the side out with three pitches," said Koosman.

"The difference between the physical abilities of the players in the major leagues is not that great and, something going hand in hand with that, the difference between the teams is not that great," Tom Seaver surmised. "So what it comes down to is that the dividing factor between the one that wins and the one that loses is the mental attitude, the effort they give, the mental alertness that keeps them from making mental mistakes. The concentration and the dedication—the intangibles—are the deciding factors, I think, between who won and who lost. I firmly believe that. I really do."

This was Seaver's logical, reasoning mind at work. He once explained his motivation, his desire for perfection, the driving force separating him from so many others: "It's why you run wind sprints in 104-degree heat in the middle of the afternoon in St. Louis in the summer. In the ninth inning with the game on the line, you draw strength from that."

As August droned toward September, the Mets got hot, and the Chicago lead began to slip. Seaver started to think about 20 wins. It was not a selfish goal. If he could get there, it would help his team catch the Cubs. Chicago's cockiness, their bulletin board bravado, the impatience of Leo Durocher, all combined with the Midwestern heat and the all-day-game Wrigley Field schedule to drain them just when they needed resources.

1969 MVP Willie McCovey had the best year of his Hall of Fame career, but failed to propel his team to the title, unlike Tom Seaver. In later years, Willie Mac showed no grace when asked to credit Seaver with MVP consideration. *Brace Photos*

Hodges's platoon schedule, judicious use of the bullpen, and five-man starting rotation had the opposite effect on New York. In late August the Mets won six straight. In early September Chicago lost seven straight.

"We went into a composite slump," Leo the Lion was quoted by Edgar Munzel in *The Sporting News*. "It wasn't just one or two guys. It was everybody and every department. Hitting, pitching and fielding all went bad."

"Leo Durocher was doing well with his veteran ballplayers," said Rod Gaspar. "According to stories, Leo was enjoying himself at that time, but the Cubs pitching fell apart, and a young upstart team, the Mets, took their place. The majority of Durocher's starting lineup was All-Stars. Leo wore 'em out."

On August 30 at San Francisco's Candlestick Park, the score was tied in the bottom of the ninth. With a man on, New York went into the famed "McCovey shift," ceding all of the left side to the pull-hitting left-handed slugger.

Willie McCovey "hit a nine iron down the left field line, and it lands fair," recalled Gaspar. Gaspar, playing left field but shifted almost to center, took chase and discovered the baseball was stuck to the ground because the field was wet. He picked it up and fired a strike to the relay man, who in turn nailed runner Bob Burda, trying to score from first. Catcher Jerry Grote thought it was the third out and rolled the ball out to the mound. McCovey saw that and, having made it to third on the relay, tried to score. Donn Clendenon alertly picked up the ball. Grote then stayed at home when he saw he had made a mistake. McCovey, realizing he could not make it home, tried to get back to third, but

Clendenon nailed him there for an inning-ending 7-3-2-3-5 double play. New York won, 3–2, in extra innings.

On August 31 Chicago (81–52) led New York (75–53) by three and a half games. St. Louis slumped and was now out of it, nine games back. In a matter of a couple of weeks, New York had gone from nine and a half back to three and a half, and while those games obviously represented a mathematical advantage for the Cubs, the psychology of momentum worked in New York's favor.

With friends and family from Fresno in attendance (as a kid, Seaver and his kin made roughly an equal number of trips to Los Angeles to see the Dodgers, and to San Francisco to see the Giants), Tom tossed an 8–0 shutout at the powerful Giants, who were battling hard for the Western Division crown.

The Giants had sluggers, namely, McCovey, who was enjoying his best year, Willie Mays, and Jim Ray Hart. They had two excellent starters, Juan Marichal (21–11) and Gaylord Perry (19–14). One-year manager Clyde King had a personality problem with Mays, which spelled his doom.

However, in 1969 San Francisco and the entire Bay Area suffered from a social malaise emanating from cross-bay Berkeley. At the University of California, sports were viewed as bourgeois capitalism. This general attitude made its way over to San Francisco, where the "Summer of Love" epicentered the decade at Golden Gate Park in 1967, ironically in the shadow of Kezar Stadium, where those rough, tough football players performed for the 49ers. Overall, sports fell by the wayside at all levels in San Francisco. Its high schools stopped producing prospects. Cal was a punching bag for their dominating rivals. The Dodgers developed a dynasty of sorts, with the Giants mere fodder for their big guns. Dodger Stadium symbolized all that was glamorous, Candlestick all that was low rent.

At least as far as the Giants were concerned, they were in the early process of becoming a second-rate National League team. The once lowly Mets, on the other hand, were ascending to the heights of glory, not just on the field but at the gate, via TV ratings, and in all ways that imprimatur is given to professional franchises. Whereas the Dodgers had obviously made a good move relocating to L.A., the Giants may well have looked at the Mets' success and concluded they should have stayed in the Big Apple.

In August 1969 New York beat the Giants in home-and-home series, winning four of six and symbolically accepting the passed torch. Those four losses would prove to be the deciding factor in San Francisco's eventually losing the West. When the Giants series concluded, the Mets finished 21–10 in August, but they weren't done yet.

Back in New York, Seaver won his 20th, 5–1, in the first game of a doubleheader with Philadelphia. New York took the last two games of the Philadelphia series, 3–0 behind Don Cardwell and 9–3 behind Nolan Ryan. The Cubs came to town, now leading by a mere two and a half games on September 8. Chicago had a four-game losing streak and was ripe for the picking. Koosman and Seaver were perfectly aligned to oppose them in the two-game set.

It rained the first night, but the enthusiasm level of the 49,000 people at Shea was off the charts. The New York Jets had nothing on the Mets. Pro football, despite the buildup of a single game played each Sunday, was no more electric than each individual Mets game. The Mets had saved baseball, possibly the city, and maybe even Mayor Lindsay's bid for reelection. By this point, he was sticking to the Mets like glue, football fan or no football fan.

☆ ☆ ☆

Leo Durocher had broken into organized baseball in the early 1920s. He had been part of some great clubs: the Murderers' Row Yanks and the Gashouse Gang Cards. He had managed Brooklyn's Bums and Willie Mays's Giants to pennants, tasting ultimate victory in 1954. He had coached on winners in L.A. and had now taken Chicago from last to first. He was the epitome of the crusty "baseball man." Leo had seen it all, done it all, and bragged to anybody who would listen about it. According to him, Sinatra called *him,* and he scored "every broad who counts."

So it was that in a situation like this, it seemed logical that a man of Durocher's experience knew what buttons to push. He had been on the other side of the coin, leading the Giants' "creeping terror" comeback run in 1951. It was the other guy who flinched. Leo's style was aggressive. The war metaphors are valid: Grant because "he fights," Patton never paying "for the same real estate twice."

In game 1 at Shea, Leo looked at his starter, 20-game winner Billy Hands, only he did not see Hands. He saw Sal Maglie. He sent Hands out to the mound with marching orders: a "contract" was out on the Mets. Maglie had been the perfect guy to do it. They called him "the Barber" because of all the "close shaves" administered using horsehide instead of a razor (which he apparently did not own, considering his perpetual "five o'clock shadow"). But Billy was what was expected of a guy named *Billy Hands.* A job like this required somebody named "Iron Joe," "Big D," Gibby . . . or Sal.

But Billy Hands went out to the lion's den, the middle of the Roman Colosseum, armed with a whip and a chair against lions and gladiators, surrounded by a frenzied crowd out for blood. He gulped, took a deep breath, and threw his best fastball right at Tommie Agee's head.

"Stick it in his ear," Leo yelled.

Who knows why a strategy that works in one time and place does not work in another time and place? In this time and place, it *did not* work. The Mets were not intimidated, and who knows how he thought the New York fans would react? They were only the loudest, most boisterous crowd in the entire history of sports, up until that time at least, but apparently he had not thought that far ahead.

Koosman got the ball and immediately retaliated. He did not low-bridge Ron Santo; he plunked him hard just above the wrist. "Koosman could throw the ball right through you," Santo said.

"They threw at Tommie, and I had to do it to end it right there," said Koosman. "If Tommie doesn't think I'm working for him, he won't work for me—and I want Tommie Agee working for me. He and Cleon, they're the two best hitters I have out there. I want both of them working for me."

"Our pitchers can't let us get run off the field," said Agee.

The next time Agee faced Hands, with Buddy Harrelson on base, he took him deep. The crowd was ecstatic, and New York led 2–0. In the sixth, Chicago scored twice to tie it, 2–2. The bean ball war was over, replaced by tense, pennant-fever baseball. In the bottom of the inning, Agee doubled. Wayne Garrett singled to right field. Star outfielder Billy Williams charged the ball, hop-stepped, and fired home. Agee, the former football player, barreled past Randy Hundley, stepping on home just before the tag. It was a bang-bang play. Umpire Dave Davidson called Agee safe.

Hundley argued the call, and Durocher came out, which was too perfect. The crowd went utterly ballistic, catcalling him every step of the way after he inevitably lost the appeal. From that point, Koosman dominated, finishing with 13 strikeouts backed by solid defense, winning 3–2.

"The Mets are on their way," the fans chanted and sang, like Brazilian soccer fans after Pelé led them to their first World Cup in 1957. Placards were produced: WE'RE NUMBER ONE. Trailing by a game and a half still was immaterial, especially with Tom Seaver on the mound the next evening.

A crowd of 58,436 came out to see Seaver vs. Jenkins in a game that defined why baseball still was and remains to this day Our National Pastime. The day-to-day tension, the spectacular hopes and expectations, the ebb and flow of a pennant chase cannot be duplicated, not by basketball with its 50 teams making the play-offs, not by soccer and its endless 0–0 scores, and obviously not by football and its need for a weekend climax followed by six days of wound licking/war preparation.

In baseball they *play for real* every day, not a press conference, not an injury report, not practice in full pads. They strap it on, the fans pay real money to see 'em play real ball, and on September 9 they got it in spades.

Now, the score tells us New York won, 7–1, behind Seaver's dominant pitching. The standings tell us the Mets trailed by a half game afterwards, with Montreal coming to town and Chicago headed for the "City of Brotherly Love"—Philly—where "fans" in a foul, stinking, about-to-be-demolished ballpark had about as much "love" in them as the Germans in the closing days of World War II.

But the fact is that, despite the standings, the division was won on September 9. Furthermore, with Seaver at the full height of his powers, mowing Chicago down with the sheer velocity of a cannon mixed with the accuracy of a Special Forces sharpshooter; the crowd, the atmosphere at Shea Stadium surpassed even the imperfecto of exactly two months earlier. If on July 9 the crowd witnessed the birth of George Thomas Seaver as a true New York Sports Icon, then on September 9 he had his confirmation.

Poor Ferguson Jenkins, one of the greatest pitchers of all time, was reduced to playing the Washington Generals to New York's Harlem Globetrotters. It was not a baseball game, it was a coronation, a celebration, and in all the years that the New York Yankees built their reputation as the most dominant of all sports franchises, never had they played in an atmosphere like this.

In the middle of the game, the crowd was hooting and hollering. Little kids told their dads they loved them, thanking them for buying tickets for this game. Young men proposed to young women, who said yes. Maybe a few other young women were saying yes, but not to marriage. People who had not been to church in years found their faith again. It was a Billy Graham revival, a Rollings Stones concert. Then, out of nowhere, a black cat, hearing all the noise, the foot stomping, the thunderous ovations, darted out onto the field, right in front of the Cubs dugout. Durocher just stared at the thing, as if to say, "What next?"

Not a white cat, or a beige cat, or a striped cat. A black cat, and not in front of the Mets dugout, or out in the bullpen; no, in front of the Cubs. Mocking them, a scaredy-cat; the crowd, the buzz, the lights freaking it out. Apparently, feral cats lived in the catacombs of Shea. The insane pounding had forced it out of its hole, and here it was. After that, the Eastern Division was clinched. All that was left was to play out the calendar.

"It's almost a legend now," Swoboda said, laughing. "But then it was the most incredible thing you ever saw. It was like we hired the cat and trained him to run back and forth right in front of their dugout. . . . This cat . . . looked like he was right off a Halloween poster, had the hair up on his back . . . it's like the Cubs can't buy a break. . . . This was like

Hollywood. This happens in movies about baseball. You know what I mean?"

Santo, who was "very superstitious," said the cat "just stared at Leo. It freaked me out a little."

"The look on the Cubs' faces was priceless," recalled Grote.

"I thought that was a little eerie," recalled Ferguson Jenkins.

Some people accused the Mets of setting it up, but Pete Flynn, a member of the groundskeeping crew, said nobody had "anything to do with that cat coming onto the field. As a matter of fact, I never saw that cat before that game or anytime after."

"Mr. Leo Durocher, a baseball manager who on this night is reduced to being a wax house prisoner; a dugout denizen of ghostly superstitions; the leader of a doomed crew playing not at Shea Stadium, but on a different kind of diamond in a ballpark known only as . . . *The Twilight Zone*."

Do-do-do-do-do-do-do-do do-do do do doooooo . . . do-do-do dooo.

The crowd sang *"Good night, Leo . . ."* while waving handkerchiefs. It was surreal. The swing in momentum was so total that Chicago, while mathematically up by a half game, was theoretically at least eliminated. This is a premise that is easy to make in hindsight, but teams have withstood similar onslaughts. Seventeen years later, the St. Louis Cardinals led the defending World Series champion Mets. New York rallied in September 1987, but the Cardinals regained their footing to win the East. But the 1969 Mets were a team of destiny. *Nobody*, in New York at least, and probably around the country (including much of Chicago, truth be told), doubted them at this point.

The Mets felt the Cubs were tired from all those day games in the Chicago summer, but more to the point, Durocher had ridden this horse until it was dead—emotionally, physically, and despite "Mr. Sunshine," poor old Ernie Banks, spiritually.

On September 10 Montreal came to Shea Stadium. Yes, the 110-loss Expos. Yet right to the end, those guys played the "team of destiny" for all they were worth. While Ken Holtzman and the Cubs were losing their sixth straight game, 6–2, at decrepit Connie Mack Stadium in Philadelphia, New York and Montreal battled to a 2–2 tie in the 12th inning. The crowd was scoreboard watching as Ken Boswell drove Gaspar home with the winning run, 3–2.

By September, every day was a day for smiles.

John Rogers Photos

Don Cardwell made history when he and Koosman pitched shutouts with the pitcher driving in the winning run in both ends of 1–0 double-header wins.
Brace Photos

At the precise moment New York won, their record stood at 83–57. The Cubs, still toiling away in Philadelphia, were now officially 84–58. The Mets were in *first place* by .001 percentage point.

"Look Who's No. 1" read the scoreboard. The metaphors continue to be apropos: Mardi Gras, Octoberfest, you name it. When Philadelphia held the lead, New York went to bed and woke up in first place for the first time. They would not relinquish it by a long shot. The weather began to cool in September. After battling through the summer heat, it was very refreshing.

The *New York Times*: "Mets in First Place" in letters about the same size as "JFK Murder Solved." A telegram was received at the Mets offices: "Congratulations being number one. Am rooting for you to take all the marbles. As a New Yorker I am ecstatic, as a baseball person I am extremely pleased, and as a Yankee I consider suicide the easy option." It was sent by Michael Burke, the chairman of CBS and, at the time (pre–George Steinbrenner), owner of the Yankees.

"By September 10, we began to feel that nobody could beat us. Period," said Ed Charles. "We were sky high."

There was no letup. Gentry shut out Montreal. At Pittsburgh's Forbes Field (another relic in its last season), the Mets won both ends of the doubleheader, 1–0. In each game, the pitcher (Koosman in the first, Cardwell in the second) knocked in the winning run in addition to holding the powerful Bucs of Roberto Clemente, Matty Alou, Willie Stargell, and Al Oliver scoreless for 18 innings. When it was over, the two pitchers had a playful argument over whose knock was harder hit, both seeming to care more about swinging the bat than throwing shutouts.

Art Shamsky took the day off to honor the Jewish High Holy Days. When he entered the clubhouse the next day, somebody posted a sign, in jest: WHY DON'T YOU TAKE OFF EVERY DAY? It was similar to something Don Drysdale said to Walter Alston. Sandy Koufax did not pitch the first game of the 1965 World Series because of Yom Kippur. Drysdale started but was batted around. Afterward he said to the manager, "I bet you wish I was Jewish, too."

Later in the Pittsburgh series, Swoboda's grand slam knocked the Pirates back in the 10th inning.

The season was typified by a win over Steve Carlton, an all-time great, who set the big league record with 19 strikeouts but lost to New York. In 1970 Tom Seaver tied Carlton's record. *Brace Photos*

Then the Mets traveled to St. Louis and faced Steve Carlton, who, like Tom Seaver, was coming into his own and would define pitching greatness in the next decade and beyond. He was an unhittable force of nature, striking out an all-time record 19 Mets (breaking the previous mark held by Sandy Koufax). The Mets made four errors. With the Cubs losing their third straight and 11th of 12, it was a good "off day" for the Mets to accept a rare defeat at the hands of a future Hall of Famer . . . except that Swoboda, who "never hit Carlton well" (who did?), powered two two-run homers, and New York knocked him off, 4–3.

"How do you figure something like that?" Swoboda said of the game, but he may as well have been asking about the whole magical year. Al Weis throwing out a Dodger runner on a bang-bang play in a 15-inning, 1–0 Mets win; the July 8 comeback against Fergie Jenkins; Seaver's imperfecto, arm ailments, and strange healing; the black cat; two 1–0 wins with pitchers' RBIs winning 'em; now beating one of the greatest ever on one of his best nights . . . ever. Chance? Luck? Or destiny?

After the game, Swoboda was on Harry Caray's postgame show. Caray "looked like something just ran over his dog." As talkative a man as has ever been associated with baseball, Caray was almost speechless, at least by his standards, by this point. After beating Carlton, New York led Chicago by four and a half games. They had won 10 of 11 and were at .605.

"My God, the Mets have a 'magic number,'" said Tom Seaver.

John Lindsay, who had lost the Republican primary but was running behind as the Liberal Party candidate, was slowly moving back into the race, on the strength of you-know-what.

On September 19 Pittsburgh swept New York in a doubleheader. The next day, Bob Moose of the Pirates threw a no-hitter against them. The Cubs made no advancement despite the slight setback, losing two straight to St. Louis. On the first day of the fall, September 21, Koosman and Cardwell repeated their doubleheader act (minus the game-winning hits), beating Pittsburgh 5–3 and 6–1.

St. Louis came to Shea, enormous crowds simply exuding electrical, religious energy. Seaver dominated the Cardinals for his 24th victory. The next game, Tug McGraw picked up the 3–2 win over Bob Gibson, with Buddy Harrelson driving in the winning run in the 11th.

"Before 1969 I never saw any improvement in the team," said Ed Kranepool. "You knew you were going to be eliminated from a pennant race by the All-Star Game."

On September 24, 1969, before a packed Shea Stadium throng in the last home game of the year, Donn Clendenon and Ed Charles homered. Gary Gentry pitched his best game of the season, a powerhouse four-hit shutout that just amped the crowd up even more as he went along, mowing down Cardinal after Cardinal. Steve Carlton, the Hall of Famer in his prime, fresh off a 19-strikeout performance against this same club, was bombed out early.

The stands were filled with signs: QUEENS LITHO LOVES THE METS, YOU GUYS ARE TOO MUCH. People grinned idiotically at each other, and programs were torn into confetti. The crowd continued to

It was all glad-handing on the road to glory. *John Rogers Archives*

sing, "Good-bye, Leo," wrote Roger Angell, "rendered *capella*, with the right field tenors in especially good voice."

A little after 9:00 p.m., Joe Torre grounded into an inning-ending double play. Pandemonium ensued, with ecstatic fans taking to the field, stealing bases, tearing up the pitcher's mound and home plate (no mean feat, as these are drilled deep into the ground and they lacked pickaxes; they had to dig with their hands). The turf was torn up. It was a sight never seen before.

Ed Kranepool, who had been there from the beginning, douses Tug McGraw. The Mets and their fans turned the victory celebration into an art form.
John Rogers Archives

When the Jets beat Oakland to clinch the AFL title at Shea in December 1968, there was nothing like this. In the old days at the Polo Grounds, fans would use the stadium to leave through the center field gate, but it was just a shortcut to the subway.

The closest anybody had ever seen to this was when Boston won an exciting, last-minute game to clinch the NBA title a few years before, but the basketball crowd was already almost on top of the floor as it was. No baseball crowd had ever done this; certainly not at Yankee Stadium. Ebbets Field never let loose like this. When Bobby Thomson hit the "shot heard 'round the world," the crowd stayed in the stands.

Fans at Dodger Stadium were too laid-back for this kind of thing. Cardinals supporters were too polite. When Detroit won it all in 1968, they did it in St. Louis. They had crazy fans who may have tried something, but nothing like *this,* and it was only for the division.

"When the crew saw what was happening to the field when the people all ran out, we didn't know what to think," groundskeeper Pete Flynn told Art Shamsky in *The Magnificent Seasons.* "When we saw all the torn up turf afterward, we knew we had our work cut out for us."

The clubhouse was sheer bedlam, of course. The Mets had broken out champagne when they went into first place for the first time. Now, simply winning the division, they celebrated as if they had captured the World Series. Roger Angell wrote that it was "clubhouse water sports (Great Western, Yoo-Hoo, Rise lather, beer, cameras, interviews, music, platitudes, disbelief)."

"Beautiful, baby," said Ed Charles. "Nine years in the minors for me, then nine more with the Athletics and Mets. Never, *never* thought I'd make it. These kids will be back next year, but I'm 36 and time is running out. It's better for me than for them."

Rod Kanehl and Craig Anderson, two original Mets, met in the clubhouse and shared in the glory.

"It was wonderful," recalled Shamsky. "There was dousing of champagne everywhere. Everyone entering the locker room got it."

"I've gone full circle," declared Kranepool.

Toasts were offered "to Leo" and "to Casey."

George Weis hugged Gil Hodges. "Nineteen sixty-two," he said to the manager.

"Nineteen sixty-two," Hodges replied to the front office man.

"Our team finally caught up to our fans," said Donald Grant. "Our fans were winners long ago."

The papers treated it like . . . a miracle: "How could this team have done it?" At the heart of it all was Seaver, who now wore a new nickname over and above his "Tom Terrific" moniker: "The Franchise."

There was no letup after the clinching, as often occurs. As Frank Sinatra sang, Chicago is "my kind of town," and when the Mets came in there with the division wrapped up, it was for all practical purposes their colony, having been won in battle. The Cubs fans pulled a purple funeral crepe and dropped it over the Mets dugout, to which Swoboda told them, "You're pissing in the wind, and the wind is blowing in your face."

The Mets won the first of the two-game season-ending set at Wrigley Field, running their winning streak to nine games and reaching the pivotal 100-victory mark. Finally, on the last day, the Cubs beat the Mets; almost a cruel joke at that point.

"Who were the Mets of 1969?" wrote Jack Lang for *The Sporting News*. "A bunch of nobodies. A bunch of kids. Outside of maybe Tom Seaver and Jerry Koosman and perhaps Cleon Jones, there wasn't a regular on the club that anybody coveted." Lang stated that it was "a miracle."

"For me, personally, I thought it might be my last chance to get into the play-offs or World Series," Ernie Banks recalled. "It was really disappointing for me, and as far as the city was concerned everyone was looking forward to a World Series in Chicago. It was pretty sad three or four months after the season ended."

"Maybe we did run out of gas," growled Leo. "But if the Mets had played only .500 ball, we still could have hung on. But they just kept winning, winning, winning."

At 100–62, the Mets finished eight games ahead of the 92–70 Cubs. They won an astounding 38 of their final 49 games (29–7 when it counted), a record matched by few teams in history. Periods of relative success include the 1946 Red Sox, who captured 41 of their first 50 games. The 1984 Tigers opened 35–5.

In coming back from nine and a half games out on August 14, the Mets did something that is worth mentioning with the 1951 Giants (13½ out on August 13) and the 1978 Yankees (14½ behind on

July 17). Similar comebacks include the 1914 Boston Braves, who were in last place on Independence Day but won the pennant. In 2004 Houston came out of nowhere to win 36 of their last 46, getting into the wild card berth. Teams that were simply great, dominating the schedule from start to finish, include the 1906 Cubs, 1909 Pirates, 1927–1928 Yankees, 1929–1931 A's, 1954 Indians, 1961 Yankees, 1969–1970 Orioles, 1986 Mets, 1998 Yankees, and 2001 Mariners.

The Cubs have been painted as "choke artists," and they certainly did their share of clutch losing, but the picture is not cut and dried. With the Mets making a major run in late August, Chicago won four straight games. This included one over the contending Reds, three over the powerhouse Braves in Atlanta, and another at Cincinnati.

What was really remarkable was not simply that New York came from almost 10 out with a month and a half to play, but that they rallied, tied, and sped past their rivals to win by eight; a 17½-game swing between mid-August and October 2. The season can be compared to both the 1951 and 1962 seasons. In 1951 the Dodgers really did not blow the pennant. The Giants won 37 of their last 45 games to tie, but Brooklyn played fairly well, even winning a clutch regular season finale at Philadelphia on a crucial Jackie Robinson grab to stay alive.

"Freckle-faced" Wayne Garrett was just one of a cast of characters in this drama for the ages.

Brace Photos

Tom Seaver was seen as a modern Lancelot, riding a white steed to the rescue of a team, a city, and indeed a whole country. Subsequent reports of his ego, his human flaws, while few and far between, were magnified because in that one year he was seemingly flawless. There were some indications that his image was not quite what people perceived.

"Such a combination of Galahad-like virtues has caused some baseball old-timers to compare him to Christy Mathewson," wrote Roger Angell in *The New Yorker.* "Others, a minority, see an unpleasantly planned aspect to this golden image—planned, that is, by Tom Seaver, who is a student of public relations. However, his impact on his teammates can be suggested by something that happened to Bud Harrelson back in July. Harrelson was away on Army Reserve duty during that big home series with the Cubs, and he watched Seaver's near-no-hitter (which Seaver calls 'my imperfect game') on a television set in a restaurant in Watertown, New York."

"I was there with a couple of Army buddies who also play in the majors, and we got all steamed up watching Tom work," Harrelson said. "Then—it was the strangest thing—I began feeling more and more like a little kid watching that game and that great performance, and I wanted to turn to the others and say, 'I *know* Tom Seaver. Tom Seaver is a friend of mine.'"

Angell put it this way:

Most of the Mets, it seems, are equally susceptible to enthusiasm. Young and alert and open, they are above all suggestible. And this quality—the lead-off hit just after a brilliant inning-ending catch; the valiant but exhausted starting pitcher taken off the hook by a sudden cluster of singles—is what made the Mets' late innings worth waiting for this year. It is also possible that these intuitive, self-aware athletes sensed, however vaguely, that they might be among the few to achieve splendor in a profession that is so often disappointing, tedious, and degrading. Their

Tom Seaver called Gil Hodges "infallible" in 1969. Every move he made seemed to work out. Donn Clendeneon's "Cheshire cat" smile seems to say he, too, knows Gil made the right move.

National Baseball Hall of Fame Library

immense good fortune was to find themselves together at the same moment of sudden maturity, combined skills, and high spirits. Perhaps they won because they were un-bored.

Angell had a "sense of unreality" when visiting the Mets clubhouse, writing that the team less resembled a true big league ball club, and more the cast of a Hollywood set about a big league club. They were "younger and more theatrical," the drama "hopelessly overwritten," with players right out of central casting: "Bud and Ken"; the "freckle-faced" Garrett with a "sweet smile"; the "broken-nosed scrappy catcher" (Grote); Agee and Jones ("silent, brooding big busters"); the "cheerful hayseed" (Koosman); the "philosophical black elder" (Charles); at least one "Jewish character," indispensable in New York (Shamsky); "seamy-faced, famous old-timers" (Hodges and Berra); "and Tom Seaver, of course, the hero. And who can say that the Mets didn't sense this, too—that they didn't know all along that this year at Shea life was imitating not just art but a United Artists production?"

Koosman was lucky in that he was simply viewed as a fine pitcher. The weight of all the expectations Seaver carried never fell on him. He just went out and pitched. His first half was a mixture of spectacular success, a few nagging injuries, and some mediocrity mixed with a lack of support. In the second half, down the stretch, he was almost as good as Seaver, and this statement must be understood in its full meaning. *Almost as good* as Seaver was like an actor who was *almost as good* as Olivier, a writer who was *almost as good* as Hemingway, a political figure who was *almost as good* as Churchill.

Koosman finished 17–9 with a 2.28 ERA, with 180 strikeouts in 241 innings pitched. Gary Gentry was 13–12, and everybody expected him to someday be a 20-game winner. Don Cardwell was 8–10, and Jim McAndrew finished 6–7. Somehow, the starting staff does not add up to the concept of a 100-win team. One conjures the image of Baltimore's four 20-game winners in 1971, or Oakland's three 20-game winners of 1973. Where did those 100 wins come from?

Cal Koonce's name might not be remembered if he hadn't played for the '69 Mets. *Brace Photos*

Certainly Gil Hodges's use of the bullpen explains much of it. Tug McGraw, used in various capacities, was 9–3 with 12 saves. Nolan Ryan was 6–3. Cal Koonce (6–3) and Ron Taylor (13 saves, 2.73 ERA) were effective late in games. In later years, McGraw and Ryan were stars, but they were not at that level yet. The 1969 Mets bullpen was not as spectacular as Oakland in the early 1970s, when a host of "stopper" pitchers held opponents until Rollie Fingers closed the door, or the Yankees of the late 1990s, when Mariano Rivera would do the same thing for Joe Torre.

New York's 2.99 ERA was quite insane, especially when compared to modern records in the age of designated hitters, "juiced" balls, small parks, and steroids. However, St. Louis was better (2.94). They threw 28 shutouts on the year with 35 saves. In the American League, Baltimore's ERA was 2.83. The American League as a whole: 3.63. The NL: 3.60. With expansion teams, there was a dilution of talent. Better NL teams tended to get better against Expos and Padres pitching, put up numbers against Expos and Padres hitters.

Offensively, the Mets numbers do not logically figure to a 100-win season, especially in a pretty good year for hitters. It was a vast improvement for baseball over 1968; a year of solid, even, competitive achievement, individually and for teams—pitching and hitting—in both leagues. Cleon Jones had a breakout year, hitting .340 to finish third in the league with a modest 12 home runs and 75 runs batted in. Jones's run production is worth noting. Today, .340 hitters are generally expected to be power guys with 90 to 100 RBIs.

Agee hit a respectable .271, supplying more clout than his Mobile friend with 26 long balls and 76 runs scored from the leadoff spot. Clendenon was one of the strongest .252 hitters in memory, or so it seemed. He hit 12 home runs with 37 RBIs after coming over in the June trade. Shamsky was quite solid: .300, 14 home runs. Swoboda was nobody's idea of Harry Heilman or any all-time greats, with a poor .235 average, 9 homers, and 52 RBIs. Kranepool's .238 with 11 homers made nobody forget or remember Lou Gehrig. Ed Charles was anemic (.207). Bud Harrelson (.248), Al Weis (with the exception of two games at Wrigley Field in July), Wayne Garrett, Bobby Pfeil: all field, no hit. Ken Boswell? He could not even field. Jerry Grote went from .282 in 1968 to .252 in 1969. J. C. Martin was mainly a pinch hitter, Rod Gaspar was a defensive replacement, and Duffy Dyer caught in the second games of twin bills.

The Mets hit 109 home runs. Eight of the 12 National League teams hit more. They batted .242, behind six other clubs (10 points below the league average). Some people have tried to compare the Mets to the Dodgers teams of Maury Wills and Lou Johnson, who stole bases at a great clip, manufacturing runs that way. Not so. They bunted and played a lot of "little ball," but stole only 66 bases. The Mets scored 632 runs, compared to 720 for Chicago. Eight teams scored more, including every team in the Western Division except San Diego. Their .980 fielding percentage (a nebulous statistic) led the division.

How did they do it? Again, if one looks at it in a logical way, it was the pitching of Seaver and Koosman, with some luck. But considering it all, the hand of destiny played its role, too. It was like the miracle of life itself; too perfect to be a coincidence, like a windstorm blowing parts all over the place until they settle into a perfectly constructed fighter jet.

Seaver was easily voted the Cy Young award, but a major controversy came in the awarding of the National League MVP, which went to McCovey. Tom Seaver was unquestionably the deserving winner of the 1969 MVP. Pitchers had won MVP awards on numerous occasions in the past. This included Hal Newhouser of Detroit in both 1944 and 1945 and Brooklyn's Don Newcombe in 1956.

In 1963 Koufax was the National League's Most Valuable Player. In 1968 pitchers represented both leagues: McLain and Gibson. This probably was too much for some members of the media, who began to clamor that, especially since the Cy Young was now awarded in both leagues (instead of to just one pitcher, as it had been between 1956 and 1966), they had their own trophy.

Two writers on the selection committee simply ignored Seaver on their ballots altogether. The vote consisted of 10 places, with 10 points awarded for first place, 9 for second, 2 for ninth, 1 for 10th, and so on. McCovey finished with 265 points, Seaver with 243. They both had 11 first-place votes. Had both of the writers voted Seaver second, or if other writers who penalized him for being a pitcher had voted him higher, he would have beaten McCovey.

It caused a howl in the New York press, and caused *The Sporting News* to editorialize that pitchers were the "step-children in the MVP poll," reminding the Baseball Writers' Association of America members that indeed hurlers are eligible. It caused the rules to be changed so that the vote would no longer be kept secret; writers would face accountability.

Seaver never complained, expressing only class and admiration for "Stretch." McCovey has held

Tom Seaver won the first of his three Cy Young awards in 1969. Here he is pictured after his second (1973). Seaver also won the award in 1975. He should have been the 1969 MVP as well.

John Rogers Archives

popular elder statesman status in San Francisco, but he and Willie Mays, in truth, became (if they were not all along) egotistical blowhards. In 2001, Mays was asked a question about Joe DiMaggio. He bluntly stated that, "You can't compare Joe to me." Mays may be the greater all-round player, but DiMaggio is certainly worthy of being "compared" to Mays, and in 1969 was voted the Greatest Living Ballplayer.

At the same time, McCovey was asked about the 1969 MVP vote. "Seaver shouldn't have finished as high as he did," said McCovey unapologetically. "I should have won it the year before when they gave it to [Bob] Gibson." McCovey had a solid year in 1968 and a great one in 1969. In '68 Gibson was inhuman, his 1.12 ERA pushing St. Louis to the pennant while McCovey's efforts were not good enough to push San Francisco beyond their usual 1960s bridesmaid status. In 1969, Seaver was as good as Gibby, and in head-to-head matches, when it counted, dominated Big Mac and his teammates; a major reason the Mets won and the Giants were left holding the bouquet again.

Seaver should have won the MVP.

11

THE MARCH TO THE SEA

I'll make Georgia howl!

—General William T. Sherman

In October 1969, a well-equipped army of Braves awaited the Mets in the hostile land of Atlanta, Georgia. The fact that the Atlanta Braves met the New York Mets in the 1969 National League Championship Series was ironic on many levels. First, there was the Tom Seaver connection. It was the Braves who drafted Seaver in 1966, the Mets who scooped him up when the Braves made perhaps the biggest mistake in that franchise's history.

Had Seaver been a Brave between 1967 and 1969, Atlanta may well have won National League pennants. The 1969 Braves, adding Seaver's 25 wins to the 93 they did achieve, would have been one of the best teams in history and may well have gone all the way. The club probably would have had a successful decade after that instead of getting lost in the wilderness until 1991.

Then there was Hank Aaron, the man Seaver "chose" as his favorite baseball player. Seaver was awed to face "Bad Henry" and to be his teammate in All-Star Games. Plus, there was the "Mobile connection." No less than four residents of Mobile, Alabama, were participating: Aaron and his brother, Tommie, who were close friends with Cleon Jones and Tommie Agee. To top it all off, the NL's MVP that year, Willie McCovey, was from Mobile.

There were also the strange social contrasts. First, the Braves franchise was presumably named after Indian tribes in Massachusetts, or perhaps because the participants in the Boston Tea Party dressed themselves as Indians. This name followed them to Milwaukee and Georgia, where other Indian tribes in both states made the name stick in a way that "Lakers" might not have been quite right for the desert that is Los Angeles.

Hank Aaron was Tom Seaver's boyhood idol. Now Aaron stood in the way of his first trip to the World Series. *Brace Photos*

This was a franchise that went from the bastion of the Union during the Civil War to the symbol of the Confederacy, the town famously burned in *Gone with the Wind;* a liberal Northeastern city to a conservative Southeastern one; a franchise in search of an identity. It was the first time a Southern city hosted postseason baseball, featuring two cities that might as well have been in different countries, not to mention they seemed headed in different directions.

Manager Gil Hodges faced the baseball version of Union general William T. Sherman's task in 1864–1865, which was to enter the state of Georgia, wreak havoc, and thus achieve ultimate victory.

"I'll make Georgia howl," Sherman famously told Abraham Lincoln. Hodges and his team intended to do the same thing.

The South hated Northern, that is, government, meddling with their "states' rights." Sporting events between Southern and Northern teams always carried with it a political and social edge: the 1966 "Catholic vote" awarded Notre Dame the National Championship over Alabama, an event that still stuck in the craw of Dixie. But most of these events were college-related, infused by the local pride that comes with seeing players, mostly from the same geographical region, play against young men representing another region.

The 1969 Mets–Braves matchup did not have that. New York featured the two "Mobile boys," although that carried certain connotations. Tommie Agee and Cleon Jones left a segregated world to enter pro baseball, eventually ending up in the most diverse of all cities, New York. The Georgia they found in 1969 was legally integrated, but its residents were still struggling to get there.

The Braves featured black and Latino players, from south of the border, from the American North and South. Their fans were not quite sure how to deal with this "Brave" new world, but they did know that the "magic" team coming to play them wore shirts that read NEW YORK on them. That was enough to fire them up.

Gil Hodges had no intention of burning cities, pillaging villages, or destroying crops, but he aimed to replicate Sherman's "march to the sea" in the baseball sense if he intended to win this "war."

All the social angst and history lessons revolving around the Braves franchise and the city of Atlanta could not compare to the bizarre nature of the games themselves. The Mets might have been nominal favorites, since they won seven more regular season games and had the pitching. Despite their success, installing the Mets as favorites—anytime, anywhere—was a hard concept to grasp. Atlanta was a 13–10 favorite, despite the fact that Seaver was 3–0 against the Braves, while Atlanta ace Phil Niekro was 0–3. Atlanta had finished 93–69, but they were just as hot toward the end as New York (17 of their last 21, almost every one of them clutch). It was possible that the Braves were worn out from their Western Division death struggle with San Francisco, Cincinnati, L.A., and Houston. This always brings up the debate, which is whether it is better to coast in, as the Mets had basically done, or to come in all hot and bothered, as the Braves still were.

"Let's get one thing straight at the start," 79-year-old Casey Stengel stated. "The Mets will play all the way to the end of the World Series because they have more pitchers and they throw lightning. And you can look it up, that's best for a short series. . . ."

Stengel clarified his "all the way to the end of the World Series" statement: "Don't forget, I say it goes the limit to the World Series for the Mets."

A three-game sweep did not seem likely, but since New York had won 38 of 49, the heat of their momentum did not make that such an impossibility. What made the series bizarre was the complete lack of adherence to form. The Mets were a light-hitting team, winners of 1–0 and 2–1 games. They did it with pitching, speed, and defense. Their pitching was 90 percent of their success. If their pitching failed, they would fail.

"Our attitude going in the series was that we just didn't want to get embarrassed," said Swoboda.

Their pitching failed. They still swept the series. *Amazin'.*

The 1969 postseason was a first in a number of ways. The advent of play-offs coincided with what by then was universal color television. Over the course of the decade, baseball and other sports revolutionized via color TV. Many people had old black-and-white sets, but by 1969 most had color. The play-offs opened on a Saturday, meaning it was a sports extravaganza. Some felt ratings would suffer all the way around, since viewers would be forced to choose between two baseball games (Baltimore and Minnesota in the early play-off), meaningful college football (the conferences were in full swing), and on Sunday the NFL.

The Mets opened in a place where college football has been called "religion." Atlantans had transistor radios pressed to their ears during the baseball games, listening to Georgia beating South Carolina, 41–16; Clemson knocking off Georgia Tech, 21–10; and on Sunday the Falcons losing to Baltimore, 21–14. The lobby of the Regency Hyatt House featured a band and majorettes. Television interviewees featured mostly college football coaches.

Most people still needed to physically get up to change stations, unlike the "channel surfing" that goes on today, but the combination of sports was and would continue to be a huge success. Stadiums were full, ratings good. Football seemed to play off of baseball, and vice versa. One thing was for sure: baseball had not taken a back seat to football, as people feared it would in 1968.

The cover of the Braves game program featured an Atlanta player descending from a lunar module onto a home plate resting on the moon, with the legend, "One Step for the Braves, One Giant Leap for the Southeast."

The Mets beat the Braves 8 of 12 times in the regular season, but the Braves had a bunch of guys who could beat you. The opener was as unpredictable as snowfall in San Diego. Tom Seaver, fresh as a daisy, with Gil Hodges having lined up his rotation perfectly, took the mound. Was any pitcher, ever, hotter at that point in time than Seaver? He had won 10 straight, but they were not just wins. They were masterpieces, artistic concepts, clinics. He was so devastating that Mets fans simply assumed he could throw his hat on the mound, and two hours later another shutout was accomplished. Jerry Grote never moved his glove, Seaver's control was so good. His slider was wicked, his curve buckled knees, and his fastball broke bats. Measly grounders were gobbled up, "can o' corn" pop-ups gathered in like so many nuts at harvest. Umpires' arms shot up time after time: strike one, strike two, *strike three* . . . and you are outta there!

Batters gave up, as they had when Koufax was at his best, Gibson took control. It was "good night, Irene." See ya. Bye-bye, time. Just avoid embarrassment. Take your strikeout, your oh-fer, and be glad not all the pitchers were such gods, such immortals. Seaver was not a pitcher, he was a Hall of Fame plaque built out of flesh and blood.

So what did this living embodiment of pitching dominance do in game 1? He got hit around like a Little Leaguer, his mighty fastball reduced to straight batting practice fodder. Instead of 99 mile an hour heat, it came in steady and straight around 87, or so it seemed. His breaking stuff didn't. Dennis Hopper had better control on the set of *Easy Rider.* The Braves teed off on him. He wound up, dropped, drove, then strained his neck watching his fielders scramble for Braves line drives and home runs that traveled so far they needed a stewardess.

It was a perfect example of the very nature of unpredictability, the human element of sports, why athletics are so much darn fun. You just never know. It was just like the opener against the expansion Expos, when Seaver and his "high hopes" were batted about in a foul barrage of "bad feedback," in the form of well-hit shots off Montreal bats.

Oh, one more thing. Seaver was the winning pitcher. It was that kind of year.

Seaver woke up the night before the opener with a severe case of Aaron-induced insomnia, rolling around his bed at the Marriott Hotel. In the morning he ate lightly. For some reason, Seaver was incredibly nervous pitching in Atlanta. He kept thinking about "Bad Henry," how he got him out the first time he faced him only to give up a homer the next time up. His worst fears, it turned out, were justified.

It was hot in Atlanta. Seaver and the Mets battled the summer weather in New York, Chicago, and St. Louis but had gotten used to the mild Northern climes of September. Plus, the game started at four o'clock for TV, so Seaver was off his usual pattern; neither a night game nor a day game.

Warming up, he felt jerky and panicked. His mouth was dry. He could not spit. He had this terrible nightmare that he would wake up in a boxcar in Fresno, packing raisins. Some wizard would emerge and tell him, "None of it was real, boy. Not the Mets, not the pennant. Ha, ha." Rod Serling would be off to the side and Seaver would be like some cautionary tale on *The Twilight Zone.*

Felix Millan stepped to the plate. Seaver had no plan, no stuff, nothin'. He tossed up a batting practice fastball, hoping it would be over the plate by chance and that Millan's liner would be hit at somebody. By no reason other than luck, really, despite bouncing curves and throwing fastballs that had Grote leaping out of his crouch, he somehow retired the side. The Mets scored two runs, and Seaver thought maybe this would be the catalyst, he would recover and be *Tom Seaver,* for God's sake.

The crowd of more than 50,000 cheered, oddly puzzled that the man they heard so much about, the man they expected to dazzle them with this legendary heater and marksmanlike control, looked like a guy in the Sally League. Seaver struggled, his body totally discombobulated, and gave a run back in the second.

In the third Millan jumped on him like a hobo on a ham sandwich, slapping a "fastball" for a double. His curve—more like a wrinkle—was like a ball on a tee for Tony Gonzalez, who roped a double off the wall to tie it. When Aaron came up, Seaver felt like the Wehrmacht general ordered to "stop Patton at the Rhine" despite a lack of gas or ammunition. Double off the wall, 3–2.

With the bases loaded, he got lucky when Bob Didier missed a fastball down Main Street for a strikeout. But Niekro was no more effective. The pundits had seen the two best pitchers in the league and predicted a low-scoring affair, but Harrelson got a cheap hit, and they scored two cheap runs to take a cheap 4–3 lead.

In the fourth Tom changed from the pitching motion that had earned him success at Fresno City College, the Alaska Goldpanners, USC, Jacksonville, and New York City. Grote came out and said something like, "Are you out of your mind? What's the matter with you? Is this an act? Did gamblers pay you off?"

Gil Hodges turned to Rube Walker as if to say, "Do you see what I see?" Twenty-four Mets and 25 Braves just looked out at the car wreck that was Tom Seaver. It was not the beginning anymore, but he was literally choking from nerves. He was the embodiment of all that athletes despise the most, the man whose courage fails his team. In the fifth, Seaver threw a "fastball," maybe 83 miles an hour. NASA scientists could not have centered it in Tony Gonzalez's kill zone any better than it was. It took off like Apollo 11, over the left field fence. 4–4.

J. C. Martin's key pinch-hit single spurred New York to a win in game 1 of the National League Championship Series. *Brace Photos*

The game droned on. In the seventh, Seaver threw a slow curveball to Aaron. It was the kind of pitch he specialized in when he toiled for the Fresno High junior varsity in 1961. Aaron's homer landed in the middle of a Civil War battle reenactment somewhere. 5–4.

Seaver entered the dugout. If anybody still thought he was "perfect," he made sure the part about "swearing" when he said, "I drank beer and swear" was made perfectly clear. Niekro was still out there in the eighth. His knuckleball was more like a lame duck. The Mets jumped on it like it was skeet practice, pushing two runs across. Seaver got up from the on-deck circle, waiting for the inevitable. Hodges pinch hit for him with J. C. Martin. In keeping with the theme of the whole year, Martin hit a single, driving in two, and an error let a third in. Five runs scored, and the Mets led, 9–5. By nothing less than a miracle, Seaver stood to be the winning pitcher. Somehow, Niekro was worse than he was.

Ron Taylor entered the game. He was everything Seaver was not: effective, good, a worthy big league pitcher. He closed out the 9–5 win, perhaps the ugliest on record, with the "great" G. Thomas Seaver credited with the "victory." Then again, a win is a win. Truer words have never been spoken. To a team that had turned losing into an art form like the New York Mets, this was especially true.

Seaver's sudden postseason mediocrity was by no means unheard of. Don Newcombe was a regular season ace for years, but he was deemed so unreliable with the chips on the line that managers went with rookies and second-tier guys instead of him. Don Drysdale won 25 games for the 1962 Dodgers, but when his team needed him at the end, exhausted physically and mentally, he failed. One year earlier, Denny McLain set new standards of pitching excellence, but he got bounced around in his first two World Series starts against St. Louis.

"We got five runs off Tom Seaver," Hank Aaron, slumped before his cubicle, said disconsolately to the writers. "That should win it for us. There is something wrong."

"Could there really be 'Met magic?'" one writer asked him. Henry suggested an anatomical location for the "Met magic," but the Braves were stunned. Fate was not on their side.

Seaver spoke to the press as if he were the losing pitcher, trying to explain why he had pitched so poorly. Theories were propounded that he was rusty from not having pitched between September 27 and October 4. But Seaver had no excuses.

"I tried to control my nerves, and I couldn't," he said in a frank confession. "I couldn't get my fastball and curve together. It is very hard to explain."

Seaver thought about it some more. "It rubs me, it frustrates me," he continued. "I know what I can do, but I just couldn't do it. It happens to me all the time, except that the tension dissipates itself after my first pitch usually. . . .

"I was more tense than usual and more nervous. It's a progressive thing that happens to me all the time . . . but today my state mentally led me to rush my pitching motion physically. My hips were more open when I was throwing the ball, and my arm dropped lower. Jerry came out to the mound several times and told me to get my arm back higher. It just seemed that I couldn't throw that many good pitches in a row. Some of them were good, and I guess that's what made me keep my sanity. The crux of the whole thing, though, was that I just felt more nervous than usual."

Then Seaver smiled. "Mind if I ask a question?" he said to a reporter.

"Feel free," was the reply.

"Who won?" Seaver asked rhetorically, and everybody chuckled. He had a point. Then Seaver stood up and announced, "I gave up five runs and still won the game. God truly is a Met." It was a variation on a theme gaining more support daily.

So what happened in game 2? Jerry Koosman, every bit Seaver's equal down the stretch, came on and blew Atlanta away with a brilliant display, right? Wrong. He was worse than Seaver, and yes, the Mets *won anyway.*

Another huge crowd showed up at Atlanta–Fulton County Stadium to see Koosman square off with 18-game winner Rick Reed. Atlanta was shakier than the Mets, making three costly errors in an 11–6 loss. New York knocked Reed out early and took a seemingly insurmountable 8–0 lead in the fourth, 9–1 in the fifth. All that was left was to watch Koosman cruise along and complete his October masterpiece, but after the Braves nicked him for a run in the fourth, they scored five in the fifth, all after the first two Braves had been retired. Aaron homered, but after that Koosman came totally unglued—a walk, a double, and that was just the beginning. Hodges was forced to relieve him before he could get the required five innings to get credit for the victory, bringing in Taylor. Koosman's line was poor: four and two-thirds innings, seven hits, six runs (all earned). Aaron went yard on him. It was a terribly sloppy game. The Mets made physical and mental mistakes, but Atlanta played like bush leaguers: missed cutoffs, throwing to the wrong base.

Suddenly, with the game not yet half over, a blowout had become "nervous Nellie" time. In the seventh inning, with New York hanging on with a 9–6 advantage, Agee was on third with Jones at bat. Cecil Upshaw, a side-arming right-handed reliever, delivered while Agee took off for home plate. Jones took a mighty cut and hit a searing line drive that missed Agee's head by a foot.

Some people thought it was a missed sign, a mix-up in which either Agee thought he got the steal sign or Jones missed a "suicide squeeze" sign. Oddly, it was neither. Agee went on his own. Jones claimed he swung, intentionally trying to miss to "keep the catcher occupied." Agee could have been killed. They just stood and glared at each other after the play, too stunned to contemplate what could have been. In this year of "Met magic," the ball missed him. Of course, Jones then homered to make it 11–6, which stood up. Taylor got the win. McGraw came in, shut the door, and picked up the save.

Despite Seaver and Koosman pitching bad games, the Mets won two on the road in Atlanta. It was that kind of year. *John Rogers Archives*

The Mets had played poor, sloppy ball two days in a row. Their two aces had been hit around. They still led two games to none and were headed home. Their bright spot had been their bats, a real surprise.

Braves–Mets action at Shea Stadium. *John Rogers Archives*

"We've got one foot in the grave, and the grave-diggers are going for their shovels," said Atlanta manager Luman Harris.

"The Mets are unconscious," said Braves third baseman Clete Boyer, a veteran of many Octobers with the Yankees. "They don't know where they are. They don't understand the pressure." Hank Aaron, for instance, had been to two World Series early in his career (1957–1958), then struggled for 11 seasons to get back, only to be denied by these upstarts.

The flight from Atlanta to New York was "sweet," according to Art Shamsky. The Mets were one win away from the *World Series.* The creation of the play-offs had disrupted the usual routine, whereby a team won the league, as New York would have done with the best record absent divisions. They had not allowed themselves to think such a thing. The Series, the highest mountaintop in sports. Just like Joe Namath's Jets in the Super Bowl. The Jets' victory over Baltimore had *made* the Super Bowl what it is today. The World Series was the ultimate sporting event long before the Mets sniffed it.

When the team arrived in New York, the excitement was off the charts. Every radio and TV program featured the Mets. The newspapers could not get enough of them. Every little detail was covered. Students, teachers, parents, cabbies, bartenders, waitresses, corporate execs, whites, blacks, Puerto Ricans, gays, straights, hardhats, Republicans, Democrats: *everybody* was taken with a full case of Mets fever.

The third game was played the very next day, a Monday, with no off day for the Braves to rest or the Mets to contemplate a sense of reality. It was sunny and cool, a contrast to the muggy Georgia heat, and more to the Mets' style. Pat Jarvis started for Atlanta against Gary Gentry. A frenzied capacity crowd arrived hours before the game. Gentry was no more effective pitching at home than Seaver or Koosman on the road. It was the same kind of sloppy game, with the lead changing hands three times on homers in the first five innings. Cepeda went deep. Agee and Boswell homered for New York.

Gentry never made it out of the third inning. Hank Aaron, playing on national television, had one of the best play-off series of all time in 1969. It is not remembered because his team could not win, but he was red hot, homering again in the third game, this time off Gentry. This game might be considered the "debut" of Nolan Ryan, the first time he displayed his true brilliance, also on national television. Atlanta took a 4–3 lead, but Ryan pitched out of a bases load jam to hold it down. In the fifth, Ryan got a hit. Then Wayne Garrett homered. Ryan pitched the last seven innings, giving up just two runs on three hits in the 7–4 victory. The last out was a grounder to Garrett, who threw to Kranepool, and the Mets were the champions of the National League, three games to none in what in those days was a best-of-three NLCS format.

"When Nolan pitched those great seven innings of relief, it was huge," said Koosman. "It gave us another guy on our roster that we could go to with confidence, another body developed on our ball club. Nolan had been up and down all year, his season interrupted by both injury and military service. But Gil was doing these things throughout the year, showing us how to play the game, and because of him we found out we were capable of doing more than we knew we could."

"Our pitching got battered in that series, but it was amazing the way we outhit them," said Swoboda. "Gil stuck to his guns and platooned, so I didn't get a single at bat in the Atlanta series because of their predominantly right-handed pitching." The Mets, he said, "weren't great players who will go on to the Hall of Fame," but "just guys who made themselves useful."

Ryan was "untouchable," added Koosman. "It was a laughing matter. Every pitch he threw was intimidating."

It was also an example of Hodges's playing all the right hunches in this year of magic. He kept Ryan in the game instead of pinch hitting for him and did not remove Garrett when he faced left-hander George Stone. Everything paid off. It was amazin'. At a hundred to one, the Mets beat those odds.

"We couldn't do anything wrong," said Koosman. "We couldn't lose a game."

"The Mets really are amazing," said a gracious Hank Aaron, who no longer told writers what kinds of physical contortions they could do with "Met magic."

"We ought to send the Mets to Vietnam," said Atlanta general manager Paul Richards. "They'd end the war in three days." They had taken care of Atlanta faster than General Sherman had.

Thousands of fans poured onto the field, tearing everything up, undoing all the work done by the grounds crew after the division clinching of September 24. It was absolutely out of control; a wild, chaotic, celebratory scene infused by an utter sense of disbelief. People grabbed each other, asked whether they could believe it, was it real, how did it happen? In bars and homes and schoolrooms all over the city, the state, and the nation, people cheered and expressed jubilation and total shock. It was unreal.

The clubhouse was a mad scene of champagne mixed with machismo and awe, grown men rendered unable to contemplate the glory of it all. Into this mix arrived Mayor Lindsay, presumably wearing a suit he had chosen as one he could afford to get messy, because the bubbly was flowing and spurting in every direction.

"I poured the champagne on him, and Grote was scrubbing his head," recalled Rod Gaspar. "I got in the limelight doing it, and it helped get him reelected."

When Mrs. Payson entered the clubhouse, she was intimidated, smiled, and left before taking a champagne shower. Writers struggled to get quotes and protect their notepads amid the sea of champagne. The celebration lasted for three hours. It was a day game, so the press had enough time to delve into every story without being rushed by a deadline. When the players finally showered and dressed, 5,000 fans were waiting for them in the parking lot area beyond right field.

In Manhattan, mass hysteria was the order of the day. Churches were filled with people praying for miracles, because the Mets were living proof of such things. Men and women kissed each other on the streets like those old V-J Day photos. Bars were filled, confetti dropped from office buildings, Wall Street was awash with people dancing in the streets. Bus boys and corporate chieftains shared the glory equally. Probably because baseball is a game played daily, in which victory builds over time, each step on top of the other, the reaction by the city was even more spectacular and spread over a longer time than it had been for the Jets.

Lindsay's reelection probably could be traced to the next day's front-page pictures showing him doused in champagne by Grote and Gaspar. He attached himself to every public celebration of the team. Angst over racial strife, Vietnam, and New York's fiscal crisis faded in the light of the Mets' victory. Union members found common ground with city negotiators.

"They beat the hell out of us," said Luman Harris.

"Now I've done it all," said first base coach Yogi Berra. "I've played, managed, and now will coach in a World Series. That is all, isn't it?"

"I had them [the Mets] a lot of times this year, but this was the greatest thrill," said umpire Ed Sudol. "They're appropriately named the Amazin' Mets. They've come from the depths of despair to the celestial. I studied literature and made that up myself."

"The team has come along slow, but fast," was Casey Stengel's inimitable description.

"We're gonna beat Baltimore, and then I'm goin' fishin'," said Cleon Jones of their World Series opponents.

"We've come this far, we might as well fool the whole world, including Baltimore," said Buddy Harrelson.

"I'll walk down the street in New York now and people will say, there's Art Shamsky of the Mets," Shamsky was quoted in the *New York Daily News*. "People used to laugh. They won't anymore."

"After beating Atlanta, I think the Mets had a feeling they could beat anybody," recalled Ralph Kiner.

"The Mets made people care again," wrote Larry Merchant in the *New York Post.* "They hadn't for so long, they had forgotten they once did."

"We were being toasted by Mayor Lindsay, Governor [Nelson] Rockefeller, and it was exciting," recalled Swoboda. "Everything was happening at Shea."

"The tension of the world was on us," said Koosman. "Everybody wanted to be on the bandwagon. Rockefeller and Lindsay and numerous big names were suddenly appearing in our clubhouse."

New York did it by slugging the ball. In the Championship Series, Agee hit .357, Jones .429, Shamsky .538, Garrett .385, and Boswell .333.

"The play-off series against the Braves was one of the few times our pitchers had faltered like that and allowed an unusual number of runs," said Ed Charles.

Certainly, the Atlanta series was important because it allowed the entire team to truly share in the incredible run. Until that time, there was a strong sense that New York was an updated version of the 1948 Braves: "Spahn and Sain and pray for rain." Call them "Seaver, Koosman, or lose 'em." It separates them from the Dodgers of the mid-1960s, who won pennants and World Series on dominant pitching with little else. The Mets were—and after this series it was very apparent—a *team.* Seaver, the king of the hill, their hero who stood head and shoulders *above* his teammates, had been picked up *by* them when he finally faltered.

"The feeling of having clinched the pennant was great, especially because none of us had ever been there before," said Harrelson. "We knew we would have a very tough nut to crack in the World Series, but there was a feeling of momentum building among us. It was almost spiritual, that we were just moving forward to the next place, that it was meant to be."

God may not have been a Met, but He was looking to buy some Manhattan real estate.

Twenty-five groundskeepers immediately went to work on the Shea Stadium turf, described by one writer as resembling a "World War I battlefield." Because the Mets had made it to the postseason, the Jets had to play a "home game" in Houston instead of the baseball-occupied Shea. Also, the week in between the play-offs and the World Series, the New York Knickerbockers won their fifth exhibition game in preparation for the 1969–1970 NBA season.

Despite all the joy over the Mets, life went on. A big dose of reality was the bombing of the Army Induction Center in lower Manhattan, the site of so-called pacifist demonstrations over previous months.

12

DAVID VS. GOLIATH

So David prevailed over the Philistine with a sling and with a stone, and smote the Philistine, and slew him; but there was no sword in the hand of David.

—1 Samuel 17: 50

In the Bible story, a mere boy named David steps forth to do battle with the giant Goliath. Against all odds, he hurls a rock from a sling, slaying Goliath, and leads his people to victory.

Just like the Chosen People, the New York Mets had emerged from their seven-year wandering in the wilderness, invaded Chicago, prevailed in battle with the Giants, Pirates, Braves, and other dwellers of the National League, only to face a modern Goliath: the Baltimore Orioles. Winners of 109 regular season games and fresh off a sweep of the Minnesota Twins in the American League Championship Series, Baltimore must have looked indomitable. Manager Earl Weaver's team included future Hall of Famers Frank Robinson and Brooks Robinson and pitcher Jim Palmer. Mike Cuellar and Dave McNally were 20-game winners. First baseman Boog Powell was the Most Valuable Player in the league. Experts compared them with the 1927 and 1961 Yankees; the 1930 A's; the greatest teams in the history of baseball, indeed in all of sports.

New York City mayor John Lindsay was not to be one-upped by New York governor Nelson Rockefeller, who suddenly jumped on the Mets' bandwagon. Lindsay showed up at LaGuardia Airport with an eight-piece band. He read a cheesy poem by Jeff Greenfield that mentioned everybody from Koosman to the batboy, but somehow omitted Tom Seaver. It did not matter. The Mets made Lindsey look so good the poem sounded like "The Gettysburg Address."

The Mets arrived in Baltimore and thought they were in triple-A. Then they arrived at the Sheraton-

Mike Cuellar bested Seaver in the first World Series game. He shared the 1969 American League Cy Young award with Detroit's Denny McLain.
Brace Photos

Belvedere. It was as old as the Confederacy, or so it seemed; shabby and run-down. The team complained to traveling secretary Lou Niss, and in the backs of their minds they tucked away the thought that, if possible, they did not want to come back. The Orioles that day were having a parade, as if they had already won.

Baltimore's Memorial Stadium held 52,137 fans, but there were empty seats on Saturday, October 11, game 1 of the 1969 World Series between the Orioles and the New York Mets. In the stands were 50,429 Bird loyalists who came out to see a matchup between the fireballing college boy Tom Seaver and the junk-throwing Cuban émigré Mike Cuellar.

In the top of the first inning, Cuellar retired the Mets with little effort. Seaver removed his jacket and walked, plowboy-style, to the Memorial Stadium mound. Up stepped Don Buford, a left-handed hitter and not a power threat.

Seaver's first pitch was a ball, but as Grote returned it, he suddenly felt himself again. He had the confidence to give Buford his best inside heat. He went into his windup and delivered just that, right where he wanted it in on Buford's letters. Seaver was stunned to see Buford turn on it, his rising bat meeting the ball and sending a drive to right field. It would be an easy fly ball to Ron Swoboda, finally in the lineup against the left-hander Cuellar. Swoboda drifted back a couple of steps, pounded his glove, back a couple more, then his back was against the fence, and the baseball, as if driven by unseen forces, drifted over the fence for a home run. Not a homer by F. Robby, B. Robby, or Powell, but by Buford. One batter, two pitches, 1–0 Baltimore. Here we go. It was like fumbling the opening kickoff, and the other team recovers it in the end zone for six points.

"Confirmation" of Baltimore superiority, "seemed instantaneous when Don Buford, the miniature Baltimore left fielder" took Seaver deep, wrote Roger Angell. Swoboda said he could have caught the ball, but he did not time his leap, the ball touching his glove "at my apogee."

Swoboda's back was to a fence with a gate that actually could be pushed back 2 or 3 feet, but he was in unfamiliar territory and did not take advantage of it. Swoboda watched film of that play many times and was always disappointed at his stutter-step approach, letting a catchable ball go over the fence. Swoboda told writer Bill Gutman that he was totally disoriented by the first game of the World Series, comparing it to parachute jumps that he later made. He was "petrified." Over time, Ron became aware of his surroundings during a jump and compared that eventual orientation to playing in the Series. He said he felt like "a mechanical man" going back on Buford's drive.

At least against the Braves, Seaver got out of the first unscathed. Seaver retired the next two hitters, but Powell found no mystery to him, rapping a jarring base hit. Brooks Robinson tapped out to end the inning.

Baltimore's Don Buford homered off Ron Swoboda's glove in the first at-bat of the World Series. Swoboda would later atone for his misplay.
John Rogers Archives

Cuellar was untouchable, mainly because he induced half the Mets to hit grounders gobbled up by Brooks Robinson. Seaver knew he needed to be at his best in order to give his team a chance. He settled into a rhythm and set Baltimore down in the second and third in the same fashion as he dominated the National League all year. He was back. However, his legs, weakened by the inability to run between starts as usual, were giving way. In the fourth, he got the first two men out but lost the hop on his fastball.

Elrod Hendricks stepped to the plate. All season, hitters like Hendricks were unable to get around on Seaver's heat, but Ellie stroked a single, pulling it to right field. Brooks and Frank just saw a blur. Buford and Hendricks were all over him. Go figure.

Davey Johnson came to the plate, an unthreatening pose, but Seaver worked him like he was Hank Aaron. Four balls later, and there were men on first and second. Then Mark Belanger came up. Prior to 1969, he could not hit his way out of a paper bag, but in that year he improved from .208 to .287. Seaver pitched to him like he was still the .208 Belanger, but the .287 Mark delivered a single on a hanging curve, and it was 2–0. Then, the unforgivable sin: a chest-high nothing pitch to Cuellar, of all people, who drilled it into center field for an RBI single. Un-bee-lievable!

Buford up. Little Don, tired of the golden boy getting all the USC praise, slapped one down the right field line. The runners advanced, all station-to-station baseball that Earl Weaver normally eschewed, but on this occasion he welcomed 4–0, and the crowd, as they say, "went wild."

"When Tom is pitching and giving up hits like this, I feel like a voodoo doll," Nancy Seaver explained. "I feel as if someone is sticking a needle in me with every hit."

In the Mets fifth, Brooks retired Al Weis on a tough, deep chance. In the bottom of the fifth, Seaver felt like a man who had just finished a marathon after running a triathlon. He was completely jarred by the entire experience, the crushing blows of Oriole hits coming on the heels of such excitement and anticipation. Laboring, his knees buckling, the exhausted Mets ace gave all he had to retire Baltimore, knowing he was done for the day via a pinch hitter in the next inning.

Cuellar was a mystery all afternoon. The game had no further excitement except for the seventh inning. New York scratched a run. With runners on first and second with two outs, Rod Gaspar pinch hit, producing a "swinging bunt" roller toward third. Brooks Robinson came swooping in, barehanded it, and threw the man out at first base. It was a spectacular play but as common in Baltimore as crab cakes and beer.

Robinson put pressure on right-handed batters "with his aggressive stance (the hands are cocked up almost under his chin), his closeness to the plate, his eager appetite for the ball," wrote Angell. "His almost supernaturally quick reactions are helped by the fact he is ambidextrous; he bats and throws right-handed, but eats, writes, plays ping-pong, and fields blue darters with his left."

That was that. Cuellar completed the six-hitter, a dominant performance by Baltimore as a team with one small blip, not considered particularly noteworthy at the time. The two Robinsons and Powell were a combined 1 for 12. Mets fans had a difficult time finding much solace. If they were to have a chance, it had to be with Seaver,

Defensive wizard Brooks Robinson's clutch play preserved Baltimore's 4–1 game 1 win. *Brace Photos*

and now he was gone, a loser having pitched two straight underperforming games. The pipe dream of a Shea celebration was as distant as *Apollo 11* on July 20.

But confident Ed Charles walked up to Baltimore pitching coach George Bamberger after the game, telling him, "George, this is the last game you guys are gonna win."

"[B.S.]," replied Bamberger, a skilled member of the Earl Weaver School of Oratory.

"Whoa, this isn't going to take long," Swoboda remembered thinking. The Baltimore native had relatives at the game. He said the whole experience was a "strange feeling . . . *woo*, baseball of this magnitude is *very* different."

Seaver was a stand-up guy in the postgame clubhouse, admitting that he "ran out of gas." That night, Tom, Nancy, his parents, brothers, sisters, and their families went out to dinner at the Chesapeake House. His relatives were surprised at his cheerfulness. The fan in him could not be contained. He had *pitched in the World Series!*

As Tom made his way to the table, he saw Rod Dedeaux, his coach at Southern Cal. His son, Justin, who roomed with Seaver at USC, was with him. They were dining with . . . Don Buford.

"Front-runner," Seaver hissed. In jest.

The other half of the "Robinson boys" duo, Frank Robinson was hard-nosed but gave the Mets little respect. *Brace Photos*

On Sunday, the Mets picked up the papers and read Frank Robinson's cutting remarks. The veteran showed little respect for the Mets. After all, this was a man who had earned his living doing battle with Aaron's Braves, Mantle's Yankees, Mays's Giants, Koufax's Dodgers, Yaz's Red Sox, and McLain's Tigers, veteran teams all. Worthy opponents. Rod Gaspar? Ron Swoboda? Al Weis? The Mets had sat on their hands in the dugout, too, Robinson wondered aloud. He thought these youngsters would at least be enthusiastic.

Gaspar, probably high on champagne and in a moment of temporary insanity during the play-off celebration, told somebody the Mets would sweep four straight. It got back to the Orioles. "Bring on Ron Gaspar," said Frank.

"Not Ron," Merv Rettenmund corrected him. "That's Rod—stupid."

"Okay, bring on Rod Stupid," said Robby.

"Robby was one of those guys who was all business, all the time, once the game started," stated Art Shamsky. "He played hard, and the opposition knew it. If he didn't like a player on the other team, particularly a pitcher, he would get on his case, usually from the dugout. He was tough."

Robinson and Bob Gibson were among that breed of ballplayers who frowned on pregame or postgame fraternization. Even at All-Star Games, Robinson was hard to talk to. He gave nor took no quarter. Off the field he was fair to everybody, but he was like one of those linebackers who pretend the opposing running back impregnated his little sister, even if he did not, just for extra motivation.

Donn Clendenon tried to stir things up a bit. He knew Robinson from the National League. During batting practice, he tried to introduce Rod Gaspar and Robinson. They just stared at each other. Gaspar took off for the outfield, trying to avoid trouble.

Shamsky and Robinson had been teammates in Cincinnati. During a series, ironically enough against the Mets in 1965, the Reds held a big lead. Robinson taunted the Mets and was retaliated against by being hit by a pitch. When New York brought in a right-handed sidearm reliever known for hitting right-handed hitters, Reds manager Dick Sisler did not want to risk injury to his star. He sent Shamsky in to pinch hit for Robinson.

"You talking to me?" Shamsky asked Sisler, incredulous that he might be asked to hit for *Frank Robinson.* "This was like a scene right out of the movie *Taxi Driver,*" was Shamsky's description of it. Shamsky grabbed a bat. He always called Frank "Mr. Robinson." Somebody told Shamsky, "Good luck." He was not talking about the at bat. F. Robby was kneeling in the on-deck circle, unaware of Sisler's move.

"What the hell are you doing here?" Robinson asked Shamsky.

"Dick wants me to hit for you," said the rookie.

"You can't be serious," Robinson said, managing to sound like John McEnroe would a decade or so later. "Get out of here!"

Shamsky went back to the dugout. "G-g-go back out there and hit," Sisler, who stuttered but was also nervous about pinch hitting for Robinson, said to Shamsky.

"He doesn't want me to hit for him," Shamsky replied.

"J-j-just go back out there and hit," Sisler, who certainly did not want the job of replacing his star face-to-face, said to Art.

Shamsky made the trek back to the on-deck circle, whereupon Frank said, "Get out of here."

"But, Mr. Robinson, he wants me to hit for you," said Shamsky, not sure if he was going to get swung on. He also had a bat in his hands, and that was the year Juan Marichal clobbered John Roseboro over the head with one.

Sisler made some inaudible sound. Robby looked at him in the dugout. The manager touched his forearm, a sign for a pinch hitter. Frank said something unsuitable for publication, then turned to Shamsky and said, "You better not embarrass me."

"Talk about pressure," recalled Shamsky.

Shamsky hit the first pitch over the center field fence for a home run. He was on cloud nine. In the dugout, his teammates all glad-handed him, except for Robinson. Finally, Art sat down, and Robinson appeared before him.

"Okay," said Robinson, smiling and extending his hand. "Now you can call me Frank."

It was like being initiated into the Rat Pack. "It's a day I will never forget," was Shamsky's memory of it.

Earl Weaver "was one of those guys like Leo and Gene Mauch, who took so much obvious glee in beating you and worked so hard at it," recalled Swoboda. "You loved to beat him because you knew how much he burned inside. You knew Earl had no graceful acceptance of losing, that it ate him up . . . you knew he died a little inside."

Shamsky had played against Weaver when he was with Topeka and Earl managed at Fox Cities. "Earl was a fiery little guy with sort of a gravelly voice, the complete opposite of Gil Hodges," Shamsky recalled. Hodges carried a beef until it could be aired behind closed doors. Weaver would get in a player's face, an umpire's mug, and especially a pitcher's grill . . . *especially* if his name was Jim Palmer.

Chain-smoking Earl Weaver was an old-school baseball man. *Brace Photos*

Writer Peter Golenbock, author of *Amazin': The Miraculous History of New York's Most Beloved Baseball Team,* wrote that the Mets harbored the feeling that theirs was the better league. Hodges made a point of reminding them of this, telling them he had managed in Washington and knew it for a fact.

The odds after the first game were now 5–16 in favor of Baltimore. "I was a little worried," said Ralph Kiner. "I thought [the Mets] could lose in four."

"Doesn't four of seven mean that you have to win four games?" asked Yogi Berra, putting it all in perspective.

"Seaver couldn't blacken your eye with his fastball" in game 1, said Clendenon, "but we had Koosman" ready to go in the second contest.

"Baltimore wasn't intimidating," said Cleon Jones.

"Two things came to my mind after the first game," said Seaver. "We were this group of so-called brash individuals that had no right to be in the World Series against the big, bad Baltimore Orioles with all the big names on that team. After we lost the first game I remembered here were these big, bad Orioles and they were jumping up and down in celebration. For some reason I expected them to be much more serene in victory. I was thinking, 'Why are they so jubilant?' Donn Clendenon came walking toward me, put his arm around me walking toward the clubhouse and said, 'We're going to beat these guys.' It was the same thought I had in my mind. I pitched lousy relative to how I pitched during the regular season, yet Clendenon was feeling the same thing I was."

The Mets had none of the wide-eyed wonder of World Series fans by this point. They were grim, prepared to play a grim game, and they did just that. It was a matchup of pitching and defense.

Baltimore came with their A game in this regard. B. Robinson made some fine plays. Belanger executed an extraordinary catch-and-throw. The Mets responded, with Harrelson making a hit-robbing grab. Angell wrote that Harrelson was "gaunt," noting that the "tensions of the season had burned Harrelson down from a hundred and sixty-eight to a hundred and forty-five pounds."

Jerry Koosman, the young southpaw, opposed McNally, the veteran lefty control artist. McNally entered the game with 21 consecutive scoreless innings in postseason play, going back to the 1966 Series with L.A. Donn Clendenon reached McNally in the fourth for a wrong-field homer to make it 1–0, Mets. From there, New York was determined to hold their ground.

Grim.

Amid this, Koosman had everything he did not have against Atlanta. In the seventh, he was nursing a no-hit game and a perilous lead. His stated goal since he was a kid watching Don Larsen's 1956 masterpiece was to pitch a perfect game in the World Series. Paul Blair ended Koosman's no-no dreams, leading off with a single, but Koosman worked two more outs. The Baltimore crowd urged action. They were strangely mystified that the rout they expected was not forthcoming. Blair seemed to pick up on the exchange between Grote and Koosman, stealing on a changeup curve. Brooks Robinson singled up the middle. It was tied.

Now what?

A LET'S GO METS! banner was unfurled in the aisle behind home plate, carried by Mrs. Pfeil, Dyer, Ryan, and Seaver, "smashers all," wrote Angell. The Mets derived some motivation from the fact their wives had been given bad seats out in right field. Some threatened not to play unless they were given better seats on Sunday, which the Orioles accommodated.

Grimly, the game wore on. In the ninth, faced with the obstacle of winning a late, tied game on the road, the National League champions made their move. It was pure station-to-station ball, little ball, Mets ball. Charles and Grote singled off McNally, finally tiring. In this era before Mariano Rivera and Lee Smith changed baseball strategy, Weaver just figured McNally was better than whoever was warming up in the bullpen. Al Weis, hitting .215, stepped in. On the first pitch he slapped a go-ahead single.

Koosman lost his heat and went to curves, but he walked two O's in the bottom of the ninth. With two outs, Ron Taylor came on, retired the last man, and in "a game that would have delighted John McGraw," wrote Roger Angell, it was on to the Big Apple. New York City let loose in ecstatic hope. Baltimore gave a collective, *Not again!*

Weis was typical of the 1969 Mets: a mediocre player who stepped up and had several extraordinary moments (Chicago in July, now this). "It is a segmented experience, so you aren't as bad or as good as you show," said Swoboda of the World Series. "Anything can happen, and it is an ideal opportunity for lesser athletes to shine, because you don't have to do it for three months in a row. . . . The real accomplishment is in not allowing the aura of the World Series to change you in a negative way."

Winning the second game gave the Mets confidence. "It was a close game, and if we could have beaten Koosman, it would have been a different story in the Series," said Brooks Robinson.

"We're not going to have to come back here," Jones flatly told Tommie Agee.

"I knew we had to win in Baltimore," said Koosman. "I certainly felt the weight on my shoulders about going out and doing my bit without screwing up."

The official World Series program. *National Baseball Hall of Fame Library*

"Me, one of the heroes of the game," said Weis. "How sweet is that?"

"I figured if I walked Weis to get to Koosman, then Hodges would pinch hit for Koosman and whoever he sent up there would be a better hitter than Weis," Weaver told the *New York Times*.

Koosman was a "cool cat," according to sportswriter Dick Young, because he would tell jokes on the bench before pitching a game. He and Ron Taylor held Boog and the Robinsons 1 for 10, making them 2 for 24 on the weekend. "It was an ominous note for the Orioles," wrote Ben Henkey of *The Sporting News*.

The Mets gladly boarded a plane for New York. Down deep, they knew something the Orioles only suspected. The reaction of the city would be as intimidating to the O's as their team had been to the Mets. Baltimore had heard about the crowds, the frenzy, the media, the pure adrenaline of 12 million people pumping as one, but they had not experienced it. Most of these Birds either could barely remember or had never experienced a truly meaningful baseball game in New York, what with the demise of the Yankees. A few—Brooks Robinson, Boog Powell, Dave McNally—had been on the team when they battled Mickey Mantle and company down the stretch in 1964, but Yankee Stadium was no comparison to the noise chamber they were entering.

New York had gotten the split they needed. They had a 10th man, maybe even an 11th or 12th, at Shea in the form of the crowd. It was like putting an extra shortstop up the middle, an extra outfielder to guard the line. They were suddenly confident, almost ecstatic. On the plane they practically salivated at the prospect of playing for "their people" again. The Mets had clinched the division in their last home game of the regular season on September 24, then played a pennant-clinching home play-off game. New York had played nine games on the road and one at home beginning on September 26, yet the stars were aligned.

The city had watched on TV, listened on the radio, read in the papers, but now *they were here* against the Baltimore Orioles in the World Series. It had all seemed like a myth, a rumor, but now it was for real.

On Monday, October 13, the town was in a state of utter frenzy. It was the most exciting sporting scene the city had ever known, and probably the most fevered sense of anticipation for an athletic event in American or even world history. The Mets story was more incredible than any of Babe Ruth's October moments; equaled or overshadowed Lou Gehrig's "luckiest man" speech or Joe DiMaggio's 56-game hitting streak; aroused greater passions even than Bobby Thomson's "shot heard 'round the world" or the Dodgers' "wait till next year" 1955 world title; or any of a number of mythologized events: the "Four Horsemen" of Notre Dame, the Dempsey-Tunney fight, the 1958 Colts-Giants NFL title; even Broadway Joe's Super Bowl event that was still fresh in New Yorkers' minds.

Upon serious reflection, it had all the earmarks of the biggest sports story ever, and while some earth-shaking events have occurred since (the Muhammad Ali–Joe Louis fight at Madison Square Garden occurred two years later, just for starters), it may very well still rank as number one. But to get there, to truly be as world-shaking an event as all that, *the Mets had to win.*

Everything, everywhere, took a back seat to the World Series. The shifting from Baltimore to the New York stage had a cataclysmic effect. How the Mets were able to concentrate amid all the craziness was a miracle in and of itself. The grounds crew had slept at the park, working night and day to get the field ready after it had been torn up after the pennant-clinching win over Atlanta.

The Mets left-handed hitters got their chance in the third game, since right-handed Jim Palmer was the Baltimore starter against rookie Gary Gentry. This was the one New York was "supposed" to lose. Seaver and Koosman could beat anybody, but Palmer vs. Gentry?

"I was psyched up enough against the Braves," Gentry told the *New York Times*. "I should have been a little nervous, but I wasn't because we won the first two games and all we had to do was win one of the next three games."

Gentry seemed to have trouble controlling his approach; he was either too excited or not excited enough. He had a year under his belt, and by game 3 of the Series, he felt he had a handle on how best to deal with the pressure.

"I didn't feel a lot pressure starting game 3, but anytime you pitch in the World Series it's pressure," said Palmer. "I was aware that it was Shea Stadium and not like pitching at home."

The crowds arrived early on Tuesday (it was still an era of day World Series games, even during the week), and the atmosphere was off the charts. The weather was cool with a slight chance of rain hanging in the air, but good autumn ball weather. The Mets were folk heroes, nothing less.

"After batting practice that first day in New York, as we were going to the outfield to shag for our hitters, I met Jim Hardin, who used to be in the Mets organization," recalled Jerry Koosman, "and as I was going out, he was coming in, and he said, 'What are you doing here?' I said, 'What do you mean?' He said, 'You guys don't belong on the same field with us. What are you doing here?' I said, 'You'll see.'

"So after batting practice I went into the clubhouse, and I told everybody that. Which really helped charge the ball club more." As if these guys needed additional motivation.

Jackie Kennedy Onassis and her son, John F. Kennedy Jr., attended, as well as Governor Nelson Rockefeller, Mayor John Lindsay, and Joe DiMaggio. All rooted uproariously for the Mets (well, maybe not Joe D., who probably resented cheers not reserved for *him*). Steve Lawrence sang the national anthem. Roy Campanella threw out the first ball.

In the first inning, Gentry retired the side to thunderous ovations. It grew louder when New York came to bat in the bottom of the inning. With the count two and one, Agee set off an earthquake of sound by homering over the center field fence.

In the third, Grote walked and Harrelson singled. Then Gentry drove a Palmer fastball toward right-center for a double, driving in two runs to make it 3–0. Shea was not a baseball stadium anymore; it was a tent revival.

In the top of the fourth, Frank Robinson lined one to left field. Jones made a fine play, but it was ruled a trap. Powell singled. Were the Orioles' big guns finally shooting? With one out, Gentry blew a third strike past Brooks Robinson. Pull-hitting Ellie Hendricks stepped up, and the outfield shifted toward the right. Then Hendricks, like Yogi Berra in the 1955 World Series, went to the opposite side, hitting a dangerous drive to left-center with both runners off with the crack of the bat.

Agee ran 40 yards and caught up with the ball at the warning track. Reaching up backhanded, he caught it in the edge of his glove webbing, one of the best plays in World Series history. The white of the ball could be seen through the webbing, "snow cone" style. It immediately reminded fans of "The Catch" by Willie Mays off the bat of Cleveland's Vic Wertz in the 1954 World Series at the Polo Grounds.

"When the ball was hit, I looked over at Tommie," recalled Jones. "I knew right away that he could make a play. He learned that when attending Grambling. They taught him that to make sure the crease in the glove was not up so the ball wouldn't pop out of his glove. When I saw Tommie pound his glove, I started to let up in order to play the ball off the wall just in case he didn't get to it. But I had a feeling he was going to make the play. I kept yelling to him that he had lots of room."

"I almost didn't make the play," said Agee. "The ball nearly went through the webbing of my glove."

The crowd cheered him as if he were Neil Armstrong having returned from orbit. He "carried it all the way back to the infield like a trophy, still stuck in the topmost webbing of his glove," wrote Angell. . . . "The eerie crowd—all 56,335 of us—jumped to its feet in astonished, shouting tribute as he trotted off the field."

In the sixth, Ken Boswell singled and was moved over on a grounder, a typical Mets play all year: sacrifice, fundamentals, team play. Grote then doubled to score him. In the seventh, Gentry began to tire. He walked three batters, and with two outs, Paul Blair came to the plate. Hodges brought in Nolan Ryan. Despite his having pitched so well in the play-offs, bringing in Ryan was thought to be a risky move. With his control problems, he was likely to walk a run in.

"Maybe Gil knows something I don't know," said Grote. That was precisely the point in 1969.

"As a player, I never questioned Gil Hodges' judgment," said Jones. "He made all the right decisions that year."

Ryan got two strikes on Blair. The tension was unbearable. Then Blair got one to his liking and hit a shot to deep right-center. Agee and Shamsky went after it, but neither seemed to have a chance. They looked to be on a collision course at first, but Agee was faster and got close, pounding his glove. Then the wind got to it and drove it downward. He dove, skidded, and snagged it. At that moment, the New York Mets, the City of New York, and the Baltimore Orioles knew the Mets were going to be world champs. If Agee did not make those catches, Baltimore would have won the game, "and I don't think I want to be down to the Orioles," said Swoboda.

It was probably the defining moment of the whole, improbable extravaganza. The emotions, the sound; mere words on a page cannot explain what it was like. It was phantasmagoric, almost hallucinatory. Blair was shocked. Later he was so frustrated he made light of Agee's two catches. Baltimore was a whipped crew. From that point on, everything that happened was a Mets parade, which is not to say there was no more drama remaining. But this was the last miracle. It was foreordained.

In the bottom of the eighth, having disposed of one of baseball's all-time greats—Palmer—as if he were a busher, the Metsies added a run on a homer by Ed Kranepool. Once booed, he now symbolized Mets' redemption. In the ninth, the O's loaded the bases again. Hodges, continuing to make every perfect call, stayed with Ryan, who buckled Blair with a called strike 3 curve ball to end the game.

The press treated Agee as if he had just discovered the cure for cancer. "To me, he was our MVP," said Jones, "the way he hit in 1969 and the way he played center field, particularly at Shea Stadium."

"I thought the first catch was the hardest because I had to run farther," Agee was quoted as saying in the *Daily News*.

"I thought the second catch was harder," said Hodges, who added that it was "the greatest I've ever seen in the World Series."

Jim Palmer was an all-time great. In later years he replayed the '69 World Series again and again, causing his friend Tom Seaver to advise that he "get over it." *Brace Photos*

The immediate talk after the game continued all off-season, and in fact is debated today by fans. In a 5–0 victory, Agee unquestionably saved five runs from scoring. From a clutch standpoint, Agee's plays are hard to argue against.

"The final score was 5–0, or, more accurately, 5–5—five runs for the Mets, five runs saved by Tommie Agee," wrote Angell. "Almost incidentally, it seemed, the Orioles were suddenly in deep trouble in the Series." It actually may have been 5–6. Blair's drive, had it skidded past Agee and considering his speed, might have been an inside-the-park homer.

Palmer said the scouting reports on New York were all wrong. Gentry was said to have "average" stuff, but he was not average in game 3. He was also said to be no offensive threat. Based on that, Palmer felt Blair was out of position on his double. After that game, Palmer began to famously move his outfielders around, a constant source of frustration for Earl Weaver. Agee's home run would prove to be the only one Palmer ever surrendered to a batter leading off a game. Curiously, he and Seaver—two of the star pitchers of the next decade—both allowed leadoff homers in the World Series.

"I thought the third game of the Series was the most important," recalled Frank Robinson. "We had Palmer going against Gentry. I didn't even think about losing. It was a perfect matchup for us."

"We were all surprised when Gentry pitched so well," said Davey Johnson. "I definitely think that was a key game."

"I've never seen two such catches by the same player in the same game," said Weaver afterward.

"I knew Tommie from the American League," Ed Charles said. "He had a lot of talent, but above all, he was always a go-for-broke type of player. Because of that, he never gave up on a ball in the outfield and had a propensity to make that great catch."

The crowds at Shea during the 1969 postseason were a revelation, in that previous World Series crowds did not resemble regular season ones. There is a famous photo of Chuck Hiller hitting a home run for San Francisco against New York in the 1962 World Series at Yankee Stadium. The fans behind home plate are easily identified. The men and women resemble sunglass-wearing stockbrokers and heiresses.

When Carl Yastrzemski emerged from the Fenway Park dugout before the first game of the 1967

Paul Blair was also stunned by the Mets, and at the time downplayed Tommie Agee's two catches to save game 3. *Brace Photos*

World Series, he looked at the people in the stands and asked, "Where *is* everybody? These aren't the people who were here all year."

The Shea crowds were "uncharacteristically elegant" yet boisterous, according to Roger Angell. There were a fair number of men in suits, at least in the best, most expensive seats, but more women than usual, certainly more minorities than were ever seen at Yankee Stadium, and, of course, the unprecedented placard wavers. Karl Ehrhardt, the "Sign Man of Shea," captured what many were now allowing themselves to believe: That with Tom Seaver and Jerry Koosman slated to pitch games 3 and 4, the Series just might end here. One of his placards asked a sardonic question of the Birds: LEAVING SO SOON?

13

THE PERFECT GAME

Sandy Koufax: "Tom, is God a Met?"
Tom Seaver: "No, but He's got an apartment in New York."
—TV interview during the 1969 World Series

Wednesday, October 15, was a perfect day for baseball: a little cool, blue skies, what New Yorkers almost self-righteously call "World Series weather."

Tom Seaver, the starting pitcher, arrived at Shea and was immediately distracted. Tug McGraw approached Seaver with a pamphlet. "Hey, have you seen this?" he asked him. "They're giving it out outside the park."

The front of the pamphlet showed Seaver with the legend "Mets Fans for Peace," with a reprint from a *New York Times* article headlined "Tom Seaver Says U.S. Should Leave Vietnam." It read:

BALTIMORE, Oct. 10 (UPI)—Tom Seaver, the New York Mets' starting pitcher for the opening World Series game here tomorrow, believes the United States should get out of Vietnam. He says he plans to buy an advertisement in the New York Times saying: "If the Mets can win the World Series, then we can get out of Vietnam."

The Mets would have to defeat the Baltimore Orioles before Seaver could place such an ad, but the 24-year-old Californian who electrified the baseball world by winning 25 games for the Mets, helping them to the National League pennant, thinks he can carry out the plan in any case.

"I think it's perfectly ridiculous what we're doing about the Vietnam situation," he said. "It's absurd! When the Series is over, I'm going to have a talk with Ted Kennedy, convey some of my ideas to him and then take an ad in the paper. I feel very strongly about this."

According to Seaver, the UPI story "wasn't exactly accurate—but it did reflect my feelings." Prior to the play-offs, he was contacted by the antiwar Moratorium Day committee, asking if he would sign on to an ad stating if the Mets could win the Series, then "We Can Get Out of Vietnam."

Seaver signed the ad. His opinion, at least at the time, was that the war was not helping the American image abroad, was splitting the country apart at home, and was not "adding much to our national security."

Seaver was not "opposed to all wars. I wasn't a confirmed pacifist," but Vietnam was in his view wrong. The Moratorium Day committee wanted to combine Seaver's star power with either Senator Kennedy's or Senator George McGovern's. Seaver was asked to wear a black armband in solidarity with the process, but he declined because it could disrupt his team. He felt a dual "obligation" to concentrate on baseball but also express his rights as a citizen.

Seaver was upset about the pamphlet because he had not authorized use of his name. The Moratorium Day committee had not issued it. The Chicago Seven, the people who were on trial at the time for starting the riots at the previous year's Democratic national convention, were responsible. They were headed by self-described "yippies" Abbie Hoffman and Jerry Rubin. The pamphlet showed a B-52 and the Statue of Liberty in an attempt to paint America as a warmongering country.

"It's terrible," said McGraw. Like many of the Mets, he was a Reservist, but an impish one not likely to hold a hawkish attitude. Seaver certainly was viewed as a person who was "qualified" to speak since, as an ex-Marine, he had not dodged the draft, as so many of the protestors had. Seaver had to put the pamphlet and the war out of his mind. He had business at hand.

★ ★ ★

Three hours later, Seaver took the mound. Buford stepped in. Well, if nothing else, this would determine who got the honor of dinner with Rod Dedeaux. Seaver delivered the same piping fastball that had stood him in good stead from July to September. He was on. His butterflies disappeared. Buford stared at it; it wasn't the same stuff he had seen at Memorial Stadium. Seaver worked the leadoff man, then struck him out on a curve. In the Baltimore dugout, a light panic set in. They *had* to win this game, but any hope that the below par Seaver of Saturday was on the hill Wednesday disappeared.

Seaver was not just throwing hard, he had fabulous movement, mostly sinking action that seemed to flow perfectly in the cool October air. Blair worked him to a two-two count. Seaver's legs felt strong, and with it the confidence to blow heat past the hitter. Blair managed to connect and singled. Seaver's perfect game was not to be, at least not in the traditional sense.

Seaver felt he got away with one to Frank Robinson, who skied a 395-foot out to Agee, but Powell was helpless, striking out to end the inning. In the Mets' first, Jones grounded into a double play. Cuellar looked to be as strong as he had been in the opener.

In the second, Brooks Robinson grounded out. Seaver, who said the first thing on his mind when he woke up that day was, for some reason, Elrod Hendricks, walked the Orioles catcher. Johnson grounded into a force, then was thrown out by Grote trying to steal.

Trudging in from the mound, Seaver looked for his family in the box seats. His sister Katie, her husband, Mike Jones, and their two sons, Eric and Bryan, lived in Minnesota and were staying at Croton-on-

Hudson. Also in attendance: his other sister, Carol, her husband, Bob Baker; plus brother Charles (the East Village sculptor/social worker and teacher in Brooklyn's Bedford-Stuyvesant section), with his wife, Juliette. According to Tom, Charles was perhaps the most athletic of the Seavers. He was 6'4", an excellent swimmer at the University of California. He often brought his students to Tom's games.

The Seaver family was a picture of 1960s' American youth. Brother Charles had lived in Europe for a while, studying the art of sculpting. Carol had spent time in Nigeria with the Peace Corps. Katie had gone to Stanford (Charles Sr.'s alma mater). Carol went to Tom's USC archrival, UCLA. "It took a World Series to bring them all together," wrote Seaver. Seaver spent $2,500 on Series tickets.

In the bottom of the second, Clendenon got hold of one from Cuellar, hitting a monster homer to give Seaver a 1–0 lead. When Seaver went out in the third, he told himself not to let down, that he was "the best pitcher in baseball." Seaver threw a called strike 3 to Belanger on a pitch that manager Earl Weaver deemed low. Weaver came out of the dugout to argue with Shag Crawford, apparently a calculated move since to purposely come on the field to argue balls and strikes is cause for an automatic ejection. Weaver had seen enough. His team was losing and needed a kick start. He was frustrated and let Crawford have it. The fans gave him what for, the camera zeroing in on him while legendary NBC announcer Curt Gowdy described the semihumorous sight of the little Oriole manager in the ump's face.

With Weaver banished to the visitors' clubhouse to smoke cigarettes, Belanger and Cuellar managed hits off Seaver. It was a tightrope the pitcher walked throughout the early part of that game, great stuff when he needed it but lapses. But Buford hit a high hopper that Clendenon speared over his head, throwing to second for a force. Paul Blair tried a surprise bunt but popped it back to Seaver. Then Frank Robinson was retired to end the inning.

The TV camera showed Nancy, wearing a tan tam-o'-shanter, almost as much as Tom. She was a sensation. It was like John Kennedy, who once introduced himself as "the man who accompanied Jacqueline Kennedy to Paris." A large banner was unfurled for television: CORTLAND STATE LOVES NANCY SEAVER.

When Weis singled, Seaver tried to bunt him over, but his normally good technique failed him. He bunted the third-strike foul and was out. In the fourth, Seaver retired the side one-two-three, but on the third out, covering first on Hendrick's grounder to Clendenon, the Orioles catcher spiked him. Seaver required a little medical care from trainer Gus Mauch but was okay.

From the fourth to the eighth, Seaver and Cuellar matched each other. Only Paul Blair reached base, on a walk in the sixth. After throwing two balls to Frank Robinson, Grote came to the mound. Seaver felt he got away with a hanging slider that F. Robby popped to Harrelson. He fell behind Powell, three and oh, but threw strikes to make the count full. With Blair running, Powell fouled a couple off before flying to center.

Johnson almost got him, blooping one to left that Jones ran in for, making the catch. With Cuellar on, Seaver figured this was a typical 1–0 Mets game. He and the staff were used to them. The strong New York pitching, in a complete reversal from the Atlanta play-off series, had dominated since the fourth inning of game 1. In 30 innings the Orioles had scored only once. They had been put into a severe slump by Mets arms.

Seaver felt "nervous, apprehensive, and eager" as he took the mound in the ninth. The crowd was on edge. It was not a game of spectacular hits and catches, like the previous day. It was a typical Roger Angell–type of pitchers' duel; the slow, building tension of a 1–0 contest reaching a crescendo. The Mets were *so close.* Seaver could taste it, a 1–0 complete game victory in the World Series. It was almost too good to be true. He began thinking of his near-perfect game on July 9. On that date Tom said he felt just as tense entering the ninth. Today even though he did not have a Don Larsen–style perfect game, the concept of winning 1–0, with his whole family in the stands, to give his club a near-insurmountable 3–1 Series lead with Koosman pitching at home the next day—well, this could be the *perfect game.*

But an actual perfect game was "almost a selfish goal." He wanted this Series win for his teammates. He also wanted to prove himself the team leader everybody said he was. The previous year, Denny McLain was the unquestioned star of the Detroit Tigers, but it was Mickey Lolich and his three Series victories who was the hero against St. Louis. Seaver had no trouble with Koosman being a hero, too, but he certainly wanted to atone for his game 1 loss and for two mediocre postseason performances prior to this.

Seaver glanced out at right field. He was surprised to see Swoboda still in there instead of his usual late-inning defensive replacement, Ron, er, *Rod* Gaspar. Apparently, Hodges was not going to "bring on Ron Gaspar" or "Rod Stupid."

"If Gil made a move, it was going to turn out right; if Gil didn't make a move, that was going to turn out right, too," Seaver assessed. "If, as some people said, God was a Mets fan, Gil was His prophet."

Blair led off. Pitching carefully, Seaver induced a fly to Swoboda, the first action he saw in right field all day. Frank Robinson worked a two-two count, then fouled two outside fastballs. Seaver began to press a little. He was beginning to tire, but his adrenaline was pumping. Seaver decided to go with what had gotten him here: high, inside heat, attempting to overpower the slugger mano a mano; the style he made famous in numerous battles with National League sluggers over the years: Bench, Clemente, Stargell, McCovey, Aaron, and so many others. It was good ol' country hardball, but with nine innings behind him, that extra mile or two an hour he needed to get it past the cat-quick F. Robby was missing. He roped a single to left. Seaver immediately second-guessed himself but was thankful Robinson missed it by a fraction of an inch. Otherwise the game would have been tied.

Powell came to the plate. Seaver decided on breaking stuff and jam pitches. He got what he wanted, a double-play grounder, but it had eyes: right field, base hit, Robinson racing to third. First and third, one out, grim tension gripping Shea.

With Ron Taylor and Tug McGraw warming up, Hodges came to the mound. In today's era, Seaver would have been gone; he probably would not even have started the ninth. Hodges trusted Seaver when he asked him how he felt. "All right," he said. "A little tired but nothing serious." Maybe he was, just this once, fudging a little, but Hodges had a hunch and stuck with him. He almost made his first serious managerial error in this year of infallibility.

They discussed the base to throw to on a double-play ball back to the mound. Brooks Robinson was quick but not a fast runner. Hard stuff, in. They decided to pitch him. He had an .067 Series average but was clutch.

Then it happened. If it was possible that a better catch than Agee's two from the previous day could be made, better than Mays in 1954, maybe the greatest catch in Series history, or some say in all of baseball history, it was about to happen. If

Agee's catches defined the Series and the season, this would outdo them.

The crowd chanted *"DE-fense, DE-dense,"* as if the Jets were making a goal-line stand or the Knicks were trying to hold off "Earl the Pearl" Monroe with a minute left protecting a one-point lead.

Seaver jammed Robinson high, but he tomahawked a nasty, hard-sinking line drive toward right field. Swoboda raced toward it. He had no angle, no real place to turn his glove or his body to make a catch. He was like a matador trying to tackle a bull. This hit had all the earmarks of skidding past him, scoring Powell from first, putting B. Robby on third with a triple, making the score 2–1 Orioles. The third run would be 90 feet away. Seaver would trudge into the dugout with his second loss of the Series. Baltimore would suddenly be very much alive, full of momentum after tying the Series at two games apiece, knowing they were going home no matter what. Seaver suddenly turned into a fan.

"I watched, fascinated by the race between Ron and the ball," was how he described it. His "fielding instincts, everything Rod Dedeaux had drummed into me, weren't working." Not sure what to do, whether the ball would go to the wall or be trapped, he did not know what base to back up, so he went to none of them.

After delivering the pitch, he threw up his glove self-protectively when he saw Robinson's violent contact, in case he hit a shot back at him. From the mound he watched the ball start to sink, "and Ron left his feet and dove and jabbed out his glove backhanded. The ball hit the glove. It stuck."

Then, "even more remarkable than the catch, which was pretty remarkable," Swoboda rolled, displayed the glove to the umpire, who made the out call, and in one motion came up throwing home to try to nab Frank Robinson, who had the wherewithal to tag up just in case. Robinson scored to tie the game. Powell, stunned, held at first. There were two outs.

Even though Baltimore had just tied the game, Shea went ballistic cheering for Swoboda. People asked themselves if they had seen what they just thought they saw. In the dugout, Gaspar just cheered, knowing that he may have been a better fielder, but he never would have made that play. Swoboda, despite his hard work, was not a good outfielder. He had bumbled around, letting Buford's fly land for a homer in Baltimore. But Gil—hunch, intuition?—had made the right moves again, both in what he did and what he did not do.

Seaver was drained, mentally and physically. Realistically, he had no business staying in the game. His style, the opposite of the seemingly effortless grace of Jim Palmer, was one total exertion after another. There was a reason he worked so hard, ran so many wind sprints. He needed to in order to maintain the kind of physical condition necessary to sustain his "drop and drive" motion. In his head, he was disappointed, the shutout lost, victory now nebulous, momentum taken away.

But momentum was not with Baltimore, either. They had to be scratching their heads; first Agee, now *this guy*. What did they have to do to catch a break here?

Hendricks took two balls. Seaver was losing it rapidly, feeding him an easy one that Hendricks hit for a two-run homer to put Baltimore ahead, 3–1—except for the fact that it barely curved foul.

God is a Mets fan.

Seaver gathered everything he had and delivered some heat to get Hendricks to fly out. Now the Mets would need to score in the bottom of the ninth for Seaver to get the win. The faulty memory of millions of New Yorkers is that they did just that. However, just as California tied the game after Dave Henderson's homer for Boston in the 1986 Championship Series, which they won in extra innings, the Mets did not win game 4 in the ninth.

In the bottom of the inning, Jones singled with one out. Swoboda, who had on 10 occasions driven in the tying run, mostly down the stretch, stepped to the plate amid thunderous cheers. He had suddenly, inexplicably, risen to the heights of New York hero worship, his visage and announcement of his name drawing cheers previously reserved for Mickey Mantle or Frank Gifford.

"Ron, who looked to me like a small Paul Bunyan, started creating myths of success about himself instead of myths of failure," wrote Seaver, who added that with work he could be "one of the best hitters in baseball."

For the third straight time, Swoboda singled to right field. Frank Robinson, who by now was in half-belief regarding this entire episode of *The Twilight Zone* he was living in, nonchalanted the ball but scooped it up and threw it, so Jones stopped at second. Hodges called on Shamsky to pinch hit for Ed Charles, but reliever Eddie Watt induced a grounder to Johnson.

Seaver sat in the dugout, not sure of his feelings. There was no logical way he should have been allowed to pitch the 10th. He was bushed. He knew it and half wanted, expected, to be pulled. But Hodges had his hunches, and this one said to stay with his ace. Seaver trudged out

This sequence shows Swoboda's miracle diving catch to preserve game 4 for Seaver and the Mets.
John Rogers Archive

there, determined to draw on his last reservoir of strength.

The atmosphere was now a frenzy of pleading, begging, and cajoling the home team to victory, hope against hope. Seaver never looked at Hodges. He got up, took his jacket off, crossed the foul line, "and I was safe." A whole city was with him, the hero, a Prince Valiant, as Nancy described him. *Don't lose, don't be the goat, not now, not after everything we've been through together.*

Seaver told himself not to let himself, Gil, the team, or the city down. He had thrown 135 pitches, but this was the *World Series,* for God's sake. They were all going to leave it out on the field, every piece of themselves, against the 109-win Baltimore Orioles.

Things started out badly for Tom; a hard Johnson grounder to third, the difficult chance failed by defensive replacement Wayne Garrett. Belanger tried to bunt, but Seaver went with two-seam fastballs, throwing rising heat to induce a pop-up to Grote. Clay Dalrymple pinch hit for Watt.

"He was no threat to anybody—except me," was Seaver's assessment of him. The Phillies beat Seaver twice in 1968, chiefly on a homer and another hard hit by Dalrymple. He singled, and there were runners on first and second. This was the bottom of the order, but they touched the Mets ace. Now the top of the order came up.

Buford flied to Swoboda, but Johnson tagged and went to third. All 57,367 fans sweated it out; it was hold 'em time. Hodges stayed in the dugout. Blair came up. Seaver knew Blair was the last man he would face and put all he had into getting him out. A hit would score a run, and he would be lifted. An out would mean Seaver would be pinch hit for.

This was it. Seaver struck Blair out on two hard fastballs and a good curve. Relief, ecstasy, and hope mixed together.

Jerry Grote faced reliever Dick Hall, who pitched like a guy who had just had a stroke. He delivered the ball from somewhere in his chest cavity, his face contorted like one of those astronauts sitting in a G-force machine at top speed. Grote hit an easy pop to Buford, but God seemed to decide to guide the ball directly into the setting sun. Neither Buford nor Belanger could get it. The ball fell in for a double. Shea was a wall of sound.

Gaspar went in to run for Grote. Seaver surmised that somehow Gil knew he would need Gaspar to pinch run for Grote, which was why he did not use him to replace Swoboda, which was why Swoboda made the great catch, which was why the faster runner was now on second, which was . . .

Billy Hunter, managing in Weaver's place, ordered Al "Babe" Weis intentionally walked. Weis batted .215 with 23 runs batted in that year. That was an improvement over his .155 numbers from 1966. At least. J. C. Martin pinch hit for Seaver. Kranepool was a better bunter than Martin, if that was the plan, but Hodges went with Martin. More mystery.

Southpaw Pete Richert, a two-time All-Star with the lowest ERA on the Baltimore staff, replaced Hall. Hodges stayed with Martin instead of right-hander Duffy Dyer against the lefty. On the first pitch, Martin laid down a perfect bunt about 10 feet in front of home plate. Richert picked it up and fired to first base. Martin was running about a foot inside the fair side of the base line. The ball struck him on the wrist and rolled down the outfield foul line beyond anybody's reach. Martin should have been called out for interference, as replays showed, but the umpires missed it. Gaspar was waved around third and headed home with the winning run.

Seaver: "I couldn't see his face. I could only see his legs. I saw them pounding up and down, kicking up dirt, and then, as Rod Gaspar's front foot stretched out and touched home plate, in the fraction of a second before I leaped out of the dugout to welcome him, my whole baseball life flashed in front of me, the perfect game I'd pitched when I was 12 years old, the grand slam home run I'd hit for the Alaska Goldpanners, the first game I'd won as a member of the New York Mets, the imperfect game I'd pitched against the Chicago Cubs, one after another, every minor miracle building toward that one magic day.

"I never realized before that a man's whole life could be encompassed in a single play, in a single game, in a single day."

Seaver burst out of the dugout and met Gaspar at home plate. A wild on-field celebration ensued.

Duffy Dyer was pinch-hit for by J. C. Martin, whose bunt led to the play that sealed a 2–1 10-inning victory for New York. *Brace Photos*

Afterwards, Seaver and Swoboda were whisked into Hodges's office by PR man Harold Weissman, to be taken to a press conference. They were both itchy to celebrate with their teammates, who could be heard going "hog wild" next door.

It was strangely uncomfortable, the two players drinking beer. They were not friends. They were different kinds of people, opposites brought together by fate and common purpose.

Later, Swoboda found much fault with Seaver, in their off-season activities, the way he "marketed" Nancy. He eventually admitted, more or less, that it was jealousy; he would have "been smarter" had he hung out with Seaver, giving the ace his proper due and respect. But he was a young bull in those days, headstrong, saying things, teeing off on Hodges. He even expressed some remorse that some of his best plays in 1969 directly benefited Seaver more than Koosman or pitchers he liked more as people.

"Helluva catch," Seaver said to him.

"I was going after it all the way," he said. "I wasn't going to quit on it."

"If you have the right mental attitude, things go right," said Seaver.

"If you have the right mental attitude, you make a catch like that," replied Swoboda.

Eventually, they were taken by golf cart to what Seaver described as a "presidential press conference, dozens and dozens of reporters . . . television lights glaring, cameras clicking, microphones jammed against each other."

Oddly, Seaver recalled the celebrations, which had been piling up by then, as rote, "going through the motions . . . we had become public property," dealing with Howard Cosell, Dick Young, the national press, ABC, NBC. Gaspar was now a bigger celebrity than Jim Morrison. Each Met was a national figure, a hero.

Finally, the writers and camera crews left, leaving only Seaver and his teammates; exhausted warriors. Seaver told Al Weis he would be "batting cleanup tomorrow, Babe."

Seaver told Koosman to wrap it up the next day. He had no desire to see Baltimore ever again.

"That was the real Seaver today," Rube Walker said to him.

14

THE PROMISED LAND

And He said, Behold, I make a covenant: before all thy people I will do marvels, such as have not been done in all the Earth, nor in any nation: and all the people among which thou art shall see the work of the Lord.

—Exodus 34:10

For millions of New Yorkers, and millions more throughout the Fruited Plain, the morning of October 16, 1969, dawned with the kind of anticipation one usually reserves for the birth of a child, a wedding day, a long-anticipated reunion. There was religious fervor to the day, spirituality, a sense of destiny. *Everybody* was following this story.

Tom Seaver woke up that morning fatigued, aching, and exhilarated. His work was done. He could be a fan, a cheerleader. What a day! He knew that he was now a true New York Sports Icon. He had put himself in a position to walk the streets of New York, his privacy forever gone. The reality of this discomfiting notion had not yet hit home.

Gil Hodges (left) seems to know something nobody else does. *John Rogers Archives*

In truth he would not have welcomed this idolatry, but the dye was cast. He was, as he put it in *The Perfect Game,* "public property."

Game 5 featured Koosman against McNally, the dueling pitching artistes of game 2: one a flame-throwing southpaw, the other a crafty one. Both were big league stars of the first order.

Baltimore was stunned by fate but came out like professionals trying to see the bright side. For a team that won 109 games and swept the championship series, winning three straight was routine. First McNally over Koosman, then it was Gentry, and he could be beat.

That day, 57,397 fans jammed Shea, hawking with cries, shouts, and Pentecostal enthusiasm. Pearl Bailey, a big Mets fan and good friend of Mrs. Payson, sang the national anthem. While waiting to be introduced, she stood next to Koosman warming up. She told him she was into astrology and saw "the number eight," and "you're going to win the game." The contest started, and the two pitchers settled into their work, which was to render bats quite useless. Then in the third, Baltimore made their move . . . finally. Belanger opened the inning with an opposite-field single, bringing up McNally.

Dave McNally was a star of the 1960s and '70s, but was twice bested by Koosman in the Series.

Brace Photos

"With McNally up, we were expecting a bunt," Koosman said. In accord with that expectation, Koosman fired a high strike. McNally did not bunt. He was not a great hitter, not like some pitchers—Don Drysdale, Warren Spahn, to name a couple—but he handled the bat and swung away, hitting a two-run home run over the left field fence. It was a surprise that shocked the fans, but at the same time there was something unsaid: McNally was doing the hitting for Baltimore, not their sluggers. B. Robby, F. Robby, Powell: all were in slumps.

That premise only lasted a couple of batters. Koosman got the next two outs, then faced Frank Robinson, the ultimate competitor. He boasted of only 2 singles in 16 at bats. Robinson, one of the greatest home run sluggers of all time, got hold of one and drove it *deep* over the center field wall to make it 3–0, Orioles.

The massive crowd began to rationalize: no home field celebration, on to Baltimore. In the dugout, Gary Gentry began to feel the nerves that would come with pitching at Memorial Stadium against the surging home champions. What were the chances that Agee would save his skin this time?

The fan Tom Seaver began to morph into the professional hero who would have to win game 7 like Koufax and Gibson in recent years.

"Seaver could win with bad stuff," said Ed Charles. "He was such a competitor with a gift for self-analysis. He always knew just what it would take to win on a given day. Koosman was so strong that he could struggle for the first part of a game, then suddenly just start blowing you away."

Perhaps there was some chicanery involved in Gil Hodges's admonition that Cleon Jones had been hit by a pitch, which the umpire agreed upon inspection of the "shoe polish ball," followed by a homer by Clendenon (left). *John Rogers Archives*

Which is what happened. After the third, Jerry was untouchable. But could the Mets score three off of McNally? They had barely sniffed him in Baltimore. In the top of the sixth, Frank Robinson, an all-time hit-by-pitch artist, backed off an inside fastball, then said it grazed his uniform. Umpire Lou DiMuro said no. Robinson and Weaver argued vociferously, which, of course, woke up the throng.

Robinson "disappeared into the runway behind the dugout for five minutes while the trainer sprayed his thigh with a freezing medication and while everybody in the stadium waited," wrote Joe Durso. "Then he returned, was greeted by a sea of waving handkerchiefs and struck out."

Baltimore's protests were "long and ineffectual," wrote Roger Angell. DiMuro's examination of the shoe polish baseball was done with "the air of Maigret," whereupon it was pronounced "the true Shinola."

The argument was lost, Robby was set down, and Koosman was now at the top of his game, pitching better than Seaver the previous day. In the bottom half of the inning, Cleon Jones stepped in. McNally came in low and inside. The ball skipped past his foot, but Jones said he had been struck. Jones was not adamant. He wanted to hit. DiMuro again did not call it. But on-deck hitter Donn Clendenon told Hodges he had seen the ball hit Jones' shoe. Hodges casually meandered out to the batter's circle, quietly spoke with Jones, then informed DiMuro that his man had been hit. DiMuro demurred, that is, until Hodges retrieved the ball and showed it to him.

"Then, with the precarious resolve of a judge letting a guilty defendant go free on a technicality, he straightened up, took a deep breath, and thrust out his right arm, index finger pointing to first base," wrote Joe Reichler in *Baseball's Great Moments.* "The 57,397 spectators roared their approval.

"Surprisingly, plaintiff Weaver did not hotly contest the circumstantial evidence. . . . Having been found in contempt and ordered from the premises the previous day, Weaver was not anxious for another ejection."

Many in the press box recalled a similar incident involving Milwaukee's Nippy Jones against New York's Ryne Duren in the 1957 World Series. DiMuro explained that when Hodges showed him the baseball, it had a *shoe polish* smudge on it. To this day, the story has holes. Shoe polish? Yes, in those days clubhouse attendants did clean and shine the player's spikes before every game. They used an old-fashioned polish, buffing it with a cloth or brush for some sheen. In later years, the shoe polish was replaced by a liquid application. Modern baseball shoes have a different kind of leather, less subject to scuffs and dirt. Generally, these shoes are wiped clean using a wet cloth, retaining a shine.

While Jones would have been wearing polished shoes, by the sixth inning the cool air, dust, grass, and activity would seemingly have made it unlikely that polish could still be fresh enough to rub off on a glancing baseball. Many have said Hodges put

Donn Clendenon's homer sent Shea Stadium into spasmodic ecstacy. *John Rogers Archives*

polish on his fingers, smudging that ball when he picked it up, which in the strange pantheon of baseball would have been an acceptable form of gamesmanship that Leo Durocher could applaud.

Swoboda told Peter Golenbock that "it made sense for you to keep a ball with shoe polish smudges on it in the dugout somewhere, and as soon as a pitch is close, toss that sucker out there and say, 'Here's shoe polish on the ball.'"

"After the ball bounced, it came into our dugout," said Koosman. "The ball came to me, and Gil told me to brush it against my shoe, and I did, and he came over and got the ball from me and took it out there and showed the umpire, 'There is shoe polish on the ball.'"

The argument left McNally stewing on the mound. Weaver, to quote Rube Walker, had about as much chance under these circumstances "as a one-legged man in a butt-kicking contest." Not this year. Not in this place.

With Jones at first, Clendenon came to bat. With the count two and two, he got hold of one, knocking a two-run homer over the left field fence. It was 3–2, but it was over. It had been over for two days. Yogi Berra said, "It's never over 'til it's over." It was over. The script had been written. The crowd was now out of control, sensing it, the drama and hysterical craziness of it all building to the boiling point.

McNally retired the side. Then Koosman gave his best imitation of Lefty Grove. He was not going to be touched again today. In the bottom of the seventh, "Babe" Weis stepped in. Improbably, many actually thought about a home run. He had done it in Chicago. It was that kind of year, that sort of environment. McNally just figured his best swing would result in a "can o' corn." Weis took him deep. As the ball left Shea, the concept that this was indeed an inspired act of God presented itself to the eyes of spectators, at the park and watching on TV, changing from a possibility to manifest truth. It was insane!

Koosman took the mound. This time he resembled Warren Spahn. One-two-three. The Birds was dead, 3–3, bottom of the eighth. Eddie Watt came in. If New York scored, they only needed to hold the O's one inning, and it was theirs. Delirium built, people edging to their feet, anticipating a riotous on-field celebration. Cleon Jones met Watt with a hard drive over Blair's head for a double. Weaver and his team looked like Napoleon when he sees the Prussians come to Wellington's aid in the late afternoon glare at Waterloo. Baltimore was the loser of history, at least this history.

Clendenon tried to bunt, but it was too hard. He was thrown out, and Jones held. Swoboda took the stage again. He slammed a hard-sinking liner to left, not unlike the ball Brooks Robinson hit to him the previous day. Buford got there but trapped it. Jones alertly waited halfway between second and third, then raced home with the go-ahead run when the catch was not made. The place was a madhouse. Charles flied out, but Grote hit a grounder to first. Powell bobbled it and threw late to Watt covering the base. Swoboda was hustling. He scored the insurance run that Koosman, now imitating Sandy Koufax, did not need anyway. Still, it electrified the audience. This was it. A done deal. The picture of Koosman hugging Swoboda as he scored appeared in *Life* magazine.

Koosman took the hill. The crowd was screaming, incomprehensibly noisy, edging toward the aisles. New York's finest nervously eyed the crowd, who were about to explode.

"It was so noisy at Shea you couldn't hear yourself think," said Koosman. "And the cops and the

After the Mets captured the World Series, the field at Shea Stadium more resembled the running of the bulls at Pamplona than a baseball game. *National Baseball Hall of Fame Library*

specials were already coming down the first row so people couldn't mob the field. It was so noisy you couldn't even hear the bat on the ball."

Koosman nervously worked Frank Robinson too carefully, walking him, but quickly got Powell to ground into a force. Brooks Robinson flied to Swoboda. Davey Johnson came to bat. Koosman was in the maelstrom, something out of a poem about keeping one's head when everyone else is losing theirs. Calmly, he delivered to Johnson and induced a high, lazy arc to Cleon Jones in left field.

"With all the noise, you couldn't hear the crack of the bat," said Koosman. "I didn't think it was going out, but the fans were going *nuts* when the ball was in the air, and I thought it was going to be a home run, but when I turned around and looked at Cleon, I knew right away. . . ."

Johnson later said he got all of it. Swoboda in right felt at first that it could carry. "What stopped it from going out?" he asked, implying unseen forces. It was 3:17 p.m. Jones camped under it, made the catch, and like the Southern Baptist he was, sunk to one knee in prayer.

Jones then sprinted to the infield for his life while the world exploded. The Mets quickly celebrated on the mound. Koosman jumped into Grote's arms like a little kid, and then "here come the fans," he said. "They came right through the cops, and my mind immediately went from celebration to running for your life!"

Fans were coming over the top of the dugout, falling on top of each other. Koosman tore one guy's leg with his spikes, stepping on and over him. The players quickly made for the dugout like youths running from bulls at Pamplona. Each member of the grounds crew was tasked with "saving" a base, but they quickly gave up. Jones never made it in. He jumped a fence. Fans were grabbing everything: hats, gloves, bats. It was sheer bedlam.

"They did it with a full dose of the magic that had spiced their unthinkable climb from ninth place in the National League—100-to-1 shots who scraped their way to the pinnacle as the waifs of the major leagues," wrote Joe Durso in the *New York Times.*

"Children, housewives, mature men, all swarmed onto the field where the Mets beat the avalanche by a split second."

TV star Ray Romano was on the field after the division clincher. "I got hooked on Mets magic," he said.

"I ran on the field three times," director Spike Lee said.

Later, Swoboda came out to see what was going on; fans were digging up the bases, the mound, home plate, the turf. "It was the most appropriate loss of institutional control I can ever recall," he said. "The fans had a right to do that. Besides, they had to re-sod the field for football anyway. What difference did it make? Let them go out and have some fun."

After several hours in the clubhouse, Seaver and Gentry ventured out on the now-empty field. Gentry's uniform was still intact, but Seaver looked disheveled. Little clods of turf lay all about, resembling Old Testament frogs having fallen on ancient Egypt.

"I remember being tongue-tied and on the verge of tears," recalled Koosman. "There was so much emotion I didn't even think about the magnitude of our achievement, about the great upset and coming from nowhere. We were just so happy that we had reached that point."

"It's beautiful, beautiful, beautiful, what else can I say?" yelled Seaver. "It's my biggest thrill. The club played to win all year long. We never quit. We'd come from behind to win. We did it today." He added that pitching with this team, with these teammates, was "a pleasure."

"I never heard anyone on the Baltimore team say we were lucky," said Buddy Harrelson. "They took it like men and just said the bastards beat us." History would judge that they were ultimately champions, too, but this was not the day.

In five games, Baltimore collected 23 hits and batted .146. They scored nine runs. New York hit only .220 but scored 15, mostly in the clutch. Form played out, unlike the championship series: New York had a 1.80 ERA for the Series. Baltimore's staff was still an excellent 2.72.

"It was just one of the magical moments that can never be duplicated," wrote Bill Gutman.

"So, at last, we came to the final game, and I don't suppose many of us who had watched the Mets through this long and memorable season much doubted that they would win it, even when they fell behind, 0–3, on home runs by Dave McNally and Frank Robinson off Koosman in the third inning," wrote the redoubtable Roger Angell, perhaps the best of all Mets chroniclers. The Orioles, he added, suffered from "badly frayed nerves." One fan produced a sign that read, WHAT NEXT? Angell said he had no answer, describing Shea as "crazily leaping crowds, the showers of noise and paper, the vermilion smoke-bomb clouds, and the vanishing lawn signs. . . ." They won it with "the Irregulars" (Weis's first-ever homer at Shea, as if he had a plethora of long balls in other parks; Clendenon and Swoboda). They combined to hit .400 with four homers and eight RBIs. Powell and the Robinsons were held to a .163 average, one homer, and a single RBI.

Defensive plays that "some of us would remember for the rest of our lives" gave the "evident conviction that the year should not be permitted to end in boredom" (from Angell's chapter on the 1969 Mets, "Days and Nights with the Unbored" in *The Summer Game*).

He was prescient, too, acknowledging the "awareness of the accompanying sadness of the victory—the knowledge that adulation and money and winter disbanding of this true club would mean that the young Mets were now gone forever."

"This is the first time," said Swoboda (amid Moët et Chandon). "Nothing can ever be as sweet again."

Pearl Bailey came in the clubhouse and planted a big kiss on Koosman, which his teammates thought was more than just a little bit friendly on her part. She had predicted the "number eight." The score: 5–3. Supposedly, Jones gave the final out ball to Koosman, but that has been an ongoing question over the years.

"If the Mets can win the World Series, we can get out of Vietnam," Seaver said in the clubhouse. "I just decided to say it," he later told Shamsky. "History proved that they couldn't figure a way politically to get out."

In the corridor outside the clubhouse, Seaver met with Nancy, his father, and the rest of his family. "We'll never forget this day," said Charles Seaver. "None of us will."

"Who's stupid now?" Gaspar said to anybody who would listen. Somebody asked Yogi Berra if it was "over now." Berra said he did not actually know how many World Series rings he now had. "Too many for my fingers," he said. The postgame celebration was "the best in the history of baseball, and probably will never be duplicated," recalled Ralph Kiner.

"No team ever drank, spilled and wasted as much champagne as the Mets who, within a space of little more than three weeks, had three clinchings to celebrate as they won first the Eastern Division championship, then the National League championship, and finally the big one," wrote Jack Lang, who maintained that "through it all, the calmest man in all the world was Gil Hodges. . . ."

"I was able to bring a championship back to the greatest fans in the world," said Hodges.

The MVP of the Series could have been Seaver, Koosman, Weis, Jones, or Swoboda. Clendenon won it, having hit three long balls. What a team effort!

The city continued to go wild. Ken Boswell invited all Mets fans to the team party at Mr. Laffs, a well-known sports bar on First Avenue in Manhattan where ex-player Phil Linz tended bar. A couple thousand showed up.

On Broadway, at the Copa, Toots Shor's, P. J. Clarke's, 21, Jilly's, the Forum of the Twelve Caesars, McSorley's Old Ale House, Eamonn's, the

Central Bar, the Latin Quarter; everywhere in Manhattan, Queens, and the Bronx; in Westchester County, Long Island, way out in the Hamptons; in Albany, upstate, in western New York, in Rochester and Buffalo; in Connecticut and Jersey, from the shore and all over the Garden State, it was a celebration. From Wall Street to Main Street, America was "Mets country." "In country," which was what the GIs called Vietnam, word spread, and unless you were from Baltimore, the Mets were the toasts of Saigon, Hue, and N'Trang. From Paris to London to Berlin, expatriate New Yorkers celebrated, and Europe now knew about the Mets.

First Avenue was blocked off. Only one lane could get north to 64th and First. People were dancing in the streets. Car horns blasted all over the city. Confetti was everywhere. All bars and restaurants celebrated. Mobsters partied with prosecutors. Gays toasted hard hats. Blacks and whites, Jews and Gentiles, Puerto Ricans and Orientals, young and old, Democrats and Republicans, conservatives and liberals, Christians, atheists, Israelis, and Arabs all cheered each other—again. Even Yankees fans, people who thought baseball was boring, men and women—especially men and women—celebrated long into the night. "Luck," as Sinatra sang, "be a lady tonight."

"Never before—not for the one-time perennial World Champion Yankees, not for the Moon men, not for Charles A. Lindbergh, not for anyone," Bill Gutman quoted one writer in *Miracle Year, 1969*. "Never before had New Yorkers exploded in quite the way they did yesterday in a spontaneous, unrestrained outpouring of sheer joy when the Mets, their Mets, copped the World Series."

The city threw a ticker tape parade, and in keeping with that theme, it surpassed previous such spectacles for Charles Lindbergh, Douglas MacArthur, John Glenn, Namath's Jets, Neil Armstrong; astronauts, athletes, war heroes. In 1969 there were three ticker tape parades: the Jets in January, Armstrong and the *Apollo 11* astronauts after the July moon landing, and the Mets. The third totally eclipsed the other two. It was the biggest parade in New York City history. The motorcade went from Battery Park to Bryant Park behind the main library at 42nd Street. Banners and confetti were everywhere.

The Mets rode in open cars, fans held back by barricades. Girls threw themselves at the players as if they were Joe Namath or Robert Redford. The cops, somehow sensing that it was joy, not a riot, restrained themselves. They instinctively realized this was the last of 1960s innocence. Later New York celebrations were like jail breaks, or the overthrow of dictators. There was very little vandalism in October 1969. The people of this great metropolis were all like little children. They were in awe, like the saved entering the kingdom of heaven.

At City Hall, Mayor Lindsay presented them with keys to New York. Mrs. Payson and M. Donald Grant accepted on behalf of the players at Gracie Mansion. Lindsay announced that a street in Brooklyn was named after Hodges. It was declared "Mets Day." More than a million people lined the streets. Koosman and his wife were in the same car with Tom and Nancy. Gil and Joan Hodges were in the front car.

"The thought absolutely floors me—the World Champion Mets," Nancy told reporters. "Six months ago the thought would have made me wonder if I should consult a psychiatrist."

Sometime the most poignant moments come from the losers. When the New York Giants captured the 1951 pennant, every writer and photographer made a beeline for their clubhouse. One solitary cameraman won a Pulitzer Prize capturing Ralph Branca's despondency. In the visitors' clubhouse after the fifth game at Shea, Earl Weaver, released from the pressure and possibly pinching himself a little—after all his minor league years he had managed a team in the *World Series*—kicked his feet up and started in on the beer. He was asked about holding a late lead.

"No, that's what you can never do in baseball," said Earl. "You can't sit on a lead and run a few plays into the line and just run out the clock. You've got to throw the ball over the damn plate and give the other man his chance. That's why baseball is the greatest game of them all."

Weaver also shed doubt on the shoe polish incident, saying that the ball had somehow made its way into the Mets dugout, and that Hodges may have already had a "plant" in there, waiting for just such an event. "How did that happen?" asked Weaver. "It was just another thing that went against us."

15

FALL FROM GRACE

There are two sentences inscribed upon the Delphic oracle, hugely accommodated to the usages of man's life; "Know Thyself," and "Nothing too much": and upon these all other precepts depend.

—Plutarch

A man's got to know his limitations.

—Clint Eastwood as "Dirty Harry" Callahan, Magnum Force

All glory is fleeting.

—George C. Scott, from the Latin phrase "Sic transit Gloria mundi," Patton

The Mets' World Series share was $18,000 per man. After winning the Series on Thursday, the whole team appeared on the *Ed Sullivan Show* on Sunday. Ron Swoboda lived off his appearance fees. Donn Clendenon received a Dodge Challenger for being MVP. Little Al Weis was given a Volkswagen called "Mighty Mite." Boswell, Garrett, and Gaspar appeared on *The Dating Game.* The girl picked Gaspar, and they went to Europe, but "nothing happened." Seaver was offered $70,000 by a Florida producer to act in a stock road show touring Florida for seven weeks. He declined. Gil Hodges received a raise to $70,000 for the 1970 season. General manager Johnny Murphy tragically suffered a heart attack and died in January 1970.

"More trouble has started per square inch in Las Vegas, the gambling capital, than in any city since

Sodom," wrote John Devaney in *Tom Seaver: Portrait of a Pitcher.* "Trouble began for the 1970 Mets on a Las Vegas stage in the fall of 1969."

Shamsky, Seaver, Koosman, Clendenon, Jones, Agee, and Kranepool went to Vegas. They did two shows per evening, dinner and midnight, with comedian Phil Foster. They sang "The Impossible Dream," from *Man of La Mancha.* Each made $10,000 for the two weeks.

"We were stars wherever we went," said Koosman.

Things began to fray in Vegas. They had been asked not to include their wives, to make it just about the players. Nancy came along anyway, annoying some of the guys who probably wanted to let their hair down and "let boys be boys." The faithful wife and the faithful husband were, to them, prying eyes looking over their shoulders. They had to answer to their own spouses who asked, "If Nancy Seaver was there, how come I wasn't invited?" Nancy was always around the TV cameras, "honing in on their glory," according to John Devaney. Criticism of her was not relegated to this group. Baltimore's Pete Richert said that her carrying that banner in Baltimore had been "bush," and that his wife stopped that stuff as a high school cheerleader.

"It went to our heads," said Swoboda. "Some stars thought they were superstars, some fringe guys thought they were stars, nobody worked hard, nobody really cared.

"Those guys [who performed at the Las Vegas club] made some extra dough, but they created jealousies. We won because we had been a one-for-all-and-all-for-one team. Now we were cashing in separately. That created problems. It even created problems among that group. Seaver wanted more money than the others got, and don't forget they had to play together again a few months later."

☆ ☆ ☆

Most of the big money offers came to Seaver, who was identified as the symbol of the team. The "one for all, all-for-one" concept of the season was lost in the glare of Seaver's larger-than-life persona. At 24, he was the youngest winner of the Cy Young award and the youngest to win 25 games since Dizzy Dean 34 years earlier.

Seaver won the S. Rae Hickock Belt as the Professional Athlete of the Year. *The Sporting News* named him Man of the Year. *Sports Illustrated* chose him as the Sportsman of the Year. The two publications featured flowery, overly flattering portrayals of the Mets superstar. Glowing terminology describing Seaver, his pitching prowess, and his wife filled these pages and more. The buildup of his personality, intelligence, charm: it was over the top. He was a fictional character come to life, too good to be true.

Baseball Stars of 1970 had Seaver on its cover and as its feature story. Editor Ray Robinson repeated the Seaver quote that he was "not an All-American," that he could not be one because he drank beer and swore, but with a wink the pitcher added, "But I do keep my hair short, so I guess you could say I am an All-American boy."

"Tom is the greatest guy in the world," said Buddy Harrelson.

"Tom is as nice as everyone says he is . . . he's not just the product of an advertising campaign," said Dick Schaap.

Seaver, Robinson wrote, "contributed to the restoration of baseball glory in the battered, but unbowed, city of New York." He was a "Huck Finn of a pitcher."

"There are two things of primary importance to me, and they're both in this room—my marriage and baseball," Tom Seaver told the audience at the

Sports Illustrated luncheon honoring him as Sportsman of the Year. The audience included Joan Payson and Bowie Kuhn. "I would not do anything to jeopardize either of them." Glancing toward Nancy, he said, "I wouldn't have had the success I've had without Nancy's help. I wish you'd thank her for me."

Hearing the applause, Nancy cried.

"Gee, I told you not to cry," said Seaver.

Seaver took out an ad in the *New York Times:* "Now available: Tom Seaver, America's top athlete and sports personality, plus Nancy Seaver, Tom's lovely wife, for those situations that call for Young Mrs. America or husband and wife sales appeal."

Some of his friends and teammates said it was in bad taste. His mother was "horrified." Tom spun it: "I won't take any offer that would interfere with my career."

Tom did not enroll in USC that fall. Instead, the Seavers bought a 90-year-old farmhouse in Greenwich, Connecticut, a suburban "bedroom community" of Manhattan business executives and socialites, located some 45 minutes from New York City. The choice of Greenwich was telling. It was and still is one of the wealthiest communities in the world, but not wealthy in the nouveau riche, Malibu sense of the term. It is the ultimate "old money, blue blood" town of Bushes, Kennedys, and Walkers (as in Herbert Walker, one of the Mets' original owners and a nephew of President George H.W. Bush). By making themselves residents of Greenwich, the Seavers made a statement, about their pursuit of wealth and status, their desire for privacy, and their politics.

Manufacturers offered free furnishings for the home if Tom would make a sales pitch. He built a winery, cultivating a lifelong love of the vintner's art. He was constantly on TV that winter and began to think about a broadcasting career. Seaver appeared on the Kraft Music Hall, enduring a pie in his face. He appeared on many talk shows, including Alan Burke's. A pilot of his own show was discussed. He chatted with boxer Rocky Graziano.

"Would you believe this—here I am, an ex-middleweight champion of the world and a great actor, but it's dis kid and his wife who own their own TV show," said Graziano.

"That's because I'm better looking than you, and I've got a lovely wife," Seaver joked.

"Oh, Tom," Nancy cooed.

"Visually, you appear to be the storybook version of Mr. and Mrs. America," said Burke. "Nancy, do you feel jealous about Tom's adoring female fans?"

"No, I want everybody to love him as much as I do," she replied.

"What is the most inspiring thing that's ever happened in your life?" Burke asked Tom.

"My wife," was the answer.

"Is that the key to your success?" he was asked.

"She gives me a reason for striving," said Seaver. "Without her, I wouldn't have been as successful in baseball."

Away from the cameras, the Seavers were "very tight," according to one writer. "They just want to be alone and walk on the beach."

Sara Davidson of *McCall's* did a feature on them at their new home. In that article, which was based on several interviews with both Seavers in various locations, Tom's reputation for not bedding women on the road was first made public, at least in a wide-scale manner. This caused more than a little problem for other players. First their wives asked why Nancy Seaver could be in Las Vegas when they could not. If Tom Seaver enjoyed his wife's company in Sin City, why did their husbands prefer . . . somebody else's? Tom Seaver's faithfulness toward Nancy could not help but imply that it was an exception to the rule—but an exception to what?

On December 31, 1969, Tom and Nancy Seaver placed an ad in the *New York Times:* "On the eve of 1970, please join us in a prayer for peace."

At some point, players started to complain that Seaver had become a "different guy . . . aloof," more concerned with outside things and TV appearances. The endorsements and attention lavished on all the Mets in the immediate aftermath of the glorious victory started to fade for most, but not for Seaver.

"He was somewhat more verbally polished than Jerry Koosman, his pitching partner, and considerably whiter than Donn Clendenon, the batting hero of the Series," wrote Robert Lipsyte in the *New York Times.*

Seaver signed a new contract for $80,000 and made it clear that his goal would be to someday be the first "$200,000 ballplayer," which was seen as money hungry.

"No one roots for Goliath," Wilt Chamberlain said, and as the Orioles could attest. Seaver was no longer the peppy leader of a hungry band of underdogs. He was a superstar with all the trappings. "The cheering fades and the envy grows the nearer one is to the top," wrote Devaney.

Seaver told writer Milton Grossman that he was trying to keep his "feet on the ground," admitting he was more "introverted." Everyday situations, restaurants, places where it was "fun to be recognized" were now problems. He had become a true New York Sports Icon. The things that made Joe DiMaggio a pain, Mickey Mantle prickly, now affected Seaver. This was the Apple, not Pittsburgh. He began to question whether people saw "a human being and not just a baseball player," adding that while he owed the fans full effort, off the field it was a two-way street.

In the spring of 1970, Ron Swoboda had a blowup with Tom Seaver. The players took up a collection for a clubhouse guy. Swoboda was not there, so somebody told Seaver to "get the money out of Ron's pants pockets." Swoboda had planned to give money to the man at Miller Huggins Field anyway. Seaver announced he had taken it out of Swoboda's pants, which were hanging in his cubicle. He implied that otherwise Ron would not have contributed. When Swoboda found out, the two had a screaming match in front of the writers.

"Then he was an apple guy," Maury Allen said, referring to Seaver. "Very bright, articulate, honest, if a little dull with his detailed description of pitching mechanics. From 1970 on Seaver really has been a different guy. He is bright, articulate, easy to talk to but still aloof. . . ."

"Following the winter of his great content, writers covering the Mets—and they are the closest that anyone could be outside of his own teammates—detected a certain aloofness in Seaver very early in spring training," wrote Jack Lang in *The Sporting News.* "Tom frequently did not have time to sit through long periods of questioning like he formerly did and there were many times he was in a hurry to get out of the club house."

Seaver set 30 victories as his goal for 1970. Denny McLain had done it pitching on a four-day rotation in 1968. It was not an outlandish prospect. As good as Seaver was in 1969, he had not yet reached his full potential. It was a frightening, awe-inspiring notion that the best was still yet to come. Seaver probably did not reach his full, mature physical peak until 1970–1971.

He struck out 19 against San Diego on April 22 at Shea Stadium. That tied the big league record set by Steve Carlton in a 4–3 loss to the Mets in 1969. Seaver won his game, 2–1.

He began the year 6–0, running his regular season winning streak to 16 straight games. Seaver finally lost to Montreal, 3–0, on May 11. Later he lost again to Expos pitcher Carl Morton, 2–0, on May 20.

"We beat Seaver last week, and maybe he was trying too hard to make up for it," Morton said.

"Is that what he said?" Seaver spouted when told in the heat of a postgame defeat. "It just shows how stupid he is."

"Losing appears to be getting to Seaver," Lang wrote in a biting *Sporting News* piece, shocking readers whose expectations of Seaver as a pitcher and man were sky high. Only perfection was expected of him, on and off the field. "He is not reacting to adversity as well as he did to success. He appeared in his first three seasons to be impervious to faults, but in his fourth season he is showing another side of Tom, a not-so-pleasant side."

Hodges selected him to start the All-Star Game at Cincinnati's new Riverfront Stadium. The ace right-hander put on a power pitching display, dominating the best sluggers in the junior circuit with a scoreless three-inning, four-strikeout performance.

But beginning with a devastating August loss to Atlanta, Seaver won only once in his last 11 starts. His 17–6 record of August finished at 18–12 in October. He still led the league with a 2.83 ERA, and his 283 strikeouts set the new league mark for right-handers. But the final symbolic indignity of the 1970 campaign came on the season's last day. Out of the race, New York played the Cubs for second place. A few thousand dollars were at stake in an age when a few thousand dollars meant something to big league ballplayers. Seaver opted not to pitch, citing arm strain. The Mets lost to Ferguson Jenkins, 4–1. His teammates bitterly complained that had he pitched, they might have won and gotten the extra money. Seaver was seen as selfish. With his huge contract, he already had his. Larry Merchant of the *Post* wrote that Seaver seemed more concerned with the "image of perfection that he has worked so hard to achieve in his professional and personal life" than he was about the team. Many players were "disenchanted" with him.

"He has always tried hard, perhaps harder than most," wrote Milton Grossman of the *Post.* "But things came so easily to him, within himself there may really have been the image of the perfect young man who finds it impossible to accept that he can be flawed with imperfection."

Perhaps the greatest evidence that the 1969 New York Mets were indeed the last miracle came in examining the 1970 Mets. They were a pretty good baseball team, but that was all they were. They were the natural progression of Gil Hodges's club, which was making strides in 1968, expected to be a .500 club in 1969, and had enough youth for a bright future.

The Eastern Division was up for grabs. Nobody ran away with it. The Mets were still in the hunt in September, but in two home-and-home series with Pittsburgh, they lost six of seven games, stranding 59 runners in the combined defeats. Seaver failed in key games, which was their ultimate death knell. Pitching on the Saturday *Game of the Week,* the kind of spotlight that in the past had always brought out his best, he lost.

Pittsburgh ultimately won the East with a pedestrian 89–73 record. Losing on the last day to Chicago allowed the Cubs to finish one game better, in second place with an 84–78 mark. The Pirates were swept by Cincinnati's "Big Red Machine" in the play-offs. The Reds were then beaten in five games by Baltimore in the World Series.

The 1970 season was a cautionary tale about success and ego, but it also evened out the law of averages. If in 1969 the Mets were just lucky, over and over and over, then it stood to reason that in 1970 they could not continue to roll aces. If the 1969 team was a team of destiny, then the 1970 squad was God's way of demonstrating that the Good Lord giveth, and He taketh away.

16

THOSE AMAZIN' METS

Ya gotta believe!

—Tug McGraw

Gil Hodges became a tragic figure, because he died young and before his legacy could be cemented. After a heart attack in 1968, Hodges seemed to recover, but he was a chain smoker. In 1972 the 48-year-old Hodges was fatally felled by a coronary during the baseball strike that spring training. It was a dark, disturbing day in Mets history. The players, the fans, the entire Mets family, were shocked. Hodges was a father figure to Tom Seaver and many of his young teammates.

Jerry Koosman may have been a Hall of Famer like Tom Seaver had arm injuries not hindered his career. On his best days, he was Seaver's equal. The difference was consistency. He finished with disappointing 12–7, 6–11, and 11–12 marks between 1970 and 1972. In 1973 the Mets were a brutal offensive team, so bad that despite a 2.84 ERA, Koosman's record was only 14–15, but he pitched brilliantly in the seven-game World Series loss to Oakland.

Koosman was the last of the 1969 Mets. He eventually signed with his home state team, Minnesota, hoping to lick his wounds and finish out his career. Instead he was among the best pitchers in baseball for five seasons. Koosman was 20–13 and 16–13 in his two full seasons with the Twins (1979–1980), later helped the Chicago White Sox win the Western Division title in 1983, and had a solid year at Philadelphia in 1984. He hung it up after the 1985 campaign, having played 19 big league seasons with 222 wins (a substantially greater number than either Mike Cuellar or Dave McNally), with a strong 3.36 ERA.

In a blockbuster trade, Nolan Ryan was sent to the California Angels, who reciprocated with their

Tom Seaver's pitching mechanics were copied by most of his staff teammates over the years, including Nolan Ryan. *National Baseball Hall of Fame Library*

greatest player, shortstop Jim Fregosi. Ryan, a quiet, unassuming Texan, had not taken to the pressures of New York. After the incredible 1969 World Championship, much was expected of the team. Seaver was one of the few Mets who responded to the Big Apple's demands.

Ryan became the greatest strikeout pitcher of all time; a Texas icon and friend of Presidents. He and Seaver were the only players from the 1969 Mets to enter the Hall of Fame.

Gary Gentry was one of the biggest disappointments in Mets history. Ultimately, arm problems ended his promising career much too soon, but in truth he did not improve on his 1969 performance—which was occasionally brilliant—with 9–9 and 12–11 records over the next two years. Gentry was 7–10 in 1972, then traded to Atlanta, where he fell by the wayside as so many other overpitched Arizona State pitchers have done.

Tug McGraw overcame his problems. He came into his own in 1971 with an 11–4 record and microscopic 1.70 ERA. His screwball had become perfected. In 1972 McGraw repeated the act—a 1.70 ERA—but his most memorable year was 1973. Perhaps that was because McGraw had been deeply affected by the shootings at Kent State in 1970, and his own "role" in the Vietnam War, minor as it was as a Reservist. After the U.S. finally pulled its troops out of Vietnam in January 1973, it was as if McGraw's personality was again free to bloom. At first, like most of his teammates, he was inconsistent, going nowhere on a nowhere team, when suddenly the club picked it up the last two months and chased down the National League East pennant. Suddenly, McGraw became the face of the Mets, his energetic mound efforts riling up capacity crowds at Shea Stadium in a marvelous resurrection of the 1969 spirit.

He would prounce around, whipping his glove against his side, and coined a catchphrase that became the team's rallying cry. *Ya Gotta Believe!* was a symbol of Mets' fortitude, but has been used by every desperate team, soldier, and situation in the succeeding years. It had a spiritual, religious connotation to it, which would have extra meaning for McGraw later.

His 25 saves, mostly down the stretch, spurred Yogi Berra's Mets to the play-offs. McGraw closed out key games in the 3–2 win over Cincinnati in the NLCS, as well as in the seven-game Series loss to Oakland.

McGraw went to the Philadelphia Phillies, where he was a key component on excellent Phillies teams, often saving wins for the great Steve Carlton. In 1980 he had a 1.47 ERA and 20 saves, keying the Phillies to a World Series victory over the Kansas City Royals. His memorable last out and leap into the air, arms held aloft, is regularly replayed on the classic sports channels.

McGraw retired after the 1984 campaign with 19 years under his belt, a 96–92 record, 180 saves in an era in which the use of closers was not perfected, and a 3.13 ERA. His play-off ERA was 2.67 in 15 games. In the 1973 and 1980 World Series (he did not pitch against Baltimore in 1969), McGraw had a 2.11 ERA in nine appearances.

Just as Koosman is not in the Hall of Fame, neither is McGraw. He probably never will be, but they could do worse. The man who once joked that he "picked up my wife in a bar" was a rube in New York City. It certainly did not positively affect his career at first. He went wild and had a reputation for being "girl crazy." One night he met some chick, had what was probably little more than a one-night stand, and later found out she was pregnant. Tug distanced himself from all of it, although he did not completely abandon the girl or his son, who eventually grew up to be mega-superstar country-western singer Tim McGraw. Tim looked more and more like his old man as he matured. The relationship was strained for obvious reasons but normalized. It certainly did not hurt that his son made more money than Tug ever dreamed of, not to mention marrying bombshell singer Faith Hill. Tim had a forgiving heart. But aside from the physical appearance, the two seemed cut out of the same cloth. Tim liked to drink and party. He had his old man's wild side.

In the film *Friday Night Lights,* Tim played a character who in many ways seemed to be Tug, or at least what Tug might have been had they grown up with each other. He portrayed a former high school football legend, still good-lookin', apparently remarried to a young hottie, whose son is now a senior on the Odessa, Texas, Permian Panthers. The two clash constantly. Tim's character drinks and even walks in shirtless on his son with a half-naked girl, maybe looking to get some. In the end, there was reconciliation.

Tug's life was a country song in and of itself; honky-tonks, wild livin', life's lessons learned, reconciliation with a Christian sense of redemption, which somehow capped the whole tragicomic story when Tug died young of cancer. He was 59, living in Tim's Nashville-area home, when he passed away in 2004.

In the end, Tim and Tug became inextricably linked by physical appearance, surname, and oddly similar life paths, but in 1969, when Tug McGraw was one of those anointed heroes of New York, Tim was just a gleam in his eye.

Jerry Grote played for the Mets until 1977, when a trade to Los Angeles made him part of two more World Series in New York (both lost to the Yankees). He retired after the 1981 season, having played 16 years and 1,421 games and in four World Series.

Donn Clendenon is remembered because he was the MVP of the 1969 World Series, but he was an All-Star in Pittsburgh and may have had his best year with the 1970 Mets (22 homers, 97 RBIs, with a .288 average). He was one of the only players to improve. It was his "last hurrah." The actual "clubhouse lawyer" took his effervescent personality with him into retirement after the 1972 campaign.

One of the most incongruous facts in baseball history revolved around Ken Boswell in 1970. He was considered so bad defensively, teammates made a "tuning fork" sound or hand motion, suggesting that his glove was made of a hard substance, not soft leather. Perhaps he was unfairly maligned, but nobody was confusing him with Jackie Robinson at second base.

Then, in 1970, Boswell set the major league record for highest fielding average for a second baseman, at .996. He also established the National League record for most consecutive errorless games, 85, between April 30 and September 26, 1970. He took 391 chances without a miscue. Boswell was a member of the 1973 National League champions. The Texas native finished his career at Houston from 1975 to 1977, retiring after 11 seasons.

Bud Harrelson remained Seaver's best friend. He led the Mets in steals in 1971, also earning a Gold Glove award. In the 1973 play-offs, Pete Rose upended the diminutive Harrelson on a hard slide into second base at Shea Stadium. The crowd loved Buddy and booed Rose unmercifully. The moment was credited with spurring New York to eventual victory.

Harrelson retired after the 1980 season, having played in the end for the Phillies and Rangers. He finished with 127 career steals and managed the Mets from 1990 to 1991.

Ed Charles's last year was 1969. His name is well remembered, and he is considered a key member of the team despite having played only 61 games with a .207 average. Jerry Koosman constantly laughs when reminiscing over Charles's looping, will-it-ever-get-there-in-time throw to first base for the last out of game 2 in Baltimore.

Cleon Jones hit .319 in 1971 but tailed off after that. He left baseball following the 1976 season with a .281 career average. He never really came close to his great 1969 performance. Ron Swoboda later said Jones was a brilliant analyst of hitting who, if given the chance, could have been a great batting coach. He certainly seemed to know Tommie Agee like the back of his hand. Jones's most unfortunate moment came a few years after the 1969 season when the cops knocked on his van in a parking lot and found him in the arms of a naked woman. The headlines were not kind and left little to the imagination.

Tommie Agee had good years in 1970 and 1971, but after 12 seasons, he retired following the 1973 campaign, having spent time in Houston and St. Louis. In 12 years he batted .255 and stole 167 bases. He died in 2001.

Art Shamsky hit .293 in 1970 but .185 in 1971. He spent eight games with the 1972 World Champion

A's but made no mark, retiring at season's end with a .253 career average. He will forever be remembered, though, for his gaudy .538 mark in 13 at bats versus Atlanta in the 1969 NLCS, a source of pride.

In 1971 Ron Swoboda was traded to the Montreal Expos. At the time, he and Seaver were barely on speaking terms, and one of them had to go. The Mets certainly had no trouble deciding which one.

"Seaver and I have never been the best fans of each other," Swoboda told Milton Grossman after the trade. "We come from different backgrounds. There are three or four people on the Mets I'm not sorry to be leaving. And they might not be sorry to see me go. I'm disappointed by one thing. Four of the greatest plays I ever made, he was pitching and three of them kept him in the game. In that respect, it bothered me a little bit.

"There were a lot of incidents after the Series that really sickened me. You can't like everybody in the world, and not everybody's going to like you. You can't get affection if you don't give affection. Tom has no such feeling for people. He's rather self-centered."

"That is spoken by one of the greatest self-analysts of our time, I imagine," Seaver said when informed of the remarks.

Swoboda was a young bull, in terms of appearance and headstrong demeanor, but it turned out that he *was* a man of "self-analysis," after all. In his candid remarks to Peter Golenbock for *Amazin',* Swoboda freely admitted that the fault was at least half his, if not more. He said that he was young, that he basically blew his chance, not realizing the enormous advantages of playing in New York. In Montreal he was a nobody going nowhere. In New York he enjoyed fleeting glory, but his name is still revered for moments of supreme Mets greatness. Swoboda admired Seaver's intelligence and gave

Arguably, Seaver became better and more dominant after 1969 (although it never seemed as easy). Here he displays the ball he used to win his 20th game in 1971 with a 1.76 ERA and league-record 289 strikeouts, breaking his own 1970 mark of 283.
John Rogers Archives

him his due as an all-time pitching great; a tough mind and true pro, albeit a different personality type.

Everything Yogi Berra ever touched turned to gold: investments, commercials, quotations. His numerous funny quotes have been made into entire books. "It's never over until it's over" is probably his best remembered line, used by everybody from Hollywood hotties to coaches and writers countless times.

But younger fans are most likely familiar with his popular statement on insurance commercials: "They give you cash, which is just as good as money."

Pat Jordan grew up in Connecticut, not far from the Greenwich home where Tom Seaver moved after the 1969 season. In the 1950s, he was a flame-throwing pitcher whose services were vied for by most major league teams. He eventually signed a sizable bonus contract with the Milwaukee Braves.

Jordan pitched several years of minor league baseball, but for various reasons he failed to achieve any real success. He never made it to the big leagues. A few years later he wrote perhaps the greatest work describing minor league life, *A False Spring*. In the early 1970s, he wrote a series of essays, much of which appeared in *Sports Illustrated.* Each concentrated on a particular pitcher. They included Cleveland fireballer "Sudden" Sam McDowell, former Angels playboy Bo Belinsky, the seemingly unlimited talents of the ultimately disappointing Dean Chance, a high school wunderkind from Connecticut who never made it, and Greenwich's own Tom Seaver. Eventually, the essays became a book called *The Suitors of Spring*. It remains a classic, probably one of the 10 best baseball books of all time.

The chapter on Seaver remains one of the most telling exposés of what made the superstar tick. By the time Jordan got together with Seaver, the angst of the 1970 disappointment had been replaced by the dominating 1971 campaign.

In 1972 Seaver again won 20 games, and when Jordan's essay and book came out, Seaver's place in the pantheon of all-time greatness was completely secure. Any psychology attached to his "too much success so fast" performance of 1969 followed by the 1970 letdown was gone with the wind. Jordan found a man completely secure in every aspect of his life. Seaver knew *precisely* what made him perform at peak levels, consistently achieving the preparation and consequent result in machine-like fashion.

There was very little personality to his mound work. Seaver was a corporate pitching mechanism, like the formula for a blockbuster movie franchise that is guaranteed to succeed every time. Asking

Tom "the Franchise" Seaver eventually had a falling out with M. Donald Grant and was traded to Cincinnati in 1977, where he continued to dazzle the baseball world. The Mets have never really regained the magic of his years (1967–77).

John Rogers Archives

Seaver why he was good was like asking a master architect why his bridges stood tall and sturdy. It was a matter of building blocks, a scientific approach resisting fallibility.

Seaver's perfections—his wine cellar, his house, every detail in his personal life—were expounded on by Jordan, who found a man who, after some tinkering, was, seemingly at least, as close to perfect as mere mortals can get.

Jordan, the failed pitcher, a little bit scruffy and, to be frank, probably a tad insecure around such greatness, displayed just a touch of jealousy, but it was overshadowed by great writing, insight, and wit, as well as the ability to capture what made Tom Seaver who he was and is. Seaver never has been a colorful character, but as an example of a human being who endeavors to get the most out of that with which he engages in—particularly pitching—he discovered a personal gold mine and worked it for all it was worth.

Seaver has been described as a Wall Street type, buttoned-down, a businessman. His college teammate Bill "Spaceman" Lee once said, "I was a pickup truck and a sixpack. Seaver was a limo, fat cigars and champagne." That said, Seaver always had a good sense of humor and enjoyed playing practical jokes. When he was a member of the free-wheeling Cincinnati Reds of the late 1970s, he held his own in verbal repartee and comedic timing with such wits as Johnny Bench, Pete Rose, and Joe Morgan. The erudite Seaver was an opera buff, too. One of his favorite performers was the great Placido Domingo, who became his friend.

When he went to the Chicago White Sox in the 1980s, Seaver invited Domingo to a game at the old Comiskey Park when he was in town for opera performances. Domingo knew none of the baseball customs, so Seaver played a practical joke on him that almost backfired. He told him that it was a tradition for guests to be a "mascot for a day." He directed the great Domingo to don a huge white sock, the "uniform" of the club's mascot. Domingo thought it odd but figured "when in Rome . . ."

Seaver held his laughter long enough to direct Domingo onto the field, where he was the object of delight in the eyes of the White Sox players. At around that time the man hired as the real mascot arrived and discovered his white-sock "uniform" was missing. He went out to the field, saw the "imposter," and directed the stadium police to apprehend Domingo. Seaver was doubled over in laughter observing this charade, and was barely able to identify himself as the true culprit when explicating his friend from this sticky situation.

Seaver won 311 games against only 205 losses in a career that spanned 1967 to 1986. Those extra six losses, all of which came in his last year (1986), when he was 7–13 while hanging on with the Chicago White Sox and the American League champion Boston Red Sox, unfortunately prevented him from becoming the first-ever pitcher to win 300 and lose fewer than 200 games. In Boston, he was with Roger Clemens on a team, ironically, that lost to the Mets in a star-crossed World Series. As it was, his final career winning percentage was an incredible .603, and his ERA was an insane 2.86 for 4,783 innings.

Seaver established a major league record by striking out 200 or more batters in nine straight seasons (1968–1976). He finished with 3,640 career strikeouts. At one point he was second all-time behind Walter Johnson. Steve Carlton and Nolan Ryan passed him during his career. Later, Randy Johnson passed Seaver. Tom finished tied with Ryan for seventh in career shutouts (61).

In addition to his three National League Cy Young awards Seaver was named to 12 All-Star teams and played in 8, tying the record shared by Juan Marichal, Don Drysdale, and Jim Bunning for the most All-Star Game appearances. In 1992 he was elected to the Baseball Hall of Fame, receiving 425 out of a possible 430 votes. That 98.84 percentage in his first year of eligibility was and remains the highest percentage in Hall of Fame history, a truly remarkable and telling indication of how Seaver stands out not simply as an all-time great, but among the true Rushmore-level icons of baseball history.

Perhaps the life Tom Seaver eventually took to—after the glory and excesses of New York, and after a long career in the public eye as a television baseball sportscaster for the Mets, Yankeees, and national networks—perhaps it is best summed up in the words of Ernest Dowson in *Vitae Summa Brevis Spem Nos Vetat Incohare Longam* (1896):

They are not long, the days of wine and roses
Out of a misty dream
Our path emerges for awhile, then closes
Within a dream.

Around 1977, while still in his pitching prime, Seaver's brother-in-law asked him what he intended to do when he retired. "I told him that I intended to go back to California and grow grapes," he said. "It just kind of emerged from the back of my mind, and I think there was an amalgam of reasons."

In 2000 it was a return, literally, to Seaver's "roots" around the agricultural heartland of Fresno, the raisin capital of the world. He started sampling wines at USC. He and Nancy also took off-season bicycle trips through the wine regions of France.

"Nancy would ask me if I was sure I would like it," Seaver told longtime *Los Angeles Times* baseball writer Ross Newhan, "and I would tell her, 'No, but I know there's an itch.' I also knew that whatever I eventually did there had to be a physical involvement. Look at my [scarred] fingers and [dirtied] nails. I call it the red badge of courage. For me, sitting in front of a computer would be instant death. Nancy has the computer. I don't."

Seaver lives in the vibrantly green, sun-splashed Napa Valley wine country of Northern California. His "neighbors," which in this neck of the woods can be people 50 miles away, include former San Francisco 49ers Hall of Fame quarterback Joe Montana and Academy Award–winning director Francis Ford Coppola. It is a land of redwood forests, Douglas fir, manzanita, tanbark oak, and madrone.

"If I had a dream, it couldn't get any better than this," Seaver said.

Seaver operates a John Deere on a little slice of paradise called Diamond Mountain, 800 feet above the fertile Napa Valley. It is his shining city on a hill. His GTS Vineyard is the smallest, specializing in Cabernet Sauvignon grapes on 3½ acres of a 115-acre maze of foliage and vistas.

"I've always said that I'd rather be lucky than good," he said. "It's like when you hang a slider with runners in scoring position and the batter pops it up and everyone says to you, 'That was a great pitch in that situation,' and you kind of laugh to yourself knowing the truth."

Seaver found many similarities between baseball and wine growing, not unlike his observations to Pat Jordan on a winter day in Greenwich some 35 years earlier. "In many ways there is a sequential rhythm and analogous nature to the two seasons, and I'm sure that was a large part of the attraction for me," he theorized.

The Seavers' move back to California came only when daughters Sarah and Anne had finished Boston College. It involved a two-year search through San Luis Obispo, Apple Valley, Mendocino, Paso Robles, and even into Oregon. When they stopped at a realtor's office in St. Helena, one of the sales clips they were given was for the parcel on Diamond Mountain.

"I suspect that other potential buyers had been here before and never got out of their car," Seaver said. "I was in the Marines. Sometimes you have to put boots on the ground. This was the classic case of needing to see the forest through the trees."

The year was 1998, and the future was set. Boston architect Kenneth Kao designed a 7,000-square-foot house, blending into the hillside beige walls merging with the soil, contours, and color of the roof, which looked just like the hills and trees. A patio and pool area oversee the panoramic view.

Nancy created a greenhouse and a rose garden. Seaver had done his research, of course. He knew that grapes grow with southern exposure. Former teammate and one-time restaurant owner Rusty Staub provided valuable advice. "How in the world did you find it?" Staub asked Seaver of his land. "This is what people are killing for out here."

"Sometimes you win, 7–6," Seaver replied.

"We're close, in year six, to a return on capital," he said in 2007 of his winery investment. "My game plan is to break even in 10 years, and we may beat that by a year.

"We're a drop in the bucket [compared to other wineries], but I'm talking quality and not quantity. It's Diamond Mountain cabernet, south-facing slope. It has the potential to be drop-dead stuff."

Seaver, the true New York Sports Icon who was idolized in the Big Apple like Joe DiMaggio and Joe Namath, said he could care less about getting his "face on the cover of *Wine Spectator* because I've had enough of all that." He wants the wine to stand on its own merits. The back of the labels read, "May you enjoy this wine as much as I enjoy the journey bringing it to you. Day to day, month to month, season to season."

Seaver continued to do public relations work on a part-time basis for the Mets and became a familiar face at nearby San Francisco's AT&T Park, where he was one of the special guests honoring Willie Mays when the Giants held a day for the great star. Sandy Koufax, Bob Gibson, Steve Carlton, and Don Baylor were among his guests, traveling to Diamond Mountain for wine and remembrance of past glories. They found the great star in repose, content with his life, his career, and his family.

Tom Seaver and Jim Palmer, the two preeminent right-handed aces of baseball in the 1970s, saw each other many times over the years. They had much in common aside from both being Baseball Hall of Famers. Each had good looks, extraordinary intelligence, a sense for history, while experiencing graceful retirements. But Palmer lamented for years what might have been in 1969. Over and over, he came up with scenarios whereby the Orioles might have pulled it out. Seaver finally had to say, "Jim, it's been a long time. You've got to get over it."

APPENDIX A: 1969 TEAM ROSTER

Player Name	Age	Pos	B	T	HT	WT	Born	Place	MLB Years
Tommie Agee	26	OF	R	R	5' 11"	195	8/9/1942	Magnolia, AL	1962–1973
Ken Boswell	23	2B	L	R	6' 0"	172	2/23/1946	Austin, TX	1967–1977
Don Cardwell	33	P	R	R	6' 4"	210	12/7/1935	Winston-Salem, NC	1957–1970
Ed Charles	36	3B	R	R	5' 10"	170	4/29/1933	Daytona Beach, FL	1962–1969
Donn Clendenon	33	1B	R	R	6' 3"	210	7/15/1935	Neosho, MO	1961–1972
Kevin Collins	22	3B-2B	L	R	6' 2"	190	8/4/1946	Springfield, MA	1965–1971
Jack Dilauro	26	P	B	L	6' 2"	185	5/3/1943	Akron, OH	1969–1970
Duffy Dyer	23	C	R	R	6' 0"	195	8/15/1945	Dayton, OH	1968–1981
Danny Frisella	23	P	L	R	6' 0"	195	3/4/1946	San Francisco, CA	1967–1976
Wayne Garrett	21	3B-2B	L	R	5' 11"	183	12/3/1947	Brooksville, FL	1969–1978
Rod Gaspar	23	OF	B	R	5' 11"	165	4/3/1946	Long Beach, CA	1969–1974
Gary Gentry	22	P	R	R	6' 0"	183	10/6/1946	Phoenix, AZ	1969–1975
Jim Gosger	26	OF	L	L	5' 11"	185	11/6/1942	Port Huron, MI	1963–1974
Jerry Grote	26	C	R	R	5' 10"	190	10/6/1942	San Antonio, TX	1963–1981
Bud Harrelson	25	SS	B	R	5' 11"	160	6/6/1944	Niles, CA	1965–1980
Bob Heise	22	SS-2B	R	R	6' 0"	175	5/12/1947	San Antonio, TX	1967–1977
Jesse Hudson	20	P	L	L	6' 2"	165	7/22/1948	Mansfield, LA	1969–1969
Al Jackson	33	P	L	L	5' 10"	169	12/25/1935	Waco, TX	1959–1969
Bob Johnson	26	P	L	R	6' 4"	220	4/25/1943	Aurora, IL	1969–1977
Cleon Jones	26	OF	R	L	6' 0"	200	8/4/1942	Plateau, AL	1963–1976
Cal Koonce	28	P	R	R	6' 1"	185	11/18/1940	Fayetteville, NC	1962–1971
Jerry Koosman	25	P	R	L	6' 2"	208	12/23/1943	Appleton, MN	1967–1985
Ed Kranepool	24	1B	L	L	6' 3"	215	11/8/1944	New York, NY	1962–1979
J. C. Martin	32	C	L	R	6' 2"	200	12/13/1936	Axton, VA	1959–1972
Jim McAndrew	25	P	R	R	6' 2"	185	1/11/1944	Lost Nation, IA	1968–1974
Tug McGraw	24	P	R	L	6' 0"	185	8/30/1944	Martinez, CA	1965–1984
Amos Otis	22	OF	R	R	5' 11"	166	4/26/1947	Mobile, AL	1967–1984
Bobby Pfeil	25	3B	R	R	6' 1"	180	11/13/1943	Passaic, NJ	1969–1971
Les Rohr	23	P	L	L	6' 5"	205	3/5/1946	Lowestoft, EN	1967–1969
Nolan Ryan	22	P	R	R	6' 2"	195	1/31/1947	Refugio, TX	1966–1993
Tom Seaver	24	P	R	R	6' 1"	206	11/17/1944	Fresno, CA	1967–1986
Art Shamsky	27	OF-1B	L	L	6' 1"	175	10/14/1941	St. Louis, MO	1965–1972
Ron Swoboda	25	OF	R	R	6' 2"	205	6/30/1944	Baltimore, MD	1965–1973
Ron Taylor	31	P	R	R	6' 1"	195	12/13/1937	Toronto, ON	1962–1972
Al Weis	31	2B-SS	B	R	6' 0"	170	4/2/1938	Franklin Square, NY	1962–1971

APPENDIX B: BATTING STATISTICS

Pos	Player Name	Age	G	AB	R	H	2B	3B	HR	RBI	SB	CS	BB	SO
C	Jerry Grote	26	113	365	38	92	12	3	6	40	2	1	32	59
1B	Ed Kranepool	24	112	353	36	84	9	2	11	49	3	2	37	32
2B	Ken Boswell	23	102	362	48	101	14	7	3	32	7	3	36	47
3B	Wayne Garrett	21	124	400	38	87	11	3	1	39	4	2	40	75
SS	Bud Harrelson	25	123	395	42	98	11	6	0	24	1	3	54	54
OF	Tommie Agee	26	149	565	97	153	23	4	26	76	12	9	59	137
OF	Cleon Jones	26	137	483	92	164	25	4	12	75	16	8	64	60
OF	Ron Swoboda	25	109	327	38	77	10	2	9	52	1	1	43	90
OF	Art Shamsky	27	100	303	42	91	9	3	14	47	1	2	36	32
P	Don Cardwell	33	30	47	3	8	0	0	1	5	0	0	0	26
3B	Ed Charles	36	61	169	21	35	8	1	3	18	4	2	18	31
1B	Donn Clendenon	33	72	202	31	51	5	0	12	37	3	2	19	62
3B	Kevin Collins	22	16	40	1	6	3	0	1	2	0	0	3	10
P	Jack Dilauro	26	23	12	0	0	0	0	0	0	0	0	0	9
C	Duffy Dyer	23	29	74	5	19	3	1	3	12	0	0	4	22
P	Danny Frisella	23	3	1	0	0	0	0	0	0	0	0	0	0
OF	Rod Gaspar	23	118	215	26	49	6	1	1	14	7	3	25	19
P	Gary Gentry	22	35	74	2	6	1	0	0	1	0	0	1	52
OF	Jim Gosger	26	10	15	0	2	2	0	0	1	0	0	1	6
SS	Bob Heise	22	4	10	1	3	1	0	0	0	0	0	3	2
P	Al Jackson	33	9	1	0	0	0	0	0	0	0	0	0	0
P	Cal Koonce	28	40	17	1	4	0	0	0	1	0	0	0	7
P	Jerry Koosman	25	32	84	1	4	0	0	0	1	0	0	1	46
C	J. C. Martin	32	66	177	12	37	5	1	4	21	0	0	12	32
P	Jim McAndrew	25	27	37	0	5	1	0	0	3	0	1	3	18
P	Tug McGraw	24	43	24	1	4	1	0	0	3	0	0	1	6
OF	Amos Otis	22	48	93	6	14	3	1	0	4	1	0	6	27
3B	Bobby Pfeil	25	62	211	20	49	9	0	0	10	0	1	7	27
P	Nolan Ryan	22	25	29	3	3	0	0	0	2	0	0	0	14
P	Tom Seaver	24	39	91	7	11	3	0	0	6	1	0	7	34
P	Ron Taylor	31	59	4	0	1	0	0	0	0	0	0	0	2
SS-2B	Al Weis	31	103	247	20	53	9	2	2	23	3	3	15	51

HBP	IBB	SH	SF	DP	AVG	OBP	SLG	OPS	GB%
1	5	6	2	10	.252	.313	.351	664	59%
0	7	2	4	10	.238	.307	.368	675	59%
2	3	4	1	13	.279	.347	.381	728	57%
3	3	6	5	5	.218	.290	.268	558	50%
2	7	5	1	5	.248	.341	.306	647	65%
3	2	6	2	5	.271	.342	.464	806	56%
7	10	1	3	11	.340	.422	.482	904	62%
2	4	1	2	10	.235	.326	.361	687	58%
3	2	2	5	5	.300	.375	.488	863	56%
1	0	2	1	0	.170	.184	.234	418	44%
1	3	0	1	6	.207	.286	.320	606	55%
2	4	2	1	3	.252	.321	.455	776	55%
0	1	0	0	0	.150	.209	.300	509	59%
0	0	0	0	0	.000	.000	.000	000	50%
0	0	1	0	3	.257	.295	.446	741	62%
0	0	0	0	0	.000	.000	.000	000	--
2	2	7	1	1	.228	.313	.279	592	62%
1	0	7	1	0	.081	.104	.095	199	61%
0	1	0	0	0	.133	.188	.267	455	58%
0	1	0	0	1	.300	.462	.400	862	58%
0	0	0	0	0	.000	.000	.000	000	100%
0	0	0	0	0	.235	.235	.235	470	50%
0	0	4	0	2	.048	.059	.048	107	54%
0	1	1	2	6	.209	.257	.316	573	61%
0	0	5	0	0	.135	.200	.162	362	70%
0	0	0	0	0	.167	.200	.208	408	69%
0	1	3	0	0	.151	.202	.204	406	59%
1	0	4	0	5	.232	.260	.275	535	45%
0	0	3	0	1	.103	.103	.103	206	63%
2	0	4	0	0	.121	.200	.154	354	58%
0	0	0	0	0	.250	.250	.250	500	100%
0	1	6	1	3	.215	.259	.291	550	52%

Batting Statistics Key

Pos	Position
G	Games played
AB	At bats
R	Runs
H	Hits
2B	Doubles
3B	Triples
HR	Home runs
RBI	Runs batted in
SB	Stolen bases
CS	Caught stealing
BB	Bases on balls (walks)
SO	Strike outs
HBP	Hit by pitch
IBB	Intentional base on balls
SH	Switch hitter
SF	Sacrifice flies
DP	Double plays hit into
AVG	Average
OBP	On base percentage
SLG	Slugging percentage [explanation]
OPS	On-base percentage plus slugging percentage
GB%	Ground ball percentage (whether hits or outs)

APPENDIX C: PITCHING STATISTICS

	Player Name	Age	W	L	ERA	G	GS	CG	SH	GF	SV	IP	H
ST	Tom Seaver	24	25	7	2.21	36	35	18	5	1	0	273.1	202
ST	Gary Gentry	22	13	12	3.43	35	35	6	3	0	0	233.2	192
ST	Jerry Koosman	25	17	9	2.28	32	32	16	6	0	0	241.0	187
ST	Jim McAndrew	25	6	7	3.47	27	21	4	2	3	0	135.0	112
ST	Don Cardwell	33	8	10	3.01	30	21	4	0	2	0	152.1	145
CL	Ron Taylor	31	9	4	2.72	59	0	0	0	44	13	76.0	61
RP	Tug McGraw	24	9	3	2.24	42	4	1	0	26	12	100.1	89
RP	Cal Koonce	28	6	3	4.99	40	0	0	0	19	7	83.0	85
	Nolan Ryan	22	6	3	3.53	25	10	2	0	4	1	89.1	60
	Jack Dilauro	26	1	4	2.40	23	4	0	0	8	1	63.2	50
	Al Jackson	33	0	0	10.64	9	0	0	0	1	0	11.0	18
	Danny Frisella	23	0	0	7.73	3	0	0	0	0	0	4.2	8
	Bob Johnson	26	0	0	0.00	2	0	0	0	2	1	1.2	1
	Les Rohr	23	0	0	20.30	1	0	0	0	0	0	1.1	5
	Jesse Hudson	20	0	0	4.50	1	0	0	0	1	0	2.0	2

R	ER	HR	BB	SO	WP	BK	H9	HR9	BB9	K9	WHIP	GB%
75	67	24	82	208	8	1	6.65	0.79	2.70	6.85	1.04	49%
94	89	24	81	154	9	0	7.40	0.92	3.12	5.93	1.17	47%
66	61	14	68	180	7	2	6.98	0.52	2.54	6.72	1.06	47%
57	52	12	44	90	7	0	7.47	0.80	2.93	6.00	1.16	45%
63	51	15	47	60	8	0	8.57	0.89	2.78	3.54	1.26	55%
23	23	7	24	42	1	0	7.22	0.83	2.84	4.97	1.12	57%
31	25	6	47	92	8	0	7.98	0.54	4.22	8.25	1.36	58%
53	46	8	42	48	4	1	9.22	0.87	4.55	5.20	1.53	72%
38	35	3	53	92	1	3	6.05	0.30	5.34	9.27	1.26	50%
19	17	4	18	27	2	0	7.07	0.57	2.54	3.82	1.07	59%
13	13	1	4	10	0	0	14.73	0.82	3.27	8.18	2.00	64%
4	4	1	3	5	1	0	15.45	1.93	5.79	9.66	2.36	43%
0	0	0	1	1	0	0	5.42	0.00	5.42	5.42	1.20	100%
4	3	0	1	0	0	1	33.83	0.00	6.77	0.00	4.51	75%
1	1	0	2	3	0	0	9.00	0.00	9.00	13.50	2.00	60%

APPENDIX D: FIELDING STATISTICS

Player	Age	Pos	G	Inn	PO	A	E	TC	DP	PB	SB	CS	FPCT	RF
Ron Taylor	31	P	59	76	6	13	0	19	1	-	-	-	1.000	2.25
Tug McGraw	24	P	42	100.1	6	19	4	29	2	-	-	-	.862	2.24
Cal Koonce	28	P	40	83	7	18	0	25	2	-	-	-	1.000	2.71
Tom Seaver	24	P	36	273.1	18	48	2	68	7	-	-	-	.971	2.17
Gary Gentry	22	P	35	233.2	13	41	0	54	4	-	-	-	1.000	2.08
Jerry Koosman	25	P	32	241	4	37	1	42	3	-	-	-	.976	1.53
Don Cardwell	33	P	30	152.1	9	41	3	53	0	-	-	-	.943	2.95
Jim McAndrew	25	P	27	135	10	14	0	24	1	-	-	-	1.000	1.60
Nolan Ryan	22	P	25	89.1	0	4	1	5	0	-	-	-	.800	.40
Jack Dilauro	26	P	23	63.2	6	10	0	16	0	-	-	-	1.000	2.26
Al Jackson	33	P	9	11	2	2	0	4	0	-	-	-	1.000	3.27
Danny Frisella	23	P	3	4.2	0	0	0	0	0	-	-	-	---	.00
Bob Johnson	26	P	2	1.2	0	0	0	0	0	-	-	-	---	.00
Jesse Hudson	20	P	1	2	0	1	0	1	0	-	-	-	1.000	4.50
Les Rohr	23	P	1	1.1	0	0	0	0	0	-	-	-	---	.00
Jerry Grote	26	C	112		718	63	7	788	11	4	31	40	.991	--
J. C. Martin	32	C	48		275	9	1	285	2	3	15	4	.996	--
Duffy Dyer	23	C	19		105	10	1	116	0	0	8	3	.991	--
Ed Kranepool	24	1B	106		809	64	6	879	76	-	-	-	.993	--
Donn Clendenon	33	1B	58		418	25	7	450	46	-	-	-	.984	--
Cleon Jones	26	1B	15		99	7	0	106	3	-	-	-	1.000	--
Art Shamsky	27	1B	9		75	0	1	76	5	-	-	-	.987	--
J.C. Martin	32	1B	2		4	0	0	4	0	-	-	-	1.000	--
Ken Boswell	23	2B	96		190	229	18	437	51	-	-	-	.959	--
Wayne Garrett	21	2B	47		102	97	3	202	27	-	-	-	.985	--
Al Weis	31	2B	43		73	90	5	168	23	-	-	-	.970	--
Bobby Pfeil	25	2B	11		21	17	1	39	4	-	-	-	.974	--
Wayne Garrett	21	3B	72		40	115	8	163	10	-	-	-	.951	--
Ed Charles	36	3B	52		37	86	7	130	9	-	-	-	.946	--
Bobby Pfeil	25	3B	49		32	88	3	123	8	-	-	-	.976	--
Kevin Collins	22	3B	14		11	26	3	40	2	-	-	-	.925	--
Amos Otis	22	3B	3		3	3	1	7	0	-	-	-	.857	--
Al Weis	31	3B	1		0	0	0	0	0	-	-	-	---	--

Player	Age	Pos	G	Inn	PO	A	E	TC	DP	PB	SB	CS	FPCT	RF
Bud Harrelson	25	SS	119		243	347	19	609	70	-	-	-	.969	--
Al Weis	31	SS	52		65	128	8	201	27	-	-	-	.960	--
Wayne Garrett	21	SS	9		5	6	0	11	0	-	-	-	1.000	--
Bob Heise	22	SS	3		4	5	0	9	0	-	-	-	1.000	--
Tommie Agee	26	OF	146		334	7	5	346	0	-	-	-	.986	--
Cleon Jones	26	OF	122		223	4	2	229	0	-	-	-	.991	--
Ron Swoboda	25	OF	97		163	5	2	170	0	-	-	-	.988	--
Rod Gaspar	23	OF	91		104	12	2	118	6	-	-	-	.983	--
Art Shamsky	27	OF	78		117	2	1	120	2	-	-	-	.992	--
Amos Otis	22	OF	35		46	3	0	49	0	-	-	-	1.000	--
Jim Gosger	26	OF	5		5	0	0	5	0	-	-	-	1.000	--
Ed Kranepool	24	OF	2		3	0	0	3	0	-	-	-	1.000	--
Bobby Pfeil	25	OF	2		0	0	0	0	0	-	-	-	---	--
Donn Clendenon	33	OF	1		0	0	0	0	0	-	-	-	---	--

BIBLIOGRAPHY

1963 Official Baseball Almanac, edited by Bill Wise. Greenwich, CT: Fawcett Publications, Inc.

2001 New York Mets Information Guide. New York: Mets Media Relations Dept., 2001.

Adell, Ross and Ken Samelson. *Amazing Mets Trivia*. Lanham, MD: Taylor Trade Publishing, 2004.

Angell, Roger. *Five Seasons*. New York: Simon & Schuster, 1977.

———. *Game Time: A Baseball Companion*. Orlando, FL: Harcourt, Inc., 2003.

———. *Late Innings: A Baseball Companion*. New York: Simon & Schuster, 1972.

———. *The Summer Game*. New York: The Viking Press, 1972.

Appel, Marty. *Yogi Berra*. New York: Chelsea House Publishers,1992.

Archibald, Joe. *Right Field Rookie*. Philadelphia: MacRae Smith Co., 1967.

Baseball Encyclopedia, The. New York: Macmillan, 1996.

Baseball Stars of 1965, edited by Ray Robinson. New York: Pyramid Books, 1965.

Baseball Stars of 1970, edited by Ray Robinson. New York: Pyramid Books, 1970.

Biskind, Peter. *Easy Riders, Raging Bulls: How the Sex-Drugs-and-Rock 'n' Roll Generation Saved Hollywood*. New York: Simon & Schuster, 1998.

Bjarkman, Peter C. *The New York Mets Encyclopedia*. Champaign, IL: Sports Publishing L.L.C., 2003.

Bouton, Jim. *Ball Four*. New York: The World Publishing Co., 1970.

———, with Neil Offen. *"I Managed Good, But Boy Did They Play Bad."* New York: Dell Publishing Co., Inc., 1973.

Breslin, Jimmy. *Can't Anybody Here Play This Game?* New York: Viking, 1963.

Brosnan, Jim. *Great Rookies of the Major Leagues.* New York: Random House, 1966.

Cramer, Richard Ben. *Joe DiMaggio: The Hero's Life.* New York: Simon & Schuster, 2000.

Creamer, Robert. *Stengel: His Life and Times.* New York: Simon & Schuster, 1984.

Dearborn, Mary V. *Mailer.* New York: Houghton Mifflin Co., 1999.

Devaney, John. *Tom Seaver.* New York: Popular Library, 1974.

DiMaggio, Joe. *Lucky to Be A Yankee.* New York: Grosset & Dunlap, 1947.

Drucker, Malka with Tom Seaver. *Tom Seaver: Portrait of a Pitcher.* New York: Holiday House, 1978.

Eig, Jonathan. *Luckiest Man: The Life and Death of Lou Gehrig.* New York: Simon & Schuster, 2005.

Einstein, Charles. *Willie's Time.* New York: J. B. Lippincott Co., 1979.

Enders, Eric. *100 Years of the World Series.* Barnes & Noble Publishing, Inc., 2003.

Fox, Bucky. *The Mets Fan's Little Book of Wisdom.* Lanham, MD: Taylor Trade Publishing, 2006.

Fox, Larry. *Broadway Joe and his Super Jets.* New York: Coward-McCann, Inc., 1969.

From Cobb to Catfish, edited by John Kuenster. Chicago: Rand McNally & Co., 1975.

Golenbock, Peter. *Amazin': The Miraculous History of New York's Most Beloved Baseball Team.* New York: St. Martin's Press, 2002.

Grabowski, John. *Willie Mays.* New York: Chelsea House Publishers, 1990.

Graham, Jr., Frank. *Great Pennant Races of the Major Leagues.* New York: Random House, 1967.

Gutman, Bill. *Miracle Year 1969: Amazing Mets and Super Jets.* Champaign, IL: Sports Publishing L.L.C., 2004.

Helyar, John. *Lords of the Realm.* New York: Villard Books, 1994.

Hodges, Gil, with Frank Slocum. *The Game of Baseball.* New York: Crown Publishers, Inc., 1969.

Holy Bible. The National Publishing Co., 1970.

Honig, Donald. *The National League.* New York: Crown Publishers, 1983.

Jordan, Pat. *A False Spring.* Winnipeg, Canada: Bison Books, 2005.

———. *The Suitors of Spring.* New York: Dodd, Mead, 1973.

Lee, Bill, with Richard Lally. *The Wrong Stuff.* New York: The Viking Press, 1983.

Lichtenstein, Michael. *Ya Gotta Believe!* New York: St. Martin's Griffin, 2002.

Leventhal, Josh. *The World Series.* New York: Tess Press, 2004.

Macht, Norman L. *Tom Seaver.* New York: Chelsea House Publishers, 1994.

Markusen, Bruce. *Tales From the Mets Dugout.* Champaign, IL: Sports Publishing L.L.C., 2005.

Mays, Willie, as told to Charles Einstein. *Willie Mays: My Life In and Out of Baseball.* New York: E.P. Dutton & Co., Inc., 1966.

Newhan, Ross. "Vintage Seaver." *Los Angeles Times* (http://articles.latimes.com/2007/jul/05/sports/ sp-seaver5), July 5, 2007.

New York Times Book of Baseball History, The, foreword by Red Smith. New York: The *New York Times* Book Co., 1975.

Official 1969 Baseball Guide. St. Louis: *The Sporting News*, 1971.

Official 1970 Baseball Guide. St. Louis: *The Sporting News*, 1971.

Official 1971 Baseball Guide. St. Louis: *The Sporting News*, 1971.

Parrott, Harold. *The Lords of Baseball.* New York: Praeger Publishers, 1976.

Pearlman, Jeff. *The Bad Guys Won!* New York: HarperCollins Publishers Inc., 2004.

Reichler, Joseph. *Baseball's Great Moments.* New York: Crown Publishers, 1974.

Ritter, Lawrence. *The Glory of Their Times.* New York: The Macmillan Co., 1966.

——— and Donald Honig. *The Image of Their Greatness.* New York: Crown Publishers, Inc., 1979.

Seaver, Tom, with Marty Appel. *Great Moments in Baseball.* New York: Carol Publishing Group, 1992.

———, with Dick Schaap. *The Perfect Game.* New York: E. P. Dutton & Co., Inc.,1970.

Shamsky, Art, with Barry Zeman. *The Magnificent Seasons: How the Jets, Mets, and Knicks Made Sports History and Uplifted a City and the Country.* New York: Thomas Dunne Books, 2004.

Smith, Robert. *Baseball.* New York: Simon & Schuster, 1947.

Stout, Glenn. *The Dodgers: 120 Years of Dodgers Baseball.* New York: Houghton Mifflin Co., 2004.

Travers, Steven. *A's Essential: Everything You Need to Know to Be a Real Fan!* Chicago: Triumph Books, 2007.

———. *Barry Bonds: Baseball's Superman.* Champaign, IL: Sports Publishing L.L.C., 2002.

———. *Dodgers Essential: Everything You Need to Know to Be a Real Fan!* Chicago: Triumph Books, 2007.

———. "L.A./Orange County Prep All-Century Teams," *StreetZebra*, January 2000.

———. *The Good, the Bad, and the Ugly Los Angeles Lakers.* Chicago: Triumph Books, 2007.

———. "Time to Give Barry His Due," *San Francisco Examiner*, April 18, 2001.

———. *One Night, Two Teams: Alabama vs. USC and the Game that Changed a Nation*. Lanham, MD: Taylor Trade Publishing, 2007.

Will, George. *Bunts*. New York: Touchstone, 1999.

Whittingham, Richard. *Illustrated History of the Dodgers*. Chicago: Triumph Books, 2005.

Zimmerman, Paul D. and Dick Schaap. *The Year the Mets Lost Last Place*. New York: The World Publishing Co., 1969.

INDEX

Note: Page numbers in **bold** include photographs/captions, and page numbers in *italics* indicate statistics.

Aaron, Henry "Hank," 13, 15, 57, 106, **107**, 109, 110, 111, 112, 113, 114, 134
Agee, Tommie
background, 57, 58, 107
batting, *25*, 64, 70, 74, 92, *103*, *116*, 127, *167*
career summary, 159
Cleon Jones and, 41, 57, 58, 67, 81, 124, 128
dangerous squeeze play, 112
feeling isolated as black player, 67
fielding, 50, 78, 81, 127, 128–29
on Las Vegas stage, 151
in NLCS, 112, 114, 116
statistics, *25*, *103*, *116*, *159*, *165*, *167*, *171*
in World Series, 127, 128–29
Allen, Maury, 16, 44, 153
All-Star break, 83–84
Angell, Roger, 44, 64, 98, 99, 100, 101–2, 118, 120, 124, 128, 129, 130, 142, 147
Apollo 11, 82, 84, 148
Ashburn, Richie, 2, 4, 5

Atlanta Braves, NLCS and, 106–16

Bailey, Pearl, 141, 147
Banks, Ernie, 49, 68, 69, 70, 77, 78, 94, 99
Batting statistics, *167–68*
Bench, Johnny, **xiv**, 37, 55, 58, 134, 162
Berra, Yogi, **xiii**, **42**, 69, 79, 115, 123, 144, 147, 160–61
"Big inning," 43, 49–51
Black cat incident, 93–94
Black players, 12, 28–29, 53, 66, 67, 79, 107
Blair, Paul, 27, 124, 128, 129, **130**, 132, 133, 134, 137
Boswell, Ken, **69**, 70, 71, 94, 103, 114, *116*, 128, 147, 151, *159*, *165*, *167*, *170*
Bouton, Jim, 85
Boyer, Clete, 113
Breslin, Jimmy, 2, 3–4
Brock, Lou, 15, 58, 64
Brushback pitches, 51, 64–65
Buford, Don, 118–19, 120, 121, 132, 133, 137, 144
Burbrink, Nelson, 77, 81

Cardwell, Don, 65, 91, **95**, 96, 102, *165*, *167*, *169*, *170*
Carlton, Steve, 89, **96**, 97, 153, 162, 164
Celebrations
  clinching division, **97–98**, 99
  NLCS, **112**, 114–16
  World Series, **145**–49
Charles, Ed, **24**, 64, 67, 77, 95, 97, 99, 102, *103*, 116, 121, 124, 129, 142, 144, 159, *165*, *167*, *170*
Cheating and infidelity, 45, 53–54, 55–56
Chicago Cubs
  "big inning" against, 43, 49–51
  black cat incident, 93–94
  first crucial day against, 68–72
  Mets taking first place from, 95
  near-perfect game against, 73–81
Clendenon, Donn
  batting/base running, **66**, 70, 71, 75, 97, *103*, 124, 133, **142**, **143**, 144, *159*, *167*
  Bud Harrelson on, 66
  fielding, 90–91, 144, *170*, *171*
  on Las Vegas stage, 151
  legacy of, 159
  to Mets, 65–67
  photographs, **66**, **142**, **143**
  Ron Swoboda on, 67
  statistics, *103*, *159*, *165*, *167*, *170*, *171*
  stirring things up, 122
  Tom Seaver and, 67, 123
  World Series MVP, 147, 150
Coleman, Choo Choo, **28**
Collins, Kevin, 66, *165*, *167*, *170*
Comeback, perspective on, 99–100
Craig, Roger, 2, **4**
Cuellar, Mike, 117, **118**, 119, 120, 132, 133

Dark Shadows, 69, 71
Dedeaux, Justin, 12, 121
Dedeaux, Raoul "Rod," 10–11, 121, 132, 135
Dierker, Larry, 73, 85, 87
Dilauro, Jack, *165*, *167*, *169*, *170*
Division, clinching, 97–99
Drysdale, Don, 13, 16, 38, 89, 95, 111, 141, 163

Durocher, Leo, **45**–47, 49, 51, 64, 65, 68, 70, 71, 73–74, 75, 79, 81, 90, 92, 93, 94, 99
Dyer, Duffy, 44, 103, **138**, *165*, *167*, *170*
Fielding statistics, *170–71*
Frisella, Danny, *165*, *167*, *169*, *170*

Gaedel, Eddie, 2
Garrett, Mike, 11, 12, 32
Garrett, Wayne, 71, 77, 92, **100**, 103, 114, *116*, 137, 150, *165*, *167*, *170*, *171*
Gaspar, Rod, 64, 65, 77, 90, 94, 103, 115, 120, 121, 122, 134, 135, 137, 138, 139, 147, 150, *165*, *167*, *171*
Gentry, Gary
  biographical sketch, 37–39, 157
  disappointing career, 157
  in NLCS, 114
  photographs, **36**, **38**, **39**, **63**, **83**
  pitching, 37–39, 62, **63**, 63, 64, 95, 97, 114, 127, 128, 129, *157*, *169*
  Ron Swoboda on fearlessness o, 65
  statistics, *102*, *157*, *165*, *167*, *169*, *170*
  wife of, 56
  World Series and, 127, 128, 129, 141, 146
Gibson, Bob, 14, 16, 18, **19**, 38, 41, 48, 75, 89, 97, 104, 105, 122, 164
Gonzalez, Tony, 110
Gosger, Jim, *165*, *167*, *171*
Grant, Donald, 22–23, 99, 148, **161**
Grote, Jerry
  as All-Star, 20, 37
  attitude of, 39
  batting, 75, 78, *103*, 124, 127, 128, 137, 144, *167*
  on black-cat/Cubs incident, 94
  career summary, 158–59
  catching/calling games, 33, 37, 48, 50, 80, 90, 109, 110, 132, 133
  as face of "New Mets," 24
  firing ball back to pitcher, 58
  fishing with teammates, 40
  Jerry Koosman and, 37, 58, 124, 146
  Lou Brock on, 48
  NLCS celebration, 115
  photographs, **16**, **34**
  statistics, *103*, *165*, *167*, *170*
  on Tom Seaver, 17
Gutman, Bill, 24, 119, 146, 148

Haddix, Harvey, **17**, 18
Hands, Billy, 48, 49, 50, 51, 92
Harrelson, Bud
  attitude of, 39
  batting, 62, 97, 110, 127
  biographical sketch, 59, 159
  on Championship run, 115, 116, 146
  on Donn Clendenon, 66
  as face of "New Mets," 18, 24
  fielding, **58**, 124, 133
  foreword by, ix–xii
  on Gil Hodges, 23
  Hodges/Jones incident and, 86
  Pete Rose and, 159
  photographs, **ix**, **25**, **58**
  physical stature, 50, 127
  post-baseball life, 159
  Ron Swoboda on, 27
  special talents, 59

statistics, *103*, *165*
Tom Seaver and, 14, 17, 29, 39, 40, 59, 80, 100–101, 151, 159
on turnaround of 1969, 64
Hart, Jim Ray, 36, 91
Heise, Bob, *167*, *171*
Hendricks, Elrod, 119, 127, 132, 135
Herzog, Whitey, **23**, 60
Hickman, Jim, 47, 68–69
High hopes, 21–22, 26, 42, 43, 45, 109
Hodges, Gil
becoming manager, 18, 22–23, 36, 60
celebrating championship, 148
changing team attitude, 23–24
Cleon Jones incident, 86–87, 88
death of, 158
Donn Clendenon and, 66–67, 142–44
Earl Weaver compared to, 123
hearth attack/recovery, 20, 26, 37, 39, 40, 42, 158
Jerry Koosman and, 37, 87, 112
management style, 46, 85, 90, 128
managing world series, 123, 126, 128, 134, 136, 137, 138, 142–44
NLCS (march to the sea) and, 107, 109, 110, 112, 114
photographs, **35**, **42**, **83**, **101**, **140**, **142**
playing right hunches, 114, 128
raise for 1970 season, 150
Ron Swoboda on, 25–26
Rube Walker and, 75
street named after, 148
temperament, 49–50
Tom Seaver and, 20, 44, 110, 154, 158
use of bullpen, 102–3
winning attitude, 23–24, 41, 42
on winning championship, 147
wrath of, 82, 86
Holtzman, Ken, 48, 51, 74, 75, 89, 94
Hubela, George, 76
Hudson, Jesse, *165*, *169*, *170*
Hunter, Billy, 138
Hurricane Camille, 84–85

Jackson, Al, 2, 44, 163, *167*, *169*, *170*
Jackson, Reggie, 8, 28, 35–36
Jenkins, Ferguson, 48–49, 68, 69, 70, 71, 72, 75, 93–94, 154
Johnson, Bob, *165*, *169*, *170*
Johnson, Davey, 119, 129, 132, 133, 136, 137, 145
Jones, Cleon
as All-Star, 83–84
attitude of, 39
background, 56–57, 107
batting, *41*, *57*, 75, *103*, 112, *116*, 132, 136, 142–43, 145, *167*
benching of, 88
career after 1969, 159
feeling isolated as black player, 67
fielding, **57**, 77, 81, 86, 127, 128, 133, 145, *170*, *171*
Gil Hodges and, 86–87
on Las Vegas stage, 151
in NLCS, 112
photographs, **56**, **57**
statistics, *41*, *57*, *103*, *116*, *165*, *167*, *170*, *171*
taken out of game mid-inning, 86

Tommie Agee and, 41, 57, 58, 67, 81, 124, 128
World Series and, 115, 123, 124, 132, 136, 142–43, 144, 145, 147, 148
Jordan, Pat, 161, 163, 164

Kanehl, "Hot Rod," 5–**6**, 99
Kessinger, Don, **47**, 70, 72, 75, 77
Kiner, Ralph, **18**, 61, 116, 123, 147
King, Martin Luther, Jr., 36, 42
Koonce, Cal, 26, **102**, *165*, *167*, *169*, *170*
Koosman, Jerry, 18
as All-Star, 83–84
biographical sketch, 34–37, 156
brushback pitches, 64
on Cubs/Mets rivalry, 51
Don Cardwell and, 95, 96
as face of "New Mets," 18
first All-Star Game, 20
on Gil Hodges, 87
Jerry Grote and, 37, 58, 124, 146
on Las Vegas stage, 151
NLCS and, 111–**12**, 114, 116
Nolan Ryan and, 36, 114
photographs, **26**, **33**, **65**, **112**
pitching, **26**, 34–37, 42, 62, 64, 68, 72, 88–89, 92, 95, 96, *102*, 111–12, *169*. *See also* World Series and
on post-season fame, 151
Ron Swoboda on, 65
Ron Taylor and, 64, 67
Rookie of the Year, 20
statistics, *102*, *156*, *165*, *167*, *169*, *170*
studying engineering, 34, 35, 67
Tom Seaver and, 25, 36, 88–89, 91, 103, **112**, 134, 139, 156
on world in 1969, 85
World Series and, 123, 124–26, 127, 130, 141–42, 144–47, 148
Koufax, Sandy, 4, 11, 13, 15, 17, 30, 31, 75, 78, 89, 95, 96, 103, 131, 164
Kranepool, Ed
batting, 50, 63, 71–72, 73, *103*, 128, 138, *167*
fans booing, 68
on Las Vegas stage, 151
Mets keeping, 66
photographs, **5**, **24**, **71**, **98**
platooning of, 66, 67
on pre-1969 teams, 97
statistics, *103*, *166*, *167*, *170*, *171*
symbolizing Mets' redemption, 128
symbolizing "old" Mets, 23–24, 71
on Tom Seaver, 77
on winning division, 99

Lee, Bill, 11–12
Lindsay, Mayor John, 22, 91, 96, 115, 116, 117, 127, 148
Lucas, George, 10, 11

Manson, Charles, 84
March to the sea (NLCS), 106–16
Marichal, Juan, 16, 89, 91, 122, 163
Martin, J. C., 71, **110**, 111, **138**, *166*, *167*, *170*
Mathewson, Christy, 8, 19–20, 32, 79, 89, 100
Mays, Willies, 6, 36, **46**, 47, 91, 92, 105, 127, 164
McAndrew, Jim, 25, 38, 58, 66, 88, *102*, *166*, *167*, *169*, *170*
McCovey, Willie, 57, **90**–91, 103, 104–5, 106, 134

McDowell, "Sudden" Sam, 16, 161
McGraw, Frank "Tug"
  biographical sketch, 29–32, 157–58
  as face of "New Mets," 18
  nickname origin, 30–31
  photographs, **29**, **98**
  pitching, 30–32, 49, 62, 97, *102*, 112, *157*, 157–58, *169*
  screwball of, 32, 157
  Seaver pamphlet and, 131, 132
  statistics, *102*, *157*, *166*, *167*, *169*, *170*
McGraw, John, 65, 79
McNally, Dave, 117, 124, 126, **141**, 142, 144, 146–47
Montreal Expos, 44–45, 82–83, 94, 95, 154, 160
Morgan, Joe, 85, 162
Murphy, Bob, **60**, 61, 78
Murphy, Jack, 61
Murphy, Johnny, 23, 37, 60, 66, 150

Namath, Joe, 22, 53, 54, 78, 79, 148, 164
National League Championship Series (NLCS), 106–16
Nelson, Lindsay, **59**, 60–61, 73, 75, 77
New York Jets, 22, 24, 71, 76, 91, 98, 113–14, 115, 116, 148
Newcombe, Don, 103, 111
Niekro, Phil, 108, 110, 111
1970 season, 153–55
1962 Mets
  Casey Stengel on, 3
  end of, 6
  Marv Throneberry and, 1–2, **3**
  as worst team in history, 1, 4, 6
Nixon, Richard, 11, 21

The Odd Couple, 6–7
Otis, Amos, 65, *166*, *167*, *170*, *171*

Palmer, Jim, 117, 123, 127, 128, **129**, 164
Payson, Joan Whitney, **35**, 37, 68, **69**, 115, 148, 152
Perry, Gaylord, 32, 62, 89, 91
Pfeil, Bobby, 70, 74, 77, 80, 103, *166*, *167*, *170*, *171*
Pignatano, Joe, **84**
Pitching duos, 88–89
Pitching statistics, *169*
Powell, Boog, 117, 119, 120, 126, 127, 132, 133, 134, 135, 141, 144, 145, 147

Rickey, Branch, 46, 79
Robinson, Brooks, 117, 119, **120**, 124, 126, 127, 132, 134–35, 145, 147
Robinson, Frank, 117, **121**–22, 126, 127, 129, 132, 133, 134, 135, 136, 141, 142, 145, 146–47
Robinson, Jackie, 44, 100
Robinson, Ray, 8, 81, 151
Robinson, Warren "Sheriff," 32
Rockefeller, Governor Nelson, 21, 116, 117, 127
Rohr, Les, 36, *166*, *169*, *170*
Rose, Pete, 15, 64, 80, 159, 162
Ryan, Nolan
  biographical sketch, 32–34, 156–57, 162
  development of, 34, 38, 114
  as face of "New Mets," 18, 24
  fishing with teammates, 40
  Jerry Koosman and, 36, 114

New York scene, 34
in NLCS, 114
photographs, **14**
pitching, 32–34, 50, 91, *102*, 114, 128, 156–57, *169*
as project, 26
statistics, *102–3*, *166*, *167*, *169*, *170*
In World Series, 128

Santo, Ron, **39**, 49, **50**, 51, 55, 75, 77, 78, 92, 94
Schapp, Dick, 71, 76, 79, 151
Seaver, Charles, 80, 147
Seaver, Charles, Jr., 15, 17, 133
Seaver, Nancy
celebrating championship, 147, 148
Donn Clendenon and, 67
fear of cheating, 14
marriage to Tom, 14, 55
near-perfect game and, 80, 81
to New York, 16
political perspective, 19
post-baseball-world and, 163, 164
public image, 133, 152
team attitude toward, 56, 151, 152–53
Tom's fidelity and, 14, 53, 55–56, 152–53
Tom's pitching and, 77, 80, 81, 120, 137, 152
Seaver, Tom, xvii–xviii
arm stiffness, 83, 88
"big inning," 43, 49–51
Bob Gibson and, 14, 16, 18, **19**, 38, 75
brushback pitches, 64
Bud Harrelson and, 14, 17, 29, 39, 40, 58–59, 80, 100–101, 151, 159
Christy Mathewson and, 8, 19–20, 100
college years, 10–13, 85, 152
Cy Young awards, 103, **104**
Dick Selma and, 8–10, 13, 14, 34, 54
Donn Clendenon and, 67, 123
draft confusion, 13
drive for perfection, 17, 89–90
Ed Charles on, 142
first All-Star Game, 15–16, 17
on Gil Hodges, 20
growing up in Fresno, 8–10
Henry Aaron and, 13, 15, 106, 109, 110, 111
high school sports, 9–10
hot streak in 1969, 89
humanitarian acts, 19
on importance of attitude, 89
Jenkins vs., 93–94, 96
Jerry Koosman and, 25, 36, 88–89, 91, 103, 134, 139, 156
in Las Vegas, 151, 152–53
legacy of, 161–64
marriage fidelity, 14, 53, 55–56, 152–53
to Mets, 13–14, 43
military life, 10–11
as modern Lancelot, 100
Montreal debut disappointment, 44–45
MVP award and, 103–5
Nancy and. *See* Seaver, Nancy
near-perfect games, 73–81, 134
New York scene, 16
nicknames, 14, 99
1970 season, 153–54
1968 season, 18–19, 20
NLCS and, 106, 108, 109–11, **112**

Pat Jordan and, 161, 163, 164
perfect delivery, **49**
Pete Rose and, 15, 64, 80, 159
photographs, **xvii**, **9**, **44**, **49**, **76–77**, **104**, **112**, **157**, **160**, **161**
professional attitude, 17–18, 89–90
Ron Swoboda and, 27
Ron Taylor on, 64
Rookie of the Year, 18, 22
statistics, *162–63*
team attitude toward, 17, 56
on team philosophy, 39–40
today, 163–64
top prospect, 14
Vietnam War and, 19, 131–32, 147
winning 20th game, 91
work ethic, 15, 16–17
youthful look in majors, 15
Seaver, Tom (World Series)
awards/publicity resulting from, 151–52
as fan, 140–41, 142
Game 1, 118–19, 120–21, 123
Game 4, 131–39
near-perfect game, 134
peace pamphlet distraction, 131–32
Segregation, 12, 28–29, 107
Selkirk, George, 23, 60
Selleck, Tom, 11
Selma, Dick, 8–10, 13, 14, 24–25, 34, 48, 54, 80
Shamsky, Art, 65
batting, *103*, *116*, 136, *159–60*, *167*
on Earl Weaver, 123
fielding, 128, *171*, *172*
Frank Robinson and, 121–22
on Hodges/Jones incident, 86
on Las Vegas Stage, 151
on NLCS with Atlanta, 113, 115
photograph, **85**
platooning of, 71
on Rube Walker, 41
statistics, *103*, *116*, *159–60*, *166*, *167*, *171*, *172*
on world in 1969, 84
on Yogi Berra, 42
Shoe polish incidents, **142**–44
Sisler, Dick, 122
Spangler, Al, 77, 78
Spring training (1969), 37, 39–42
Statistics
batting, *167–68*
fielding, *170–71*
pitching, *169*
season ERA, *103*
team roster, *165–66*
World Series, *146*
Stengel, Casey, 27, 79
bits of Stengelese, 5
"Hot Rod" Kanehl and, 5–6
inviting "youth of America," 28, 29
on 1969 Mets, 108, 115
on 1962 Mets, 3–4, 6
photograph, **2**
platoon system, 25
on 73rd birthday, 3–4
Throneberry interference call and, 1
Tug McGraw and, 31
Swoboda, Ron "Rocky"
affinity with black guys, 28–29, 67
on Amos Otis, 65

baseball history, 27–29, 160
batting, 95–96, 136, 144
biographical sketch, 27–29, 160
on Bud Harrelson, 27
"bull in a china shop, **27**
on Cleon Jones, 56–57, 86–87, 159
on Cubs/Mets rivalry, 93, 96, 99
on Donn Clendenon, 67
as face of "New Mets," 24
fielding, 65, 77, 118–**19**, 134, 135, **136–37**, 145
on Gary Gentry, 38–39, 65
on Gil Hodges, 25–26, 86–87
on Jerry Koosman, 36, 65
kinship with downtrodden, 29
mythical catch, 135, **136–37**, 139
on NLCS with Atlanta, 108, 114, 116
on Nolan Ryan, 34
personality, 26–27, 160
professional attitude, 65
on shoe polish scam, 144
statistics, *103*, *166*, *167*, *171*
straightjacket incident, 27
Tom Seaver and, 27, 65, 138–39, 153, 160
on Tug McGraw, 30
on turnaround of 1969, 88
on World Series, 119, 121, 122–23, 124, 128, 146, 147, 151

Taylor, Ron, 44, 64, 67, *102*, 111, 112, 124, 126, 134, *166*, *167*, *169*, *170*
Team roster, *165–66*
Throneberry, Marv, 1–2, **3**, 68
Torre, Joe, 66, 98, 103
Triandos, Gus, 28
Trimble, Joe, 64
Turnaround of 1969, 64, 72, 86, 88

Veeck, Bill, 4

Walker, Harry, 85
Walker, Herbert, 22, 29, 152
Walker, Rube, **41**, 74, 75, 110, 139, 144
Washburn, Ray, 41
Watt, Eddie, 136, 137, 144
Weaver, Earl, 120, 122–**23**, 124, 126, 129, 133, 142–43, 144, 149
Weiss, Al "Babe," 36, 60, 63, 75, 78, 82, 96, 103, 120, 124, 126, 133, 138, 139, 144, 147, 151, *166*, *167*, *170*, *171*
Weiss, George, 5, 29, 60
Westrum, Wes, 15, **22**, 32, 36, 58
Williams, Billy, 16, **47**, 77, 92
Williams, Ted, 80
Wilson, Don, 85, 87
Woodstock, 84
World events (1969), 84–85
World Series, 117–49
Agee's outstanding play, 127–28, 129
arriving in Baltimore, 117–18
celebration, **145**–49
crowds at Shea, 126, 127, 129–30, 141
David vs. Goliath analogy, 117
final out ball, 145, 147
Frank Robinson's cutting remarks, 121–22
Game 1, 118–21
Game 2, 124–26
Game 3, 127–29

Game 4, 131–39
Game 5, 141–45
Mayor John Lindsay and, 116, 127, 148
Mets banner in Baltimore, 124
MVP, 147, 150
player celebrity status/egotism after, 150–51
program cover, **125**
public attention on, 126–27
shoe polish incident, **142**–44
statistics, *146*
Swoboda's remarkable play, 135, **136–37**, 139
See also specific participant names
Wynn, Jim "the Toy Cannon," 85

Yost, Eddie, 41–**42**, 65
Young, Don, 47, 69–**70**

Zimmerman, Paul, 76, 79

ABOUT THE AUTHOR

Steven Travers is a USC graduate and ex-professional baseball player with the St. Louis Cardinals and Oakland A's organizations. He is the author of 15 books, including the best-selling *Barry Bonds: Baseball's Superman*, nominated for a Casey Award (best baseball book of 2002). *The USC Trojans: College Football's All-Time Greatest Dynasty* was a National Book Network "top 100 seller." *One Night, Two Teams: Alabama vs. USC and the Game That Changed a Nation* (a 2007 PNBA nominee) was the subject of a documentary (*Tackling Segregation*) and is being made into a motion picture. Steven wrote for the *L. A. Times,* was a columnist for *StreetZebra* magazine in Los Angeles and the *San Francisco Examiner*. He also penned the screenplays *The Lost Battalion* and *21.* A fifth generation Californian, Steve served in the Army; coached at USC, Cal-Berkeley, and in Europe; attended law school; and was a sports agent. He has a daughter, Elizabeth, and still resides in the Golden State.